T0342223

The Urban Commons

DANIEL T. O'BRIEN

The Urban Commons

How Data and Technology Can
Rebuild Our Communities

Harvard University Press

Cambridge, Massachusetts, and London, England

2018

Library of Congress Cataloging-in-Publication Data

Names: O'Brien, Daniel T., 1983– author.
Title: The urban commons : how data and technology can rebuild our communities /
    Daniel T. O'Brien.
Description: Cambridge, Massachusetts : Harvard University Press, 2018. |
    Includes bibliographical references and index.
Identifiers: LCCN 2018015010 | ISBN 9780674975293 (hardcover : alk. paper)
Subjects: LCSH: Urban renewal—Massachusetts—Boston. | Municipal
    Services—Massachusetts—Boston—Citizen participation. | Public
    Spaces—Massachusetts—Boston—Management—Citizen participation. |
    Public Spaces—Management—Technological innovations—Massachusetts—Boston. |
    Sustainable urban development—Massachusetts—Boston.
Classification: LCC HT177.B67 O27 2018 | DDC 307.3 / 4160974461—dc23
LC record available at https://lccn.loc.gov/2018015010

To Leslie, my original partner in the Boston project

Contents

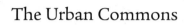

The Urban Commons

Introduction

IN LATE AUGUST 2011, Hurricane Irene struck the east coast of the United States, battering the country from North Carolina's Outer Banks to Vermont. Along with much of the rest of Massachusetts, Boston was lashed with winds and rain. I am interested in what happened next.

In the 48 hours after the storm, the city of Boston's Parks and Recreation Department received 1,045 reports of "tree emergencies," about the same amount it would typically receive in an entire year. Each of these reports was processed by the city's 311 system—a telephone hotline and associated web applications that offer direct access to nonemergency city services—creating a digital record of the damage that Irene wrought on Boston and its infrastructure, including fallen limbs, branches, and even whole trees. There were also reports of downed streetlights and signs, and requests for highway maintenance. If we map the reports, we see that they came from across the city, though they were more common in some places than in others (see Figure I.1 and video at http://vimeo.com/41535798).[1] Neighborhoods along Boston's eastern coast, such as South Boston and Dorchester, were exposed to strong winds coming off the water and saw a particularly high density of downed trees. We also see a concentration in the city's more suburban southwest corner, a neighborhood called West Roxbury, where the storm took a toll on its tree-lined streets.

Reports made through Boston's smartphone application, Citizens Connect, permitted residents to describe their concerns in detail, offering a richness that numbers alone cannot.[2] One resident in West Roxbury

1

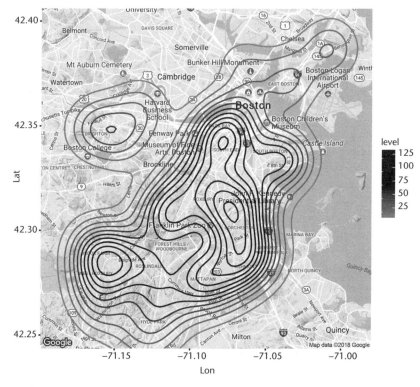

FIGURE I.1 Density of tree emergencies reported via Boston's 311 system in the 48 hours following Hurricane Irene.

complained of an "ELECTRIC POLE SLANTING Due to hurricane IRENE. This may cause major power outage in area if not attended too!" In neighboring Hyde Park, a "Bottom wire is sparking. Needs attention immediately could bring down power or start a pole fire." There was also a "tree branch blocking avondale street" and a "possible live wire hanging from pole on Codman Park," both in Dorchester. And my favorite, if only for its distinctiveness: the "huge sink hole in front of vacant church formed" on St. George Street in the South End.

More than just chronicling the impacts of Hurricane Irene, these reports tell an important story about the care Bostonians exhibited for their city in the wake of the storm. Each report contains an instance of *custodianship,* in which someone sought to counter the degradation of a space. She or he not only observed a damaged tree or downed power line but then took action to fix it. We repeatedly see this spirit of caretaking in the comments, as people fretted about a "tree down blocking Ocean street—impassable to emergency vehicles" or about a "tree fallen on car blocking side walk, two handicap persons could not pass!" There was even a case in which we see custodianship occurring twice, first when "Neighbors moved [a fallen tree] to sidewalk" and again when the individual reported that "it needs to be picked up."

What is more, the database reveals how people vary in their custodianship through user accounts. Whereas most reports regarded issues near the reporter's home, a handful of individuals reported issues more widely; one person apparently made an activity of it, calling in 24 separate tree emergencies, which spanned the southern half of the city! Similarly, expressions of custodianship varied from place to place. For example, a tree down in the Upham's Corner section of Dorchester was reported by 10 different people in two days. In sum, whether they did so locally or across the area, once or many times, the residents and communities of Boston were able to channel their custodianship through the 311 system. This in turn equipped city services employees with a precise map of the damage created by Irene, guiding their efforts to restore order.

Hurricane Irene is just one instance of how 311 systems, which are steadily growing in popularity in American cities, enlist constituents in the maintenance of public spaces and infrastructure, or what I call the *urban commons*. At its heart, the 311 system constructs a collaborative relationship between city residents and government operations. Residents act as the "eyes and ears of the city," reporting problems that they observe in their daily movements. City services departments then deploy the specialized equipment and personnel required to fix them. Though cleaning up after Hurricane Irene is a dramatic example of this teamwork, it is visible on any given day, as resident reports instigate the filling of potholes, replacement of streetlight outages, and removal of graffiti. In many cities, from Boston, to New York City, to Chattanooga, it has become the "new normal" for the upkeep of public infrastructure.

The 311 system has been lauded in recent years as a symbol of how technology can benefit municipal governance. Technology's promise is typically cast as a smarter, more efficient government that better embodies the democratic ideals of responsiveness and accessibility.[3] This book takes a different tack, focusing on the novel insights we gain from the data generated by 311 systems, as well as the research-policy collaborations that these analyses can support. Importantly, the 311 data can advance knowledge in ways that are both theoretical, or "scholarly," and practical, or "applied." Toward the first, by documenting the custodianship of the city, these data offer insights into the fundamental challenge of the commons that confronts communities worldwide. While the maintenance of shared spaces concerns everyone, it is technically the responsibility of no one. Most research to date in this area has focused on how institutions can help to manage the commons, but far less is known about how, when, and why people contribute to this process. The 311 database captures such actions in intricate detail, opening the door to a variety of understudied questions: How do people approach this shared task? How often do they contribute to it, and what are their motivations for doing so? When do the combined efforts of a community succeed or falter in staving off degradation? We might extend these discoveries to the social and behavioral dynamics that underlie the functioning of urban neighborhoods and to other types of commons more generally.

Turning to the practical, because 311 is an active government program, the data it generates provide a natural tool for evaluating how it works. This holds immediate implications for the hundreds of municipalities that have 311 systems, but it can also provide insights on broader themes in public policy and administration. Such systems are representative of a governance strategy known as *coproduction,* in which constituents are actively involved in the execution and enforcement of policy.[4] Coproduction programs, like parent-teacher organizations or community policing, create a collaborative relationship between government and the public. Analyses that reveal the nature of 311 participation also teach us what makes these other programs successful. Importantly, this applied question is linked to the theoretical one. The relationship between constituent and government facilitated by 311 depends on people's custodianship for the urban commons; any theoretical advances on the latter will help us to better understand the operation of the former.

Through these themes, I, too, argue that 311 is emblematic of a novel trend afoot in cities, though one that encompasses and goes beyond the adoption of technology by local governments. Recent years have seen the emergence of the field of *urban informatics,* or the use of modern digital (i.e., "big") data and technologies to better understand and serve the city. The field is an intellectual melting pot, bringing together academics of many stripes—from sociology, to computer science, to biology—with innovative policymakers and practitioners, private corporations, and informal communities of "hackers" and app developers. This has created a distinctive opportunity for advances in the academic, public, and private sectors alike, but more importantly, it has fueled the creation of new models of collaboration across them. To be sure, 311 is one of many examples of urban informatics, but it exemplifies the field. On the one hand, it is a technological innovation that has sought to improve the effectiveness and responsiveness of city services. On the other hand, it generates a novel database that offers a deeper understanding of both the day-to-day patterns and the long-term trends of the city and its neighborhoods. The subsequent insights can then inspire further policy innovation.

This book presents an extended study of how the residents of Boston, Massachusetts, have utilized 311. In doing so, one of my primary goals is to introduce the field of urban informatics and its potential. My approach is threefold. First, the book offers an empirical illustration of the type of work that might occur within urban informatics. It does this by leveraging the "big data" of hundreds of thousands of 311 reports, combining them when necessary with more traditional "small data," to deepen our understanding of (1) the behavioral dynamics that constitute the collective maintenance of the commons and (2) the internal workings of coproduction programs. At the second level, the studies were conducted under the auspices of the Boston Area Research Initiative (BARI), an institution that I codirect and whose mission is to coordinate efforts across universities and the public and private sectors in order to advance urban science and policy in the digital age. The BARI community represents a different type of commons, the unique ecosystem of data sharing and widespread collaboration that characterizes the practice of urban informatics within a region, and the empirical studies herein embody this collaborative spirit, articulating a cycle of learning and innovation. The result is a demonstration of how researchers and policymakers can work together to simultaneously advance scholarship and inform pressing societal issues and questions.

Embedded in these first two levels is an overarching narrative about the field of urban informatics itself. This is the third and highest level of the book. We see in the empirical studies how urban informatics research might contribute to science and policy, and in BARI we see a model for the institutional forms that can initiate and sustain such work. From these it is possible to articulate the opportunities and challenges that face the field, including broader societal trends such as the introduction of "civic technology" and the emergence of digital divides between "data-haves" and "data-have-nots." Because a main goal of this book is to introduce urban informatics and its promise, I have written it for a diverse audience, including both my fellow urban scientists and our counterparts in the public and private sectors. I have striven to make the book as accessible as possible. Thus, I provide guideposts throughout, alerting readers to sections that present the in-depth statistical analyses necessary to substantiate a given claim, and follow them with nontechnical summaries. The remainder of this chapter sets up the context and inspiration for the work that follows, and the contributions it promises to make.

Urban Informatics: Discovery and Innovation in the Digital City

Challenges and Opportunities in the Modern Urban Context

Recent years have seen a digital revolution that is transforming society. At its root has been the rapid proliferation of computer technology, and where there are computers, there are data. The icons of this so-called revolution have been things like cell phones, online shopping, and social media, but digitization is ubiquitous, providing us with a wealth of new tools and information across domains. Cities have played a special role in this trend. Leading technology corporations locate their headquarters in major cities, and city governments are most likely to have the budget, expertise, and perceived need for cutting-edge systems. At the individual level, urbanites tend to own and use smartphones at a higher rate than the rest of the population.[5] Consequently, cities have both a greater concentration of technology and data than other regions and a unique level of human capital for utilizing both. Concurrently, there is a pressing demand for innovations that can advance our understanding of the city. Cities are now home to more than half of the world's population,[6] a proportion that the United Nations anticipates will grow to two-thirds by 2050. Possibly more striking is the rate of growth hidden in these numbers: there is currently a net increase of about 5,000,000 urbanites every month. That is to say, the annual growth in the world's urban population is approximately equal to the populations of New York City,

Shanghai, Delhi, and Tokyo *combined*. This rapid urbanization emphasizes the need for breakthroughs that make cities more manageable, efficient, and sustainable.

The field of urban informatics has arisen in response to this context, with leaders across sectors leveraging modern technology and data to attack the challenges posed by the city. Policymakers have utilized these new resources to improve city services and increase civic engagement. Private companies have turned them into products that purport to increase the efficiency of urban life. Informal "hack" communities are building apps and writing blogs based on these data and tools, sometimes giving rise to start-up companies. Scientists are mining the new data for insights on behavior and society while also proposing and developing new technologies. Even local news outlets, when not recounting the advances made in the other sectors, are using the data to fuel their own investigative reporting. Altogether, these efforts have embodied the argument that cities generate our greatest problems but can also be the source of the necessary solutions.[7]

Urban Informatics and the Pursuit of Cross-Sector Collaborations

The utilization of digital data and technology in cities has already drawn considerable attention. The idea of "smart cities," originally put forward by computing and technology companies in the private sector, such as IBM and Cisco, refers to the development of new technologies that improve the overall efficiency of the city. Stephen Goldsmith and Susan Crawford have reconfigured this into a model for city management in the twenty-first century.[8] "The responsive city," as they dubbed it in their book of the same title, uses data to best target services, solve pressing issues, and make long-term policy decisions. They also emphasize the opportunity to use technology to improve the engagement between constituents and their government. My colleague Anthony Townsend, who has also written a book titled *Smart Cities*,[9] recently described "The New Urban Science" as a loose confederation of interdisciplinary urban research centers, each pursuing a research agenda based in modern digital technology and data and fueled by cutting-edge computational techniques.[10]

I agree with the basic substance of each of these perspectives, but they miss two fundamental points. First, they unnecessarily segregate the private, public, and academic sectors. I instead use the term urban informatics to encompass the efforts of each, as well as the collaborations between them, their distinct but overlapping goals, and the products that result. The term also spans the use of data and technology across numerous domains, from engineering and the physical sciences, to transportation, to public health, to delivery of basic city services, to community organizing. Second, there is a tendency, particularly in the narrative surrounding smart cities, to highlight the emergence of futuristic technologies, such as autonomous vehicles or ubiquitous sensing of environmental conditions, resource usage, and the like, as defining examples of the field. However "sexy" these advances may be, they are largely incipient and are limited to a handful of cities that have the resources to pilot them. I am more interested in the urban informatics projects that, while often less dramatic, can provide everyday value to cities of nearly any size. I highlight these underappreciated aspects of urban informatics—cross-sector collaboration and broadly attainable advances—because they arise from the ongoing proliferation of data and in turn are critical in amplifying the field's overall impact on society.

Constructing Research-Policy Collaborations around Novel Data

Though I have argued that widespread collaboration is fundamental to urban informatics, one might reasonably ask to what extent these synergies across disciplines and sectors are real. Most readers are probably familiar with partnerships that target a single topic, such as those between criminologists and police departments, education researchers and public school districts, or policy schools and social and economic programs, but there are fewer instances of broad-based, cross-disciplinary efforts to bridge the divide between research and policy. The last time this happened in a concerted fashion was in the 1960s, when municipal governments, universities, and foundations organized around the problems facing urban areas, from the complexity of managing infrastructure and services for mass society to the social ills of poverty and segregation. As recounted by Peter Szanton, these relationships eventually collapsed.[11] Now as then, a set of novel challenges created an opportunity and a need for extensive collaboration on research and policy, but a major difference in the current context is the newly available wealth of data.

Modern digital data might include resources that are entirely novel, such as social media posts, as well as others that are just updated versions of data we have had for decades, such as crime reports. Whether new or "old," however, these data offer us an unprecedented first-row seat to the *pulse of the city*—the daily rhythms and annual trends of the places, people, and institutions that constitute an urban area.[12] From this vantage point, we can ask a range of questions that transcend both disciplines and sectors: How do the dimensions of the pulse of the city differ across spaces, from Wall Street, to Main Street, to residential areas? Do they vary with racial or socioeconomic factors, and do they suggest forms of segregation? How do they respond to unexpected events, such as snowstorms, hurricanes, or parades, and when do they return to equilibrium? These and related questions have both substantive and practical implications, making them a natural catalyst for research-policy collaborations.

Logistically, access to the pulse of the city overcomes a major hurdle to cross-sector collaboration. Even when academics and public officials are interested in similar phenomena, they are often trying to answer distinct, albeit overlapping, sets of questions. But extensive data resources can provide a common basis for pursuing these questions conjointly. This is of course true for disciplines that have traditionally engaged in such partnerships, such as criminology, education, and public health, but data availability can also lower the barrier of entry for disciplines with a more theoretical bent, such as sociology. Even more notable has been the way that researchers from disciplines that have not typically had an urban focus, such as computer science, chemistry, and physics, have been attracted by the complexity of the problems and the sophisticated data that make them newly tractable. In this manner, the data themselves are a mechanism for convening across sectors, forming the basis of both a new urban science and a smarter, more responsive government.

Extracting Knowledge from the Pulse of the City

My second concern with existing narratives around urban data and technology is that they often emphasize the futuristic. Lost sight of are the less flashy opportunities that are equally valuable *and* more widely available. Many cities have little capacity to widely distribute sensors or to experiment with autonomous vehicles, but access to the pulse of the city is within reach. The skills required to utilize such data do create some hurdles, but these methodologies are becoming increasingly common. Consequently, there are opportunities right now for cities of all sizes to better understand and serve their communities, and the answers are lurking within data that already exist.

Translating modern digital data into products is not automatic, and it requires a certain amount of creativity. Often exotified for their size, most "big data" are also distinctive in that they are "naturally occurring." This means that, instead of being collected for the specific purpose of generating knowledge, they are the by-product of some administrative operation, social media platform, or other business process. This has important consequences for how they can be incorporated into research. On the plus side, they often capture events and conditions that were rarely accessible to analysts. However, because they were never intended for research, it is not always clear what they are capable of measuring and how they might inform science, policy, or practice. This has given a number of academics pause, particularly in the social sciences,[13] and raises some technical challenges surrounding measurement and validation that I will attend to in Chapter 2. Putting these concerns aside for the moment, the broader point is that it falls to the researchers and policymakers working with these data to imagine and realize how they might be valuable.

Take the example of 311 systems and the hundreds of thousands of requests for nonemergency government services they receive. This book focuses on the window these data provide into custodianship and how urbanites maintain the urban commons, but there are many other ways to use them. I will also touch on collaborations with colleagues in which we have used 311 reports to track patterns of physical disorder and deterioration (i.e., "broken windows") across the city and to evaluate the impacts of technology on civic behavior. Moving beyond the work described in this book, officials in Buffalo, New York, have used their 311 data to better target long-term public works projects.[14] In New York City, one research team used 311 reports to identify pockets of interethnic conflict between neighbors,[15] and another evaluated the effects of stop-and-frisk policing on relations between government and the community.[16] Colleagues of mine in Boston have explored whether and how the system perpetuates existing social and economic inequalities[17] and identified aspects of the tool that can encourage or inhibit certain types of reporting.[18] There are also efforts to determine how the usage of the system relates to more traditional political behaviors, such as voting, something I will discuss at length in Chapter 5 as well.[19] This is to say nothing of the dashboards that use the data to track the performance of basic city services, for example, by measuring how long on average it takes a department to fill a pothole or fix a streetlight outage each month.[20] Together, these individual examples suggest just how valuable a single data set might be. All it takes is some ingenuity, imagination, and a touch of data science.

Building a City-wide Research-Policy Agenda: The Example of Boston

Just as the manner in which a given city leverages a particular data set depends on the interests and concerns of local researchers and policy-makers, the same dynamic is magnified when we think about the broader research-policy agenda of a city. To see this in action, let us take a closer look at the pursuit of urban informatics in Boston. Boston offers a distinctive locale for urban informatics. It has long been famous for its density of high-quality academic institutions and consequent leadership in science and computing. More recently, its public sector has received considerable attention, including some awards, for its efforts to incorporate technology and data into governance.[21] There are also many technology companies that maintain headquarters there, including Google, Microsoft, and the recent arrival of General Electric. For these reasons, it is often ranked as one of the top five "smart cities" nationally, if not #1.[22] Given this rich context for urban informatics, the Boston Area Research Initiative (BARI), which I codirect, has sought to catalyze an interdisciplinary urban research agenda that capitalizes on digital data and technology to advance both science and policy. Its focus has been on convening researchers and public officials in the pursuit of collaborations that address questions with immediate relevance to ongoing questions and issues in Boston while simultaneously expanding our fundamental understanding of urban areas more generally. It also works closely with local educational programs to train the next generation of scholars, policymakers, and practitioners who will further advance the field and its applications.

The work accomplished through BARI's programs has been explicitly interdisciplinary, spanning the academic spectrum, from the measurement of the heat island effect to analyses of census data from the nineteenth century. Additionally, BARI has been distinctive in its effort to apply modern digital data and technology to long-standing questions in the traditional urban disciplines, such as sociology, criminology, and planning. This has aligned closely with the emphasis that the administrations of Mayor Martin J. Walsh and his predecessor, Mayor Thomas M. Menino, have placed on relations between government and community and on the development of innovations that facilitate civic engagement.

The 311 project arose from this merger of digital governance and computational approaches with an interest in civic behavior in neighborhoods. In 2011, the city of Boston's Mayor's Office of New Urban Mechanics (MONUM) received much attention for the success of its 311 system, including the introduction of a smartphone app called Citizens Connect, which offered new channels for requesting government services. It had also just begun to recognize how the data of the system might act as "the eyes and ears" of the city, describing conditions in real time. At about the same time, BARI was founded at the Radcliffe Institute for Advanced Study at Harvard University, in close consultation with MONUM and other city partners. In this context, the 311 system presented itself as an ideal project for demonstrating the potential of collaborations on research and policy; it could offer a new window into the maintenance of urban neighborhoods while also providing guidance for the innovative program seeking to facilitate this maintenance.

311: A Window into the Urban Commons

As already noted, the novel data resources fueling urban informatics were not collected for research purposes, and therefore many scientists view their potential for scholarly analysis with some skepticism. With the proper methodological and theoretical rigor, however, they might provide us with an array of insights on the city, ranging from the practical to the profound. This raises the question: Which aspects of behavior or society will a given data set or program help us to better understand? To answer this question for the case at hand, it would first be useful to give a brief overview of the contents of 311 data.

Boston's 311 system receives about 175,000 requests for service per year. These requests might be for any government service, from a special garbage pickup for discarded furniture, to fixing a pothole, to wanting to know the mayor's birthday (yes, such requests are on record). About half of these requests refer to issues in the public domain, such as streetlight outages, broken sidewalks, and graffiti, reflecting a collaborative arrangement between government services and residents in the maintenance of public spaces and infrastructure. Additionally, Boston is among a subset of cities in which 311 users can create personal accounts that track their cases and have status updates sent to them. In a given year, reports are made through about 50,000 such accounts, from which an analyst can measure and compare the reporting patterns of individual urbanites, including where, when, and how often each makes such reports.

By enabling the analysis of patterns of custodianship at the individual level, the 311 data offer a distinctive opportunity to closely examine the behavioral dynamics underlying the maintenance of public spaces and infrastructure. What motivates individuals to act as custodians? How many individuals actually do so, and how do they differ in their contributions? How does this activity determine a community's overall efficacy in maintaining the space? These and related questions offer novel insights on two main themes, one theoretical, the other practical. The former is the classical question of the commons and how groups maintain shared resources and spaces. The latter regards the operation of *coproduction* programs, which incorporate members of the public into the planning and delivery of government services. Of particular interest, in recent years we have seen the proliferation of "civic technologies," or *civic tech,* that use internet resources to facilitate interaction between governments and the public, highlighting the need to better understand why people choose to participate in such programs.

There are important parallels in the current state of knowledge on the commons and coproduction. Both have paid greater attention to institutional structures and less to the behaviors of the individuals that those institutions manage and serve. Consequently, they have had to employ certain assumptions about these behaviors and their motivations. As we will see, these assumptions are also similar, with work on the commons treating the participation of individuals in such activities as expressions of "cooperation" and the other referring to it as "civicness." These assumptions act as a jumping-off point for the research presented in this book, and the results that follow offer a more nuanced understanding of these two important phenomena.

The Behavioral Dynamics of the Commons

The 311 data capture a task that faces all societies: the maintenance and preservation of shared spaces and resources. Herders have communal pastures, hunter-gatherers have tightly clustered settlements, and modern suburbanites have subdivisions, to name just a few examples, and each is vulnerable to what Garrett Hardin famously referred to as "The Tragedy of the Commons."[23] He argued that despite the community's dependence on the long-term success of the commons, each individual is incentivized to shirk the duties necessary for its upkeep. Consequently, the commons is undermined by free riders, leading to its eventual collapse. Hardin called on scientists to discover and explain when and how groups can avoid this tragedy and successfully manage and maintain a set of shared spaces and resources. The 311 data set, with its detailed description of individual-level actions, offers a novel opportunity to examine the behavioral dynamics by which such maintenance occurs, advancing our general understanding of the commons. In addition to these broader insights, it can help answer allied questions about the operation of urban communities.

The urban commons is noteworthy because the high population density of the city means that residences and businesses are nestled within a continuous commons that affects everyone who lives, works, and plays there. The streets might be either well paved or can be cracked and may act as magnets for loose litter. Sidewalks are shared by all pedestrians and are home to garbage cans, mailboxes, newspaper stands, and trees or flower boxes that promise to organize and decorate but also require attention. There are parks, playgrounds, and other green spaces where members of the community might take their children, play a pickup game, or go for a stroll.

Urban scientists have long studied the maintenance of these various elements (or lack thereof) in terms of physical "disorder," or evidence of neglect or deterioration of spaces. Such work has treated disorder as symptomatic of more serious underlying problems in a community, including crime and poor social connections among neighbors.[24] One extension of this work that has entered popular discourse is "broken windows" theory, which argues that disorder leads to crime.[25] A closely related area of research that has also been highly influential among researchers and policymakers alike has focused on a neighborhood's *collective efficacy,* or its ability to accomplish shared goals.[26] This literature has focused largely on how a community establishes and enforces social norms, a capacity that can limit violations of all sorts, from violent crime to more basic infractions such as the denigration of public spaces. Following each of these lines of work, the maintenance of the urban commons is a valuable test case for a more general understanding of a community's inner workings.

A city's 311 database allows us to observe directly how the members of a community contribute to the maintenance of the urban commons. Not only does it track discrete actions, but also user accounts capture the habits of individuals, revealing the behavioral dynamics that underlie this maintenance. These dynamics are little understood, not only for the urban commons but also for commons more generally, because much of the work in this space has centered on the institutional arrangements that can motivate or coerce individuals to act in the interests of the broader public. Early research in this area emphasized privatization and regulation, but work in recent years has been driven by Nobel laureate Elinor Ostrom and her colleagues' assertion that local groups develop institutions that are uniquely tailored to the parameters of the local context without the need for formal intervention.[27] In the case of the urban commons, we might consider collective efficacy one of these local informal "institutions."

In the absence of knowledge about the individuals that commons institutions must manage and rely on, most commons research operates off of a relatively simple behavioral model that divides a population into two types of actors: "cooperators," who contribute to the public good, and "free riders," who do not. The long-term success of the commons is then a function of the ratio of cooperators to free riders. This sort of model is useful for making a complex problem more tractable, and in that regard it has been effective in facilitating a rich body of literature on commons institutions. Nonetheless, it would seem that the actual behavioral dynamics of commons maintenance entail considerably more nuance. In parallel, research in urban neighborhoods has revealed much about the variables that predict a community's level of collective efficacy—things such as affluence, higher rates of home ownership, and social ties within the community[28]—but far less about how it emerges from the actions and interactions of individual community members.

How and Why People Maintain the Commons

In this book, I will use the 311 database to advance our understanding of the contributions that individuals make to the commons through two interlocking themes: the motivations for custodianship and how custodians combine in the comprehensive maintenance of the commons. For each, I probe a set of assumptions that have been baked into institution-level studies. Taking the question of motivation first, there is reason to believe that custodianship cannot be reduced to a generalized concept of cooperation. Social and environmental psychologists have actually found that actions that prevent and eliminate disorder are rooted in our evolved capacity for *territoriality;* that is, to claim ownership and responsibility for a place or object.[29] Though the term territoriality is most often associated with work by biologists on how animals claim and defend spaces,[30] researchers have noted that humans exhibit "territorial" behaviors that go beyond defense or exclusion by also encompassing caretaking and personalization.[31] In urban neighborhoods, for example, one might observe various manifestations of territoriality, including fences, "No Trespassing" signs, holiday decorations, and the basic fulfillment of household maintenance.[32] Based on this logic, I put forward the *territorial thesis* of public maintenance, positing that the commons depends on our innate capacity to adopt and care for spaces, a premise that can be tested directly by using the 311 database.

Second, a major concern is how the actions of individual community members determine the overall condition of the commons. Traditional models calculate the condition of the commons as a function of the proportion of "cooperators" in a population. Classifying individuals in such a simple manner, however, ignores the possibility that there might be multiple ways to participate in maintenance. The urban commons, for instance, presents a variety of different tasks. Its topography is a patchwork of residential, industrial, commercial, and institutional spaces, each of which individuals might approach differently. In addition, 311 recognizes dozens of case types, from graffiti, to broken sidewalks, to pest infestations, and an individual might feel a special motivation to report some types of issues over others. This raises the possibility of a *division of labor,* in which there are multiple types of actors, each prioritizing certain tasks. In turn, their combined efforts are necessary for the overarching job of maintaining the commons. As we leverage the 311 database to analyze this premise in the urban commons, the result will be a model for considering the diversity of tasks and actors in other societies, as well as for the emergence of collective efficacy in the pursuit of a shared task.

The Coproduction of Government Services

The 311 system sits at the intersection of two lines of thought surrounding the administration of public services. The first, and more recent, is civic technologies (or *civic tech*), which use modern information and communication systems to bring government and its operations closer to the public. The second is the philosophy of *coproduction,* which seeks to incorporate the public into the governance process. Coincidentally (or not), coproduction was also originally championed by Elinor Ostrom and her colleagues in the 1970s.[33] Ostrom herself perhaps best described coproduction as "one way that synergy between what a government does and what citizens do can occur."[34] In other words, coproduction programs create a collaboration between government services and the public. Though 311 is probably the most prominent coproduction program that is powered by civic tech, it is joined by a number of other examples, including online public deliberation and participatory budgeting. As such, it gives us an opportunity to examine the operation of coproduction programs in general, which in turn will help us to consider the potential and limitations for civic tech in this space.

As with any collaboration, the success of a coproduction program requires that all parties fulfill their stated role. Thus, a critical question for such efforts is the extent to which members of the public actually participate. Analogous to existing research on the commons, most work on this question has focused on how institutions can design or manage programs to better elicit participation, for example by providing resources that are more accessible or of higher quality.[35] Much less is known, however, about the motivations that underlie such participation. Also similar to commons research, it is assumed that participation in a coproduction program is motivated by attention to the well-being of others or to the greater good. In place of "cooperation," however, proponents of coproduction treat such participation as an overtly civic or political action. It follows that such behavior is motivated by a *civic disposition* that is manifested in a broader pattern of political participation, including acts such as voting, contacting elected officials, and donating to campaigns. This perspective has given rise to a popular metaphor that casts coproduction programs as a "bridge to citizenship," by which participation will entrain and encourage involvement in civic life.[36] Borrowing from this framing and its understanding of how members of the public engage with coproduction programs, we might refer to it as the *public-as-citizen* model.

The public-as-citizen model takes a rather narrow view of human psychology. We are endowed with an array of motivations that includes but extends far beyond a capacity for civicness. Borrowing from the psychological concept of modularity, each of these motivations is oriented toward particular goals or tasks, meaning they are responsive to relevant cues and contexts, and manifest themselves in specific types of behaviors.[37] It would seem reasonable that a given coproduction program might appeal to any one of our motivations, provided its activities evoked the appropriate cues or called on its associated behaviors. This perspective fits well with the modern philosophy of "new public governance," which emphasizes collaboration across agencies and sectors.[38] These collaborations are not necessarily based on civicness or any organization-level analog thereof but rather on the facets and capacities that each entity brings to the table. Building on this, I propose a more expansive perspective that we might call the *public-as-partner* model, which takes a comprehensive approach to the motivations that lead individuals to participate in coproduction.

The public-as-partner model asks us to reconceptualize how coproduction programs operate. Instead of acting as a "bridge to citizenship," it appears more likely that they are levers that speak to specific motivations and translate them into enhanced public services. In turn, this raises two empirical questions. First, it is possible that each program might rely on its own particular set of motivations, depending on the nature of participation it requires. This would call for a program-by-program approach for implementation, evaluation, and promotion. Second, it invites a reexamination of the importance of a civic disposition to coproduction and whether this varies across types of programs. Returning to 311, we see that the coproduction literature and the commons literature have converged on the same question: What would motivate a constituent to identify an issue in the public domain that needs attention, be it a streetlight outage, pothole, or graffito, and report it to the government? I have already argued that the answer to this question is "territoriality," but most research on 311 to date conducted by social scientists has assumed that 311 reports are a proxy for other forms of political participation or civic engagement, such as voting.[39] The studies in this book will not only test the territoriality thesis but will also take the second step of comparing it directly with this alternative perspective, assessing and integrating the two under the public-as-partner model.

Summary

The studies that follow capitalize on the 311 database as a window onto the behavioral dynamics not only of the commons but also of coproduction programs, testing three scholarly theories: first, the territoriality thesis of public maintenance, which argues that the custodianship of the urban commons captured in 311 reports is rooted in a human capacity to identify with and claim spaces; second, a division-of-labor approach both to the commons and to collective efficacy, which posits that multiple types of actors contribute to shared tasks in different ways and therefore are each necessary to their overall realization; and finally, the public-as-partner model of coproduction, which proposes that the motivations for coproduction will be program-specific, going beyond a generalized civic disposition. These three lines of inquiry illustrate the dual opportunity of urban informatics. While they provide a deeper understanding of the city and of human behavior and society more generally, they also offer insights for the implementation, management, and promotion of 311 systems and other civic tech. How does a city most effectively advertise 311? How does a public official interpret differences in adoption across communities? What are the best ways to support communities that appear to be lacking in custodianship? Throughout this book, we will see how the empirical analysis of the theoretical models posed here offers a grounding for addressing these sorts of practical questions.

Overview of the Book

This book treats the 311 project on three distinct but intertwined levels that combine to tell the story of the emerging field of urban informatics. At the most basic level, it describes a research-policy agenda centered on custodianship in the urban commons, probing the reasons why members of the public contribute to the maintenance of shared spaces, and how coproduction programs operate. In keeping with urban informatics' basis in modern digital data and technology, it has leveraged the database generated by a technological policy innovation both to deepen our understanding of the city and to motivate innovative solutions to the challenges of managing urban areas. Second, as BARI's first and longest-running project, the study of the 311 system embodies the robustly collaborative vision for urban science and policy that we argue is necessary to realize a comprehensive research-policy agenda. Throughout the book, we will encounter researchers, policymakers, and practitioners, all of whom contribute to and gain from the work in their own way. At a third level, BARI is itself a model for urban informatics, and the collaborations surrounding the project reveal and engage broader themes facing the field, including not only how such projects come to fruition but also concerns about how evenly their benefits are distributed across society.

The book describes this work in four parts, which I summarize here in order to facilitate the navigation of the book by the range of researchers, students, and public, private, and nonprofit professionals interested in urban informatics, the urban commons, and related issues. In doing so, I alert readers to chapters that are heavier on theory or methodology so they might focus their attention on the content most relevant to their interests. In addition, within each chapter, I flag denser material and provide less technical summaries of each such section.

Part I (Chapters 1 and 2) presents a deeper introduction to the field of urban informatics and the challenges it faces, as well as its embodiment in BARI's 311 project. Chapter 1 summarizes the intellectual and societal underpinnings of the field and how they are manifested in the growing popularity of 311 systems. Chapter 2 then attends to a fundamental issue facing urban informatics: How do we leverage novel digital data for research, policy, and practice in such a way that we are confident in our interpretation of the knowledge they offer? In response to this question, I propose a methodology that leverages 311 reports as the "eyes and ears of the city" to track physical disorder, or "broken windows," across neighborhoods. The chapter uses the overarching conceptual challenges posed by big data to frame the methodology needed to address them.

Part II (Chapters 3 and 4) builds on the lessons of Part I to pursue the topic of custodianship in the urban commons. This portion of the book is the heaviest on behavioral and social theory. Chapter 3 presents the concept of the commons and then articulates how we might measure custodianship through 311 reports and test the territoriality thesis. This last step entails merging the "big data" from the 311 system with the "small data" provided by a survey of 311 users. Chapter 4 then examines the intersection between individual-level behaviors and group-level outcomes, assessing how the combined custodianship of individual residents determines the overall maintenance of the urban commons. This chapter introduces and tests the division-of-labor model of the commons and collective efficacy, identifying multiple types of actors and examining their distinct contributions to the neighborhood.

Part III (Chapters 5 and 6) transitions from what we can learn theoretically about the city to what such insights can gain us through their application to policy and practice. Building on Part II's discoveries around why and how people take care of public spaces, we can provide guidelines for 311 systems and civic tech more generally. Chapter 5 acts as the theoretical bridge, contrasting the public-as-citizen and public-as-partner models of participation in coproduction programs and then testing them empirically by merging the 311 reports and surveys. Chapter 6 then uses this framework to develop and evaluate three public experiments in the implementation of 311, with an eye toward the practical value offered by the discoveries in previous chapters. This includes an examination of the original Boston 311 experiment and an exemplar of civic tech, the smartphone application Citizens Connect (now BOS:311), that enables users to submit pictures and textual descriptions of issues.

Part IV (Chapters 7 and 8) uses 311 and associated programs as a vehicle for exposing a major challenge facing urban informatics: the emergence of multiple digital divides in the use and value of digital data and technology. Chapter 7 takes up the first of these, which lies between the large, well-funded metropolises at the forefront of the field and the smaller, less-resourced cities that most Americans call home. A case study of Commonwealth Connect, a program that subsidizes the creation of 311-like operations in municipalities throughout the Commonwealth of Massachusetts, reveals the hurdles that await efforts to transfer technological innovations across municipalities. Chapter 8 probes a second type of divide that plagues urban informatics. The focus of the field has been on collaborations between cities and universities, but the data are generated by the public, which has little expertise or capacity to use them. This chapter explores what a city-university-community model might look like, with an emphasis on how to empower community organizations to leverage modern digital data. This is made possible by a survey with representatives from such organizations.

The final chapter of the book forecasts the future of the urban commons, both in terms of the literal one that is managed by 311 and related programs and the more abstract one that underlies the civic data ecosystem. In this manner, it is also an opportunity to take stock of the field itself and how it might evolve in the coming years.

PART I

The Field of Urban Informatics

CHAPTER 1

A Data-Driven Approach
to Urban Science and Policy

IN 1996, BALTIMORE, MARYLAND, introduced the first 311 hotline.[1] It arrived with little fanfare or anticipation of its future influence. Rather, the goal was to solve a relatively mundane practical issue. Inner-city Baltimore was suffering from high levels of crime and blight, and the city was receiving enough reports for shooting and other serious events that calls about "nuisances," such as graffiti, abandoned buildings, and other issues of deterioration, were themselves seen as a nuisance. The 311 hotline was thus born of a need to triage 911 calls that did not qualify as emergencies.

It was not until a decade later that the advent of digital technology made apparent an additional advantage of 311: Equipped with the information from resident reports, operations departments could generate automated work-order queues that guided the daily deployment of resources. This enhanced the value of 311 systems for major metropolises, but it also raised the possibility that they could make government services more effective and efficient for municipalities of *any* size. As a result, 311 hotlines and allied programs are now in place in over 400 American municipalities in 40 states and counting, spanning the geographic and demographic range of the country.[2] Since then, 311 systems have become a de facto symbol for the field of urban informatics. They have inspired blog posts and magazine articles, including the widely distributed *Wired* essay "What 100 Million Calls for Service Can Tell Us about New York City."[3] Publications focused on governance have either trumpeted the benefits of 311 outright or coyly posed questions such as, "Is the cost of 311 systems worth the price of knowing?" (coming to the eventual conclusion that, "Yes, they are.").[4] They have stimulated research projects, including our flagship project at the Boston Area Research Initiative (BARI), which forms the main content of this book and has given rise to methodological and philosophical approaches that guide much of our other work.

The 311 systems have proliferated quickly, but, given that there are plenty of other technological innovations in cities that merit attention, why have they become so emblematic of urban informatics? I would argue that it is because, in addition to their widespread popularity, 311 systems embody each of five major themes whose convergence characterizes the field. The first two themes form the *bases of the field:* (1) the innovative use of novel data resources and (2) the utilization of crowdsourcing and sensor technologies that provide a detailed view of patterns and conditions across the city. Their value has been amplified by (3) widespread data sharing, or, in its most extreme case, "open data." This has been a critical mechanism for supporting a *civic data ecosystem* in which individuals and institutions from a range of disciplines and sectors can pursue and collaborate on questions of common interest. Finally, these collaborations have been channeled into two main, and often complementary, *products of the field,* which constitute the fourth and fifth themes: (4) technocratic policy innovations that improve the efficiency and effectiveness of city services, and (5) the scientific pursuit of a deeper understanding of the city and its people, places, and systems. Importantly, this view highlights two lessons that are often overlooked, especially by "smart cities" narratives. First, the products of modern data and technology need not be immensely expensive or flashy to be both informative and useful. Second, cross-sector collaborations are critical in generating these products.

Part II of this book presents an overview of the field of urban informatics, using 311 to illustrate how modern digital data can catalyze cross-sector research that generates both new knowledge and public value. This first chapter articulates and details the five main themes of the field, describing how 311 reflects each. In addition, because urban informatics is a young field and thus still relatively small, it is possible for me to summarize in this chapter many of the primary research programs that compose it. I do not provide a stand-alone list of these programs but instead describe various examples throughout the chapter in order to capture the five themes in action while also giving the reader a sense of the range of models for this work.[5] I will go into some depth on BARI, discussing why 311 has acted as the jumping-off point for us. Whereas the current chapter emphasizes the inspiration and potential of the field, Chapter 2 will follow with a more critical assessment of how one properly conducts research with the novel digital data resources that form the bases of urban informatics, again using 311 to demonstrate both the challenges and the possibilities.

The Bases of Urban Informatics

New Technology, New Data

At its foundation, urban informatics has emerged from recent advances in digital data and technology. These resources have generated new information that I divide into two forms for the purpose of presentation: enhanced forms of old information, and novel information produced by new technologies. In the first, the digitization of many administrative processes that previously existed only on paper has given rise to numerous data sets that capture the patterns of the city in intricate detail. This is occurring across the public, private, and nonprofit sectors, with examples ranging from credit card purchases, to rides on public transit, to entries to community centers; the tracking of energy and water usage to yearly vehicle inspections; the marriage registry, business licenses, building permits, tax assessments, and restaurant inspections; and, of course, requests for public services through 311 systems. This list is far from exhaustive, but it gives a sense of the diverse range of data generated by the individuals and institutions of the city. All told, their digitization makes newly accessible a wealth of information on the behaviors, movements, social interactions, commerce and industry, and physical and environmental conditions of the city.

As digitization increases the potential utility of administrative records, two other technologies are generating entirely new kinds of information. The first of these technologies builds off of social media and other internet sites and applications that gather user-generated content, also known as Web 2.0. The content shared with these platforms—Yelp! reviews, Picasa pictures, YouTube videos, exercise and sleep activity from FitBit bracelets, "tweets" through Twitter—are data that one might organize, map, analyze, and interpret. A subset of Web 2.0 applications also supports direct communication between a client and a service provider, be it private or public, capturing every transaction as a data record. This capacity has taken hold in 311 as well. Boston introduced Citizens Connect (now BOS:311) in 2008 as an early effort to introduce a smartphone app for a municipal 311 system, leveraging the internet and smartphones as an additional channel for constituents to request government services. Other cities have since followed suit.

The second technological advance of note is the proliferation of sensors. Some examples include GPS trackers for geographic mobility patterns; accelerometers that detect different types of physical movement; and sensors that record the density of pollutants in air and water, ambient temperature, light intensity, precipitation, noise levels, or physical vibrations. Some "sensors" we might not even think of as such. For example, wi-fi hot spots can be used to estimate pedestrian traffic by counting the number of devices that engage them. New image-processing programs translate footage from security cameras into estimates of pedestrian, bicycle, car, and truck volume through a space. Many cities have also deployed "shot spotters" that detect the sound profile of gunshots. These are just a few examples, but they serve to illustrate the broad potential of sensor technologies.

A Composite View of the City

The knowledge derived from modern administrative data, sensor technologies, and Web 2.0 applications evokes an approach to measurement that combines many narrow observations to build a comprehensive view of the world. This is not an entirely novel concept—for example, Sampson, Raudenbush, and Earls developed a methodology in which they surveyed thousands of Chicagoans about their neighborhood to create robust measures of physical and social conditions across the city—but its scale and generality in urban informatics is distinctive.[6] In the case of sensor technologies, a city or research center might deploy a set of units that track local conditions in real time. Each observes only a small slice of the world, but their composite provides detailed coverage across space. For example, the University of Chicago's Urban Center for Computation and Data, which I will discuss further in the next section, is deploying a system of sensors called the Array of Things in Chicago. The sensors track localized environmental and atmospheric conditions and activity, and the overall system is billed as a "fitness tracker for the city."[7]

In Web 2.0, human users provide the individual pieces of information. This process is referred to as crowdsourcing, a term that has entered common parlance through efforts such as Wikipedia, where the many members of the "crowd" collectively contribute to knowledge. At the intersection of crowdsourcing and sensor technologies is citizen sensing, in which members of the public are either an active or a passive vehicle for observing and recording events and conditions. At the most passive, cell phone records register the location and activity of a user every time the user engages with a cell tower. On the other end of this spectrum, in one project bus drivers voluntarily carried GPS trackers in an effort to identify the unofficial "routes" of Nairobi's informal transit system.[8]

Administrative records offer a third way to gain a composite view of the city. At times, these may be classified as citizen sensing, as the information is provided by constituents submitting forms or requests. For example, one might argue that 311 encourages residents to act as "the eyes and ears of the city." In turn, it crowdsources a constantly updating map of the potholes, streetlight outages, and downed trees that need attention. Other administrative data, such as tax assessments, are generated through internally directed processes. Whether they arise from citizen sensing or not, administrative processes, just like sensors, generate thousands or even millions of records, each describing a discrete event or condition at a specific place and time. In turn, their corpus can be aggregated to describe localized patterns.

The intertwined trends of (1) the emergence of novel data resources and (2) crowdsourcing and sensor technologies have provided a new view on the city. First, the data are diverse in their content, often capturing types of information that have never before been available. They are also endowed with unprecedented spatial and temporal precision, permitting extensive flexibility in their analysis and communication. Consequently, they are not limited to the sorts of annual indicators that are characteristic of traditional data sources—things like median income, ethnic composition, and rates of crime, poverty, and disease. Instead, they offer a window into the *pulse of the city*, or the daily rhythms and long-term trends of the places, people, and institutions that constitute an urban area.

Exposing the pulse of the city for observation, analysis, and interpretation has been a guiding inspiration for some of the oldest efforts in urban informatics. The term itself was originally coined by British planner Michael Batty in an essay of the same name.[9] Batty might be considered one of the founding fathers of urban informatics, having led the Bartlett Centre for Advanced Spatial Analysis (CASA) at University College London since its inception in 1995. It was ahead of its time, leveraging cutting-edge analytic and visualization tools to study and inform urban design and planning at a time when computer-based mapping was a brand-new technology. To this day, CASA remains at the forefront of the field, implementing advances in both methodology and theory, with a particular emphasis on complexity.

Another early leader in revealing the pulse of the city was Massachusetts Institute of Technology's (MIT) Senseable Cities Lab (Senseable), founded by Carlo Ratti. As its name implies, Senseable has been notable for its pioneering use of sensor technologies and citizen sensing to illustrate the patterns of the city. Ratti is an architect by training, and he and his team often demonstrate their scientific insights through captivating visualizations and interactive displays that are regularly featured in museums and galleries. Notably, neither CASA nor Senseable have centered their work on a single region, reflecting an interest in urban science defined broadly rather than an in-depth effort to study a single city. As we will see in the next section, this contrasts with some of the models that have emerged in recent years.

The Pulse of the City: Toward a Computational Urban Science

On the one hand, being able to access the pulse of the city would appear to hold much promise. On the other hand, because it is literally the daily patterns we each know and experience laid bare, initial work centered on it can sometimes seem obvious. I think of an article written by members of Senseable that I teach each year that shows that cell phone data usage in business districts in Hong Kong, London, and New York City differs markedly from that of residential neighborhoods in the same city across weekday, weeknight, and weekend hours, capturing the familiar shifts in activity between work and home.[10] A common reaction among the students is, "Well, of course." Indeed, we know that most people start weekdays at home, head into work, and then come home in the evening, with an extended respite on Saturdays and Sundays. It is by no means revolutionary to discover that the geographical locus of their cell phone usage reflects this rhythm.

As reasonable as the students' skepticism might be, a devil's advocate might retort: "Have you ever seen this information represented with such empirical precision?" The value of the work lies not in a fundamental discovery about the city but instead in its novel methodology and the future discoveries it promises. Instrumentation and recordings are the basis of science and its fundamental goal of building a cumulative, organized body of knowledge. Take the example of the movements of the celestial bodies. Humans surely have been paying attention to and attributing meaning to them for tens of thousands of years. Some of these rhythms are clearly visible to the naked eye: over the course of about 28 days, a full moon will gradually wane until it vanishes completely, only to wax anew; day length peaks at the beginning of the warmest period of the year and is at its shortest at the beginning of the winter. The comprehension of more complex phenomena, however, requires detailed record keeping. Johannes Kepler, for example, used extensive charts on the movements of the skies to represent the orbits of the planets with formal mathematical equations, forming the basis of our understanding of the mechanics of the solar system. In turn, these equations have since been critical to everything from space travel to the inference that there is an unseen Planet X lurking beyond Pluto.[11] Similar breakthroughs in observation are visible in myriad domains of science. Microscopy opened up the world of cells and the study of the building blocks of life. Atomic spectroscopy permitted the identification of the representation of atoms of different elements, allowing chemists to directly observe the composition of molecules. The identification of DNA and the elements of its code has given rise to the fields of genomics and genetic engineering. The list goes on, but in each case, the ability to observe and record a particular phenomenon opens up a whole new area of inquiry.

David Lazer and his colleagues have argued that the instrumentation of society with sensors and other digitized processes will be similarly revolutionary, giving rise to a computational social science that reaches across subdisciplines, including urban science.[12] Thus, knowing that cell phone usage is greater in business districts on weekdays between the hours of 9 am and 5 pm is just the tip of the iceberg. It is simply a validation exercise demonstrating that such patterns are indeed visible through cell phone records. What lies beneath these seemingly mundane observations is the ability to query the data to answer any number of more complicated questions. Do these patterns change during a rainy day, a snowstorm, a parade, or the aftermath of a terrorist attack? Does the profile of usage in a particular region of a city portend future events, such as the emergence of a new industry, the collapse of an existing one, or the gentrification of a neighborhood? The patterns might be disaggregated to the person level as well, permitting us to ask questions about individual differences in movement and communication. For example, are they different depending on a person's socioeconomic status or the industry she works in? What proportion of people does not follow the daily routine of morning-workday-evening or has no discernible rhythm at all? Where are people with these irregular patterns most concentrated? In sum, by recording the pulse of the city in intricate detail, digital technologies and data create an opportunity to know not only how it looks and operates today but also to predict and manage how it might evolve tomorrow.

Emerging in the earliest days of urban informatics, work by CASA and Senseable has not only exposed the pulse of the city but also demonstrated the potential knowledge and utility it might provide. The work of CASA pays special attention to the complexity and consequences of urban form. For example, it has used historical street maps to model how streets appear, lengthen, or become segmented over time.[13] It has also analyzed how urban form can influence energy efficiency, offering implications for the relationship between urbanization and climate change.[14] Senseable has lived up to its name through a variety of projects, including deploying GPS trackers in trash items to uncover major inefficiencies in how they are transported through the sanitation system.[15] It has also used a year of taxi rides in New York City to identify routes used commonly enough to justify ride-sharing programs.[16] In a project called Underworlds, it has placed sensors in the sewer system in hopes of detecting disease and infection at early stages with fine geographical precision. Altogether, these projects constitute first steps toward a computational urban science, or, as we now know it, urban informatics.

311 and the Pulse of the City

The 311 system offers a composite view of certain urban dynamics and, in turn, access to a slice of the pulse of the city. Hundreds of requests for service stream into the system daily, capturing the needs of communities in real time (as can be seen in the YouTube video at https://www.youtube .com/watch?v=MqEXDzlCltw, which animates all reports received over the course of 2011).[17] We might limit attention to the requests that reference issues with public infrastructure or other questions of maintenance and upkeep in order to observe physical conditions across the urban landscape. When considering the actions of the requesters themselves, the data reveal patterns of custodianship for individuals and communities. The *Wired* essay about 100 million calls for service in New York City exposed two elements of the pulse of the city, showing that requests are more frequent in densely populated areas and between the hours of 10 am and 4 pm, except for noise complaints, which balloon during the overnight hours. Going further, Figure 1 illustrates a series of other relatively obvious observations that my colleagues and I have observed in Boston, such as the burst in requests in February, driven largely by snowstorms, or the dropoff in reporting over weekends. There are also observations that are less obvious but intuitive, such as increases in reports of potholes in March when the snow melts, revealing the damage the winter has wrought on streets and sidewalks. We can also see deviations in the pulse of the city that are the signature of abnormal events, such as the nearly complete absence of reports on the Monday of the Marathon bombing and on the following Friday, when Governor Duval Patrick placed the region on lockdown during the manhunt for the bombers, or the dramatic spike in tree maintenance requests after Hurricane Irene we saw in the Introduction.

That said, there remain some unaddressed methodological issues regarding the interpretation of different case types (e.g., does a request for a special trash pickup for furniture contain the same meaning as one for removal of graffiti?) and whether the volume of calls reflects the density of issues across the city or the density of individuals who choose to report them. Such concerns exist for all of these novel data sets and will be examined more closely in Chapter 2. For the moment, the point is simply that 311, like many of the other newly available data sources, uses the actions of urbanites to crowdsource the localized needs and conditions, thereby providing one vantage point on the pulse of the city.

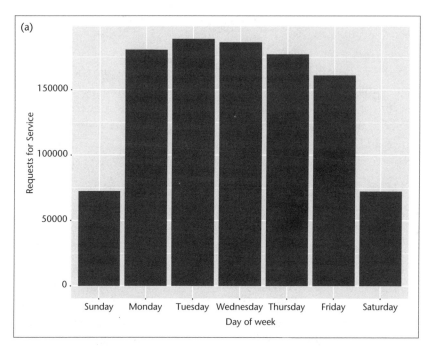

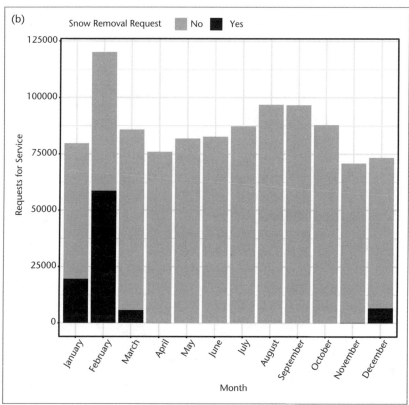

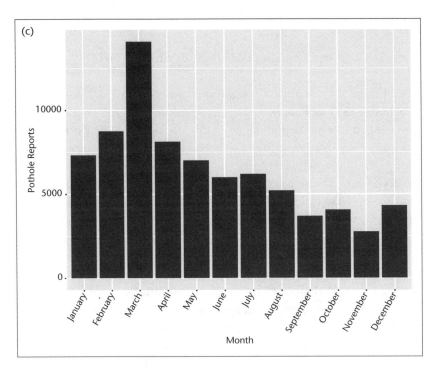

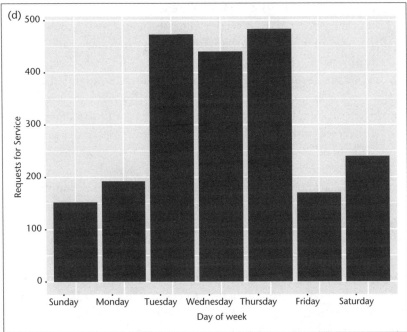

FIGURE 1.1 The pulse of the city of Boston as seen through 311 reports, including (a) differences in reporting volume on weekdays and weekends, (b) the increase in 311 activity in February thanks to snow removal requests, (c) the spike in pothole requests in March, and (d) the sharp drop in requests during the Marathon bombings (Monday) and the ensuing manhunt (Friday).

Data Sharing and Collaboration: Catalyzing the Field

"Open data" has become a buzz term and even part of the common vernacular in recent years. Generally speaking, it refers to data that a government has made publicly available, though in reality it can come from any organization willing to share data with few or no restrictions for access. One might attribute the movement toward open data to a variety of actors. There are activist groups, such as the Sunlight Foundation, that have called for the release of data as part of a broader push for government transparency. Such groups argue that these data belong to the public and that Freedom of Information Act requests create an unnecessary burden for access when it would be just as easy for the government to upload the data for all to see.[18] For its part, government has become more than just a reluctant follower in this trend, recognizing that valuable insights and tools might arise if the broader community of analysts and "hackers" gain access to these data. Private companies, such as Socrata, have also seen a market opportunity, building software for platforms that specialize in hosting data and documentation. In this manner, open data has come to offer potential benefits across sectors.

Like other aspects of the digital revolution, open data is a societal shift that has been magnified in urban areas. Many cities have passed "open data ordinances" that require departments to publish their data in machine-readable formats (i.e., spreadsheets that can be analyzed). In New York City, for example, part of the IT budget for every department is contingent on compliance with this dictum. A large number of cities have also contracted with Socrata or other vendors to implement platforms that facilitate public access to the data. "Hackathons," or whole-day events in which analysts compete to create the most compelling analyses, visualizations, and tools based on open data, are now commonplace. Indeed, 311 requests are often one of the first data sets to be released on a city's open data platform, as they were in Boston.

Though open data receives the bulk of attention, it is actually just one part of a broader trend toward data sharing, motivated largely by the potential for collaboration. Indeed, many municipal open data ordinances are as much about sharing data between departments—to better inform and integrate management across city operations—as they are about sharing data with the public. This was the explicit intent behind the ordinances of New York and Boston, the former resulting in the centralized

DataBridge, which gathers and coordinates the data from the city's many agencies and departments. Cities have also embraced data sharing across institutions and sectors in order to support projects that are either more targeted than the crowdsourced approach of a hackathon or require data sets that are too sensitive to publish through an open data platform. This was the case for an effort in Massachusetts that has lowered the legal hurdles to access for researchers to health and human services data regarding the opioid crisis in the hope of stimulating new innovations in prevention and treatment. When such cross-sector collaborations are built on a shared investment in transforming the data into insights and tools, they promise mutual benefits, and because the data in question are often updated regularly, they open the door for a sustained relationship between the collaborators, which has become a major mechanism for driving successful urban informatics projects.

From Data Sharing to Partnerships

To better understand how digital data sharing can catalyze research-policy collaborations, let us imagine a lunch meeting between an academic and policymaker during which they discover a number of common interests. As they begin to plan a study, the academic says something like, "I'll need to find funding for a graduate student. We need to write and validate a survey, and then to administer the survey and organize and analyze the data. This will all take about three years." The policy-maker might respond with some version of, "Thanks for thinking this through, but I have a newspaper headline from yesterday that needs my attention, so I'm not sure this works on my timeline." Clearly, this is a caricature, but the point stands: talks break down as a result of different institutional incentives and timelines.

Now consider how the conversation changes with the advent of large-scale digital administrative data. The academic might instead say, "You have 300,000 calls for service in that database. Give me and my graduate student a month or so; we'll do some first-cut analyses and write you a memo. We can then regroup and figure out the next steps." Suddenly, a project that produces information of common interest while *also* fitting the timelines of both parties becomes possible. These origins lead to a project with a form that is distinct from the one-off projects that often characterize research-policy collaborations. Though not a hard rule, traditional models for collaborations between academics and policymakers take one of two forms: either a researcher requests data from an agency to write a paper, or the agency contracts with a researcher to conduct a particular analysis, often a program evaluation. Even when successful, such arrangements typically do not lead to a sustained relationship. Rather, the form of collaboration I describe here entails an iterative process in which the answers to the initial questions inspire the next phase of work. Put somewhat glibly, urban informatics is driven by "partnerships not projects."

My primary focus here and throughout the book is on partnerships between cities and universities, but the same dynamic might easily involve any combination of participants, including public agencies, nonprofits, private companies, and university researchers. In addition, public agencies need not be the source of data in every case, being that each of these entities generates data. Whatever the specific nature of the project and the roles of the participating parties, digital data sharing creates the potential for a sustained partnership that grows and evolves with each new question, discovery, and innovation. Furthermore, it means that there may be multiple overlapping partnerships going on in a given city at any time, creating a network of data sharing and collaboration that is greater than the sum of its parts. This might be referred to as the *civic data ecosystem*.

The Civic Data Ecosystem

To ground the term "civic data ecosystem" more formally, let us use a relatively standard definition of the word *ecosystem* from biology: the species of organisms that inhabit a space, the physical characteristics of that space, and the interactions among them. In the current case, the space in question is not so much a physical one as it is an informational one, and the fundamental resources, much like sunlight and water for a forest, are data and data-generating technologies. In place of "species of organisms," there are different types of institutions—public, private, nonprofit, and academic—each of which contributes to the ecosystem in a characteristic way. Some generate greater amounts of data, others are particularly skilled in data management and analysis, while others are best positioned to interpret and communicate findings. Activities and interactions across these institutions then determine the products that emerge: the insights gained, the technologies advanced, the solutions proposed.

And, just as biologists recognize that organisms regularly alter the physical environment of their ecosystem, the products of these institutions will continue to shape the informational context and the activities that might thrive within it.[19]

Casting urban informatics work as occurring within and through a data ecosystem presents a distinctive view of the field. Most importantly, it highlights collaboration as the primary mechanism for translating data into products. Without collaboration, everyone is simply analyzing their own data for their own isolated purposes, creating a collection of narrow insights that do not necessarily intersect. By extension, as the teams undertaking these collaborations become increasingly inclusive, so do the products, often answering questions that are at once relevant to scholars, policymakers, and the public. Partners might even work on projects that intentionally construct and evolve the ecosystem itself; for example, cohosting workshops or hackathons can initiate desired projects, but they also support further community building. It is in acknowledgment of this spirit of collective effort and public-minded data science that I refer to this not only as the data ecosystem but also as the *civic* data ecosystem of the city, and why this might be thought of as the second urban commons in this book.

The efforts of three urban informatics programs—New York University's Center for Urban Science and Progress (CUSP), the University of Chicago's Urban Center for Computation and Data (CCD), and Northeastern and Harvard Universities' Boston Area Research Initiative (BARI)—have embodied the civic data ecosystem mindset. In each case, an academic institution has partnered closely with an active and forward-thinking city government to gain a comprehensive understanding of that city and to develop innovative solutions to its challenges. A major component of these partnerships between city and university is the amassment and integration of data from diverse sources, in turn constructing an extensive resource that might support any number of projects. Additionally, the university partner in each case has launched an educational program in urban informatics to train a new generation of scholars and public servants who are experts in the skills and concepts that constitute the field.

In New York, for example, CUSP has aligned itself closely with the Mayor's Office for Data Analytics (MODA), managing a parallel feed of the city's DataBridge and cosponsoring a number of fellowships, with students working for MODA and city employees studying at CUSP. Urban

CCD has worked with the city of Chicago on a range of projects, including the development of predictive analytic models that forecast events of major interest, from shootings to rat infestations, and the development and deployment of the Array of Things sensor system. The BARI program is similar to NYU CUSP and Urban CCD in structure and purpose but is distinctive in being an interuniversity effort that convenes faculty from the region's many institutions of higher learning. This creates an even more extensive and diverse network of collaboration.

It is worth noting that the number of centers that seek to catalyze urban informatics work within a single city has grown considerably in recent years, embodied by centers such as Metro21 at Carnegie Mellon University in Pittsburgh, Pennsylvania, 21st Century Cities Initiative at Johns Hopkins University in Baltimore, Maryland, and the nonprofit Envision Charlotte in Charlotte, North Carolina. Notably, most of these other centers do not themselves conduct data science, administer educational programs, or create policy but instead act primarily as conveners and connectors for those who do. For this reason, I group these only loosely with NYU CUSP, Urban CCD, and BARI.

Boston's Civic Data Ecosystem

The interuniversity nature of BARI goes back to its origins. In 2011, two professors of sociology at Harvard University, Robert J. Sampson and Christopher Winship, approached two institutes within the university, the Radcliffe Institute for Advanced Study and the Rappaport Institute for Greater Boston, and the city of Boston with the concept for a Harvard-Boston Research Initiative. The project was made feasible by the fact that this was more the continuation of a conversation than a completely new one. The executive director of the Rappaport Institute, David Luberoff, had long overseen multiple collaborative efforts with the city of Boston, including a highly successful summer fellowship program that embedded graduate students in public agencies. He and Christopher Winship had also had previous discussions over the years with colleagues at the city of Boston about a broader collaborative framework, though there had never before been the resources and political will to see it through. In keeping with a major theme here, though, these various activities had created trust between the institutions, laying the fertile ground that made the newly proposed initiative possible.

The Radcliffe Institute committed initial funding for the project, and shortly thereafter I was hired as a postdoctoral researcher to oversee it. In the ensuing months, we realized that the initiative needed to be inclusive if it were to fully realize its mission. The Boston area is home to the highest density of elite academic institutions in the world, housing a wealth of talent that would be key to a truly comprehensive urban research agenda. With this in mind, we hosted a symposium titled "Reimagining the City-University Connection" at Radcliffe. The unwritten agreement was that if we managed to attract at least 100 people there was sufficient enthusiasm to justify moving forward. Final counts estimated about 420 attendees.

With that, BARI was born (pronounced as in the "a" in "marker," in order to distinguish us from a prominent colleague named Barry) with the mandate of not only undertaking research projects that advance both science and policy but also fostering the collaborative relationships between researchers, policymakers, and practitioners that form the backbone of a thriving civic data ecosystem. To achieve these goals, BARI has three main areas of activity: (1) pursue core research-policy partnerships that focus on major themes and challenges facing greater Boston and at the forefront of urban science; (2) develop technologies that make emergent data sources accessible for research, policy, and practice, centered around BARI's flagship project, the Boston Data Portal, a public platform where researchers, policymakers, and community members can map and download data generated by BARI projects; and (3) convene and support cutting-edge research and policy work in the region through various mechanisms, including an annual conference,[20] workshops, a web site and network powered by LinkedIn, and seed funding for graduate student projects.

Given the richness of Boston's civic data ecosystem, we have had the good fortune to partner closely with a variety of institutions from across the public, private, nonprofit, and academic sectors, many of which will appear as collaborators in the ensuing chapters. For the moment, it is worth naming just a few to capture the different approaches to urban informatics that exist in Boston and to hint at the potential advances that lie at their intersection. Northeastern University's School of Public Policy and Urban Affairs (where I am on the faculty) has long been home to the Dukakis Center for Urban and Regional Policy, a "think and do tank" dedicated to applied research that informs effective policies. More recently, Northeastern University launched a master of science in urban informatics, a program that merges modern data science with a substantive understanding of the dynamics and challenges of the city. Through BARI, the students have the opportunity to learn through Boston-based data and collaborations with local leaders. At Boston University, the Initiative on Cities, founded by former Boston mayor Thomas M. Menino, looks both globally and locally to identify ways for researchers and policymakers to partner in the development of essential services and sustainable infrastructure. Meanwhile, both the Boston Civic Media Consortium (based at Emerson College's Engagement Lab) and URBAN.Boston (based at the University of Massachusetts Boston) are dedicated to pursuing research projects in collaboration with local community groups while also incorporating the voices of everyday Bostonians into the conversation around data science. Notably, each of these groups takes its own distinct approach to urban informatics, creating a context well suited to collaborations and projects of various forms.

On the policy side, BARI's closest partners have been the city of Boston's Mayor's Office of New Urban Mechanics (MONUM) and Department of Innovation and Technology (DoIT). MONUM is a unique entity that has played an important role in the advancement and popularization of urban informatics both locally and nationally. Its self-described role is to be an incubator for innovative approaches to improving city services and government-constituent engagement, or what it refers to as "the City's R&D team." This often entails technological solutions, but not as a rule. Boston DoIT has played the complementary role of building out the data systems and analytics team necessary to support innovations of this sort. Similar efforts have also been under way at two bordering cities, Cambridge and Somerville, and, more recently, at the Commonwealth of Massachusetts. In addition, the regional planning agency, the Metropolitan Area Planning Council, has a highly active data services department, exploring as well how such work might be extended to smaller municipalities that do not have the resources to develop such technologies themselves. In the nonprofit sector, The Boston Foundation's Boston Indicators project has sought to use data to better tell the story of Boston's past, present, and future and to identify issues in need of attention. Finally, in the private sector, there has been active engagement from some of the local technology companies, notably Microsoft New England's Technology & Civic Engagement arm.

When BARI began in 2011, the 311 system presented itself as a fitting pilot project for testing the potential for collaborations on research and policy. MONUM had recently introduced the smartphone application Citizens Connect to augment the Mayor's Hotline (as 311 in Boston was then known), and there was much interest both locally and nationally as to how this experiment would work out. Additionally, the system was already storing all requests in state-of-the-art databases that were relatively clean and research-ready. At this point, the simple vignette I described earlier ("Let us spend a month looking at those 300,000 requests for government service and we can start to figure out what questions we might answer") really did happen. In the ensuing five years, it went from a pilot project to something quite a bit more expansive, incorporating Boston DoIT; Boston About Results, the city's performance management team; the Public Works Department; and a cadre of academics from Harvard University, Northeastern University, and Emerson College. In sum, it has been an effective proof of concept, and a clear manifestation of the latent potential we believed we saw in Boston's civic data ecosystem after that first symposium at the Radcliffe Institute.

Products of the Field

Thus far, I have summarized the first three themes of urban informatics: (1) novel data resources and (2) crowdsourcing and sensor technologies, which form the bases of the field, and (3) cross-sector data-sharing partnerships as a critical mechanism for seeing the work through. What remains to be discussed are the products of urban informatics projects. Products are important because they represent the tangible results of the work but also because they reflect the motivations of the various contributors. The final two themes summarize the products of the field: technocratic policy innovations that utilize the insights and tools of urban informatics to improve city services, and the scientific pursuit of a deeper understanding of the city. One might be tempted to segregate these two elements, treating the former as indicative of "smart cities" and the latter representing "the new urban science," but this would fail to capture their mutually reinforcing relationship. New innovations depend on the conceptual advances of scholarly research, and scholarly research develops new questions based on the pressing challenges of the real world. Examining the nature of these products and their interactions will enable us to better understand the purpose and goals that energize the field and its constituents.

An important point as this section moves forward is the range of forms that the products of urban informatics can take. Of course, there are the flashy innovations that captivate the popular imagination, such as autonomous vehicles and ubiquitous sensor systems, but these do not reflect the vast majority of the everyday impacts that modern digital data and technology can have. More importantly, these futuristic innovations are only within reach for a small proportion of cities worldwide and thus fail to provide the generalized promise of the field. With this in mind, I make certain to include numerous illustrative examples that use data sources available in most if not all municipalities. In turn, this highlights how urban informatics promises insights and implications that are broadly accessible today while also laying the groundwork for the cities of tomorrow.

Innovating on Policy and Practice

As has been noted, many city governments, especially those in major metropolises, have embraced the potential of data and technology to make services, programs, and other aspects of governance more efficient and effective. Goldsmith and Crawford presaged the transformation that such innovations would bring, but rapid growth in the field since the publication of their book merits an additional summary, albeit brief, of the current state of these efforts.[21] For the sake of organization, one might loosely categorize the tools that have emerged from this work into three groups. First, there are efforts to deploy Web 2.0 applications and sensors to be the "eyes and ears of the city," capturing local conditions and patterns. The 311 system epitomizes this potential for Web 2.0, especially when a city implements internet portals and smartphone applications for reporting. Boston was a leader in this effort to leverage Web 2.0 for government services with the Citizens Connect app, but a diverse range of cities have followed suit, from New York City to Tuscaloosa, Alabama. The potential value of sensors is captured by examples such as the effort by Pittsburgh, Pennsylvania, to equip municipal vehicles with sensors that indicate when they have hit potholes, thereby saving Public Works the trouble of searching for them.

A second type of innovation has been the development of platforms, often dubbed "dashboards," that combine multiple data sets to track conditions and performance. These have their origins in New York City's CompStat program, started in the 1990s, in which the police department mapped out crimes and arrests to better grasp the trends in each precinct, and a similar cross-agency effort called CitiStat in Baltimore early in the following decade. The modern manifestations of this approach benefit from a notable expansion in data resources and statistical tools. In Chicago, for example, the city has built the WindyGrid (the public version is called OpenGrid),[22] which maps data based on custom-defined events and time periods (e.g., homicides in July, streetlight outages in 2015), representing hot spots and cool spots that had a greater or lower density of events than would be expected based on historical data and other localized characteristics. Another approach has been Boston's CityScore, which reports major indicators, such as the number of shootings and the percentage of work requests filled on time, through a public interface.[23]

A third type of innovation combines the power of the two others to create new programs and policies. These are in some ways the most powerful endorsements of the societal value of urban informatics while also being the hardest to identify and point to. Whereas the two others entail platforms and tools that can easily be trumpeted in newspapers and blogs, the impact of this third set of innovations can only be seen over time, and even then it might be difficult to communicate. There are many different examples of such programs, only a few of which I will be able to list here.

- The city of South Bend, Indiana, and the University of Notre Dame reengineered the sewer system to eliminate a major problem with sewage backflow entering people's houses during times of peak water flow. More recently, a company that emerged from this project equipped the sewer system with sensors to identify blockages in real time.[24]
- Chicago, Santa Cruz, Los Angeles, and other cities use predictive analytic models to forecast where major crimes are likely to occur, informing policing strategies.[25]

- A complementary set of programs in Boston[26] and Minneapolis[27] have used data to identify and target "problem properties" that generate an inordinate amount of crime and disorder.
- New York City has aggressively used data to drive policies surrounding transportation. They used GPS trackers on taxis to inform and then evaluate the reorganization of Times Square to be more pedestrian friendly. They also used detailed data on collisions between cars and bicycles to inform policies to limit such events.[28]

There have also been efforts to extend this sort of work into the world of health and human services, which has data that is more sensitive and problems that do not lend themselves to formulaic solutions. Though such work is less prevalent, it has gained momentum in recent years. An early leader in this area has been Actionable Intelligence for Social Policy, an initiative based at the University of Pennsylvania and centered on the construction and utilization of integrated data systems (IDSs). These link data from multiple health and human services agencies at the individual level, providing unprecedented opportunities to analyze patterns of service use, consequences of traumatic events,[29] and programs and policies that coordinate data from various sources. Examples include:

- Homelessness policy across the nation, including Philadelphia, has increasingly utilized data to distinguish between "chronic" and "crisis" homeless and target services appropriately.[30]
- In some cases, the mere access to data is the innovation. For example, Medicare workers in South Carolina have a system that uses many pieces of information about an elderly patient, including those already entered in the medical system and others entered by the worker, to suggest the necessary level of care. This permits more flexible treatment plans, with the hope of allowing the elderly to remain in their homes (rather than in nursing facilities) for as long as possible.[31]
- In Allegheny County, Pennsylvania, home of Pittsburgh, an IDS enabled an algorithm that could predict the level of risk for child abuse for a given case. This has been implemented to direct resources at the call center to cases that are more likely to lead to serious issues.[32]

Importantly, technology and data alone do not necessarily make for great policies and programs, and there is clearly a need for evaluation. Nonetheless, these and other examples illustrate the potential of digital data and technology to craft new approaches to urban governance and services.

All of the efforts listed here were realized through research-policy partnerships, with academics participating in various ways, from developing metrics, to building statistical models, to helping guide program design. One of the institutions seeking to expand this collaborative civic problem solving across cities has been the MetroLab Network (MetroLab), a consortium of city-university partnerships focused on bringing data, analytics, and innovation to city government in order to benefit local communities. MetroLab was launched by the White House's Office of Science and Technology Policy, with the city of Pittsburgh and Carnegie Mellon University agreeing to sponsor the initial phase (it is now an independent 501c3 organization). Founding members included Boston-BARI, Chicago-Urban CCD, and New York City-CUSP, as well as a number of cities that are smaller or are less prominent in this space, such as South Bend, Indiana-Notre Dame and Memphis, Tennessee-University of Memphis. MetroLab's effort to expand such work nationally is twofold. One part of its work is to support additional cities to develop the cross-sector partnerships that underpin urban informatics. The second is to construct a network that enables the learning and transfer of innovations from one city to another, thereby spreading the associated benefits more widely.

The Policy Vision for Urban Informatics

With the number of technocratic innovations in cities growing rapidly, one might ask what the overarching philosophy for this work is. In his book on smart cities, Anthony Townsend argued that rather than exotify such innovations, we should recognize that they are just modern solutions to the same problems we have always faced—sanitation, transportation, infrastructure maintenance, education, and public safety.[33] This is true on a surface level, but it does not necessarily mean that policymakers engaged in urban informatics are approaching the problems with a single-minded focus on the objective improvement of operations. The 311 system, for example, does help government to deliver services more efficiently and effectively, but it has received just as much attention for the new forms of interaction it creates between government and the public. It has been heralded as a democratizing force, making city services more accessible and responsive, while also encouraging constituents to participate directly in the governance of their own city. Thus, though technology may provide new tools for old problems, the ways in which policymakers design and implement them also reflects other societal trends.

The 311 system is not the only case in which municipal governments have leveraged technology to become closer to the people they represent and serve. In fact, the phenomenon is widespread enough to have its own name: *civic tech*. Civic tech takes many forms, most of which use Web 2.0 sites and applications to enable public deliberation and discourse. For example, the Community Plan-It platform uses an interactive virtual environment to elicit residents' ideas on development decisions in their community.[34] Participatory budgeting has become increasingly popular, especially in Latin America, giving certain constituencies more say in the use of public funds.[35] Many dashboards are explicitly pitched as public platforms so citizens can track government performance and neighborhood conditions. In this manner, civic tech reflects a reimagining of *coproduction*, an approach to public administration that seeks to directly involve the public in the governance process. Whereas coproduction has traditionally been most visible in the form of parent-teacher organizations and community policing, technology has allowed it to take on new forms and enter new domains. Part III of this book will delve more deeply into civic tech and coproduction, but for the moment the primary point is that efforts by city governments to solve well-known problems by utilizing data and technology could take on a variety of guises. The current case has been centered on a civic spirit, which in turn is building a model for public involvement in government in the digital age.

The New Urban Science: In Search of a Paradigm

Whereas the policymakers involved in urban informatics are focused on improving the efficiency of government while also making it more accessible and participatory, the goals of their scientific counterparts are not always as clear. The fundamental role of science is to advance knowledge, and it is on the strength of those contributions that academics evaluate each other. Of course, those who are collaborating with policymakers and practitioners want their research to have societal impact, but the nature of the research itself depends on the body of knowledge they hope to advance. The broad interdisciplinarity of urban informatics, however, makes it difficult to pinpoint a particular "body of knowledge" that acts as the field's primary focus. On the one hand, many of the "usual suspects" of urban science, such as sociologists, criminologists, public health researchers, and planners, have adopted modern data and methodologies as a way to further old questions about the city. At the same time, newcomers from other disciplines, such as mathematics, physics, chemistry, biology, and computer science, have been attracted to urban informatics by the opportunity to apply their computational skills and models to the complexities of societal dynamics. Consequently, the intellectual breadth of the field is wide ranging.

The diverse—or, some might say, fragmented—composition of the field poses a challenge. I am no proponent of narrow disciplinary orthodoxy (I am a biologist by training who has since worked in departments of psychology, sociology, public policy, and criminology), but there is something to be said for having a canon that at least partially unifies scholarly efforts. Without that, the result is not a collective project, which all science inherently needs to be, but rather a handful of individuals asking disparate questions about topics whose connections are not fully articulated or agreed on. Under these conditions, cumulative knowledge will be hard to come by. The great philosopher of science Thomas Kuhn argued that science is built on paradigms, or "a framework of concepts, results, and procedures within which subsequent work is structured."[36] Put another way, a paradigm codifies the overarching theoretical questions that are of greatest importance, the methods for probing them, and thus a blueprint for the research that might ensue. The question, then, is: What paradigm or paradigms are guiding scientific inquiry in urban informatics?

A Comparison of Two Paradigms

Let us apply the Kuhnian perspective to the most basic question that an urban scientist might ask: What is the city? While this question might seem exceedingly simple, how one answers it will determine what he or she deems worth asking next, thereby setting the pathway forward. There have been many answers to this question over 150 years of urban science, but here I will compare two that are most prominent in the field of urban informatics. First is the approach to urban science developed by members of the Chicago School of Sociology in the early twentieth century, which emphasizes the social organization within and between neighborhoods.[37] Second is the "social reactor" theory recently proposed by a team of physicists at Santa Fe Institute and their colleagues.[38] These examples are also instructive in that they capture an underlying tension in the field between the extension of old ideas and the adoption of new ones.

In the 1920s, Robert E. Park and Ernest W. Burgess, working at the inception of the University of Chicago's department of sociology, published a series of essays titled *The City*.[39] One of the foundational premises of their work was that the city was not a monolithic entity but rather one composed of many distinct communities, each with its own social organization— that is, formal and informal relationships, norms, and patterns of inter- action. Writing at a time when industrial cities were rapidly growing, they saw neighborhoods as a social unit similar to a village, with a social organ- ization grounded by personal relationships and localized institutions. The city, however, created a conglomeration of these many communities, requiring what Park and Burgess referred to as a secondary, or imper- sonal, set of institutions that could serve and operate a municipality of hundreds of thousands or even millions of people. This perspective has since inspired a number of lines of research, most notably work in soci- ology, criminology, public health, and others that emphasize the role of neighborhood social dynamics in shaping the mental and physical well- being of residents, thereby explaining the stark variation in outcomes we observe across the urban landscape.[40] Much of the theoretical ap- proach to neighborhood dynamics used in this book also grows out of the Chicago School.

More recently, a group of scholars based at the Santa Fe Institute (SFI), led by Geoffrey West, Luis Bettencourt, and José Lobo, have argued that the city is a "social reactor," within which increased population density results in greater interaction between individuals, in turn elevating overall productivity. They have formalized this argument using conceptual and mathematical models from biology and physics, revealing what they refer to as the universal scaling laws that relate city size to its outcomes. Empirically, they find that indeed the residents of cities with larger populations have a greater number of social connections, higher incomes, and are more productive, generating, for example, more patents.[41]

The Chicago School and SFI perspectives are similar in that they each treat the city as a social system with special properties that merit attention, but their interests are at different scales. The SFI team's social reactor hypothesis concerns itself with the processes and outcomes of an entire metropolitan area, including suburbs, positing very little about the events and conditions that differentiate neighborhoods. The Chicago School's work instead attempts to answer this latter question by focusing on the dynamics and consequences of the social organization of neighborhoods. Consequently, these two conceptions of the city inspire different lines of questioning and as such two distinct "urban sciences."

The Challenge of a Unifying Theory

Debate will naturally arise any time there are multiple guiding perspectives to the study of a broad topic. This is true even when the perspectives pose different questions of arguably equal importance, as in the case of the Chicago School's emphasis on neighborhood social organization and SFI's interest in metropolitan areas. A possible response is to privilege one perspective over the other as more important. For example, one could argue that because the social reactor hypothesis is rooted in computational methods and formal mathematical models from the "hard" sciences, it has greater merit. On the other hand, theory on social organization has remained influential for nearly a century, generating offshoots in numerous fields and having a sustained impact on our understanding of the city. Obviously, few would adhere wholeheartedly to either of these unilateral views of the field, but they are instructive because they do illustrate a broader tension within urban informatics between the traditional urban disciplines and the more recent arrivals.

Another solution is to develop a unifying theory of the city, but this is likely to be fraught with difficulties from the outset. A city is a stage for all aspects of human behavior and society, making it an ideal study site for just about any social phenomenon of interest. Furthermore, the real-world nature of the work facilitates interdisciplinary collaboration at the intersections of domains—for example, the simultaneous consideration of flow dynamics and human behavior when attempting to address traffic patterns—and offers a natural opportunity for the work to have direct public impact. Such a situation, however, does not lend itself well to a single intellectual framework. It would be difficult if not impossible to construct a single guiding paradigm that encompasses psychology, sociology, planning, political science, economics, education, public health, criminology, geography, and public policy, not to mention their respective subdisciplines *and* the components of biology, physics, chemistry, and mathematics that might also be incorporated into the conversation.

My intent is not to condemn urban informatics to be forever fragmented, a field lacking any canonical basis. Instead, the attitude that guides my own efforts and those of BARI is that there is much work to do before we get there, and that we will need to be satisfied if the "unifying theory of the city" is actually a series of interlocking paradigms, each of which sets the agenda for studying a particular class of phenomena. Returning to the foresight of Lazer and his colleagues regarding computational social science, the newly introduced data, methods, and perspectives will likely transform the way we think about many aspects of the city in the coming years, generating new theoretical perspectives and clarifying the intersections between them.[42] This will eventually result in a multifaceted synthesis that acknowledges the two paradigms I have presented here, a number of others that I have not mentioned, and, of course, a handful that are yet to be proposed. In keeping with this, BARI's activities take a catholic view of the field, supporting projects across many domains, from the mapping of bicycle collisions from police narratives, to the use of historical census data to track shifts in demography, to the integration of administrative data and parent interviews in the evaluation of the public schools' assignment system, to the detailed measurement of conditions that drive or mitigate the urban heat island effect, to digitizing Boston Public Library records to track how services are offered across neighborhoods. Our goal is to support the many disciplinary approaches to urban informatics and to create opportunities for interaction and cross-pollination across them. These are the necessary first steps to create the theoretical synthesis that promises to reshape and deepen our understanding of the city.

Integrating Urban Science and Policy

Given the distinct roles of policymakers and scientists, it is inevitable that they also differ in their motivations. The former are concerned with improving the efficiency and effectiveness of city services and programs, often with a flair for increasing interaction between the government and the public. The latter are broadly interested in contributing to our basic knowledge about the city, though the specific questions this entails depend on the researcher or program in question. These two sets of goals for urban informatics are distinct but complementary, and can be mutually reinforcing. In the one direction, nearly anything a researcher discovers about the city could, at least in theory, be relevant or useful to some agency or department. In the other direction, the current needs and trends of the city can ground research and give it a natural opportunity for impact.

The full opportunity for urban informatics to bridge the divide between research and policy, however, becomes clear in light of the other themes discussed in this chapter. First, new data resources and sensor technologies promise novel discoveries and tools, but it is not self-evident what these will be. Researchers and policymakers have a common interest in solving this riddle by developing techniques and approaches that can fully realize that potential. This symbiosis is especially apparent in the case of data generated by the administrative processes of public agencies, where the agency understands the origins and interpretation of the data, and a scientist can transform it into knowledge, much of which will be directly relevant to the agency's operations and objectives. Second, digital data sharing can accelerate collaborative partnerships that might otherwise have fallen casualty to the differing timelines and incentives of academia and the public sector. Given the various motivations of each party, as well as the diverse set of questions the available data might answer, the resulting projects might take any number of forms.

To illustrate, 311 has been a catalyst for collaboration between researchers and policymakers because its data provide a number of avenues for study, which we might categorize into four groups. First, as captured in the main theme of this book, the data bear witness to behavioral dynamics that underlie neighborhood maintenance, or the custodianship of the urban commons. Second, 311 reports can be treated as "the eyes and ears of the city," though this depends on methodologies that handle questions of measurement and validity—does the density of calls reflect the density of problems or the density of concerned individuals? Chapter 2 addresses this challenge for administrative data more generally with the test case of translating 311 reports into measures of physical disorder and deterioration (i.e., "broken windows") across the city. Third, it is a tool for tracking the interactions between the government and the public, and for evaluating the effects of certain programs on this relationship. For example, does stop and frisk discourage constituent engagement with the government?[43] Fourth, it is the most prominent case for assessing the implications of "civic tech" and the broader move toward coproduction, a major focus of Part III of this book. Studies utilizing 311 in each of these ways have the potential to produce scientific discoveries that contribute to our understanding of cities. They also offer insights for those managing 311 systems and their colleagues.

The 311 system is one of many programs and data sets, each of which merits attention. Further, the combinations of these various sources of information can support and inspire an even greater array of mutually beneficial collaborations between researchers and policymakers. This might include anything from education, to transportation, to climate change, to gentrification, to resilience and security, just to name a few. It is not necessary that each party be interested in the exact same questions, just that there be sufficient overlap in the things that each would want to learn from a particular project. Thanks to the greater incentives provided by digital data and technology, and the lowered hurdles resulting from an ethos of data sharing, the likelihood of such work is far greater than it has been historically. This promises a truly synergistic urban informatics that has the dual goals of advancing both scholarship and policy.

Conclusion: The Introspective City

I began this chapter by listing the five themes of urban informatics, broken up into three groups. (1) Novel data resources and (2) crowdsourcing and sensor technologies form *the bases of the field* by providing access to the pulse of the city with unprecedented detail and precision. (3) Widespread data sharing acts as a critical mechanism for fostering a *civic data ecosystem* characterized by sustained collaboration across disciplines and sectors. These collaborations lead to two main types of products, (4) technocratic policy innovations that seek to improve the efficiency and effectiveness of city services and (5) the scientific pursuit of a deeper understanding of the city and its people, places, and systems. This book will capture each of these five themes, but, as a product in its own right, it embodies the reinforcing relationship between the last two. The empirical work on the urban commons is rooted in the fifth theme, translating a novel data set into substantive insights on the behavioral dynamics of neighborhoods, but it also demonstrates how these insights can be translated into the policy innovations captured in the fourth theme.

I want to close the chapter by considering what happens when these five elements come together. I see it as an exercise in introspection. Each research project is an effort by a city to get to know itself, bringing some aspect of its inner workings to light. As with all good introspection, this moment of observation is also an opportunity for action. In this case, the opportunity rests with policymakers, who might capitalize on the new knowledge by designing tools and practices that can improve the city for those who work, live, and play there. It is this cycle of discovery and improvement that makes modern behavioral therapies so effective for individuals, and, by analogy, it is what makes urban informatics more than just "smart cities" or a "new urban science" but instead an integration of the two. This, however, relies on the ability to appropriately leverage the novel digital data resources that have recently become available. This is a task that, like many in the world of "big data," poses a distinct set of challenges, as we will explore in Chapter 2.

CHAPTER 2

"Seeing" the City through "Big Data"

IN APRIL 2011, representatives from BARI and the city of Boston met in the mayor's policy room to discuss the opportunities surrounding 311 data. City representatives included the director of the 311 system, the cochairs of the Mayor's Office of New Urban Mechanics, and the director of Boston About Results, the city's performance management system. This was one of an initial set of conversations about what research-policy collaborations might be able to accomplish in the age of digital data—so early, in fact, that we had not yet christened ourselves as BARI.

The agenda circulated in advance of the meeting stated the express goal of exploring directions for "the value the data might hold for improving city services and illuminating human behavior." The discussion converged on two such opportunities. One was that the data acted as the "eyes and ears of the city," tracking events and conditions in real time across Boston. The second was that they gave us an insight into how constituents engaged with government services. The problem was that if it was a pure reflection of either of these two things, it could not be the other. That is to say, if 311 reports perfectly represented the conditions of the urban landscape, then constituent engagement was robust and consistent across the city, making it a nonconcern; and if it exactly reflected constituent engagement, then one would have to assume that need was completely even across the city, in which case a map of events and conditions would be flat and uninteresting. Obviously, neither of these was the case, and the two interpretations of the data seemed hopelessly entangled.

The problem of measurement is not unique to 311 reports but is a general weakness of administrative data, social media, and the other "naturally occurring data" that are driving urban informatics and allied domains of computational social science. Because they were not created for the purposes of research, they lack many of the features that we often take for granted in traditional data. What is it that they measure? Are those things interesting? Do the data actually capture what they appear to, or are they biased in some way? At what time intervals should one generate measures (i.e., weeks? months? years?) and on what spatial scale? Such questions represent major hurdles to the potential that these data hold for both science and policy, and they need to be answered before the promised advances of urban informatics can become realities.

By the end of the meeting, we had sketched a study to be conducted that summer that would disentangle constituent engagement from objective conditions across neighborhoods, allowing us to observe "physical disorder," or deterioration of the spaces and structures of a neighborhood (e.g., dilapidated housing, graffiti, "broken windows"). Though the study began with the relatively narrow goal of generating a particular set of measures, it has had the broader impact of producing new guidelines that bring a popular methodological approach in urban science into the age of "big data." This methodology is known as *ecometrics*—that is, measuring the physical and social conditions of a space—and while we demonstrated it for the measure of physical disorder in neighborhoods, the guidelines can be further generalized to any effort utilizing naturally occurring data, whether the unit of analysis be a neighborhood, person, company, or something else.

This chapter begins with an overview of the challenges that novel digital data pose for measurement, applying them to the urban context and the development of ecometrics. I follow this by proposing a model to solve these challenges, using the case of 311 and physical disorder as an illustration.[1] Though the chapter will include substantial information on the analytic and statistical steps taken to develop the measure of physical disorder from 311 records, I have organized it such that each section begins with the conceptual basis and real-world importance of that stage of the analysis and ends with a summary of the main findings and implications, allowing readers to choose whether to dive into, skim, or skip over the deeper methodological content without losing the main points of the chapter.

"Big Data" and the Measurement Challenge

To this point, I have primarily argued for the opportunities that modern data and technology hold for research and policy in cities, only briefly alluding to their potential pitfalls. Those pitfalls, though, have been a source of considerable debate among scientists and across society at large. These discussions, which have generally centered on the buzz term "big data," clearly need to be examined in any treatment of urban informatics. I will focus here on the consequences for research and data-informed policy and practice. There are of course other trenchant questions about the ethics of modern digital data and technology. We will examine one of them, the emerging digital divide between those who can and cannot access and utilize big data, in depth in Part IV. Others, including individual privacy and the misuse of data, are tangential to the purpose of this book, and I cannot give them the space they deserve. Instead, I refer those who are interested in these questions to authors who have addressed them more thoroughly.[2]

One of the popular metaphors for the vast proliferation of information precipitated by digital technology has been the "data deluge." This metaphor is apt in that it captures not only the quantity of data but also how overwhelming it is. Just as water converts from a vital resource into a confounding nuisance during a flood, big data are rich sources of information that we do not entirely know how to utilize. There is a sense that we are wading about in data trying to figure out what exactly to do with it all. The question, then, is: What vessels and instruments will enable us to intelligently navigate the waters that characterize this post-diluvian age? Answering this question requires that we better define "big data" and how they differ from previous information sources. This will then provide the basis for how to work with them.

How "Big Data" Are Different

A colloquial meme has attempted to capture the distinctiveness of "big data" with "3 Vs": volume, or "big"-ness; velocity, or the fact that many of these data update often, sometimes in real time; and variety, or breadth of content. These features stand in contrast to traditional data from surveys, observations, and experiments, which are often limited in size, collected only once or at relatively distant (e.g., annual) intervals, and relatively narrow in content. Seeking a more rigorous definition of "big data," Rob Kitchin and Gavin McArdle compared the characteristics of a range of data sources typically granted this label.[3] They concluded that volume is a by-product of two basic distinguishing characteristics. First, velocity, with its regular updates, contributes to an ever-expanding data resource. Second, they replaced variety with its sibling, exhaustivity. Whereas variety reflects many attributes (i.e., fields or columns) describing cases (i.e., rows), exhaustivity reflects the intent to include all cases. In other words, whereas most forms of data collection rely on a sample of individuals or events in order to make inferences about the population, big data presume to document the population as a whole. Kitchin and McArdle argue that the proliferation of rows does more to grow a data set than adding columns.

Unlike Kitchin and McArdle, my intent is not to identify underlying dynamics responsible for "big data's" size but rather to describe how their distinctions will affect the advancement of science and policy in the digital age. I note three things of particular consequence. First, nearly all of these data are "naturally occurring," harvested as the by-product of some other process. In many cases, this results in a new view on some component of behavior and society that was previously more difficult to access directly. I have already argued that 311, for example, offers an unprecedented view of the patterns of urban maintenance, or custodianship. Though sensors are intentionally deployed and thus not explicitly naturally occurring, they provide unfamiliar descriptions of the urban environment. In this manner, the variety of available content acts as a substantial catalyst for research, even if it is not primarily responsible for size.

Second, exhaustivity requires that data be indexical; that is, that all elements have unique identifiers. Often, this indexing occurs at multiple levels, with each record referencing one or more uniquely identifiable units, be they individuals, census geographies, or something else, each with their own index. For example, a 311 record has a unique record ID but also references units in two other indexes: the address at which services were required and the individual who made the report (provided that person has an account with the system). When implemented in this way, indexing creates relationality, meaning data sets that reference the same unit of analysis can be merged using unique identifiers. The merger of data sets, in turn, further amplifies variety and the number of questions that might be asked about a given unit of analysis.

Third, whereas traditional data sources usually describe the characteristics of some unit of interest, such as a person, street, or neighborhood, much "big data" come in the form of records. The records of a single data set might reference a particular unit once, twice, fifty times, or not at all, creating additional detail by which one can describe all units in the population. This is not a scripted process, however, and it requires that a researcher make multiple decisions that will shape the nature and interpretation of the resultant measure. To illustrate, the average census tract in Boston generates about 1,000 requests for service per year via 311, which might be tabulated to understand the needs of a community. But how is that most appropriately done? Should all case types be included or only a subset? When should we remove duplicate cases that have been reported more than once, and how do we identify them? Should we limit the study to reports by constituents only, excluding those by city employees, in order to better understand the community's self-perceived needs? These are only a few of the considerations that might need attention, and the same would be necessary for any archive of records.

To summarize, whether we use the term "big data" or not, the distinctive analytic value of modern digital data arises in two ways. First is their ability to study events and units through an unprecedented variety of content. This is in part thanks to sources that are naturally occurring, which consequently capture information that has not previously been available, and also because they are indexed, enabling the merger of many different data sources. Second is the ability to create measures that are more precise in both their definition and scale, thanks to the specificity afforded by aggregating records. Though these features create new opportunities, they also require new approaches, both philosophical and technical, for handling them.

A Place for Theory

Identifying modern digital data's distinguishing features gives us greater understanding of the substance of the deluge but does not on its own tell us how best to navigate it. Two major camps have emerged in response to this problem, one arguing that data should lead the way, the other advocating for the role of theory as a guide. A vocal proponent of the former approach has been Chris Anderson, editor of *Wired* magazine.[4] His reasoning might be summed up in one pithy quotation from his essay

"The End of Theory": "Who knows why people do what they do? The point is they do it, and we can track and measure it with unprecedented fidelity. With enough data, the numbers speak for themselves." In Anderson's view, we now have sufficient information to obviate social and behavioral theory, which uses models of "why" things happen to approximate reality and thereby fill in gaps in knowledge. Instead, he argues, we can now fill these gaps by asking the data additional questions.

Anderson's essay has attracted numerous critics, myself included. One of the fiercest has been Massimo Pigliucci, a philosopher of biology, who wrote that Anderson misses the point that the very purpose of science is to explain why things work the way they do.[5] These insights support a broader understanding of the world, which is articulated through theory. If we limit our inquiries only to correlation and eschew explanation, we are no longer conducting science. While I am sympathetic to this philosophical point, let us also examine its practical ramifications. Using urban informatics as an example, Anderson's approach might generate discoveries that improve city services or inform a successful new business, but without theory to describe why each of these discoveries is true, they remain apart from each other and from the existing body of knowledge. More than just a way to fill in the gaps, theory is a tool for organizing and interpreting facts, creating the ligature between disparate pieces of information and imparting greater meaning to them. This has especial importance when one wants to extend or extrapolate existing knowledge to a new context. For example, this book contains many details that, construed narrowly, describe the use of 311 in Boston. Interpreting these facts through the organizing framework of custodianship in the urban commons, however, enables us to think about how and when they are applicable to other cities, other forms of neighborhood maintenance, other types of commons, and other government programs. Without theory, this is not possible.

Pigliucci also encourages Anderson to recall the maxim, "There are no data without theory." Without some theory or model of the world, one has no basis for determining which data to collect or how to interpret them. Even though naturally occurring data would seemingly be independent of a theoretically guided agenda, a researcher must still make a series of decisions that determine what will be analyzed and with what meaning. As illustrated earlier, this is true with the seemingly simple task of using 311 data to track the needs of a city's neighborhoods. Every choice that a researcher makes, from initial data access and cleaning, to variable construction, to model specification, is based on assumptions about the world and the questions at hand. To claim otherwise is to ignore the agency that the researcher brings to the data, giving the false impression that invariant truths tumble out during analysis with just a little coaxing.

An additional critique of a data-only approach to science, aptly termed by David Lazer and his colleagues as "big data hubris," is the assumption that everything we discover is "true" in an objective sense.[6] They discuss particularly the danger of algorithms that are overfit to the particularities of a data set, citing the case of Google Flu, which used regional variation in the content of Google searches to predict when and where flu cases would spike. Very quickly after its deployment, Google Flu started overestimating cases, in part because it relied heavily on search indicators that were correlated more with winter months than with actual disease. A second, potentially more insidious danger of big data hubris is the possibility that the data themselves do not represent what they would appear to. Naturally occurring data were collected not according to a systematic research protocol but rather as the by-product of some administrative or technological process. Again it is instructive to recall that there are no data without theory, though in this case the data are shaped not by the preconceived notions of a researcher but rather by the idiosyncrasies of the system producing the data. Does the system actually capture all of the events it purports to? Do some demographic groups avail themselves of a service more than others, creating an unbalanced view? Such issues can lead to bias in the data, meaning they must be probed and examined before the true meaning of a naturally occurring data set can be resolved. An even greater conundrum, though one that can be deeply interesting, is whether creating policies, programs, or services around a naturally occurring data set alters the behavioral patterns that generate these data. If this were the case, as was suspected for Google Flu, then the innovation may be premised on assumptions that no longer apply. More strikingly, the innovation itself might be driving the very behavioral change that in turn violates these assumptions. We will return to this possibility later in the chapter.

The data deluge provides a rich resource for inquiry on behavior and society. It very well might go beyond and transform some of our current theories, but it certainly does not obviate the exercise of theorizing itself. Instead, theory is as important as ever. We need it to make sense of new discoveries and the ways they advance our existing knowledge. Even before we get to that point, however, theory is essential to guiding the analytic process. The use of naturally occurring data, whether for projects scholarly, applied, or both, requires that we clearly articulate our assumptions and then properly construct the steps of data processing, cleaning and creation of variables, and model specification to be consistent with our stated goals. This diligence is as true for studying the city as for any other topic, and without it, it is hard to know what the new data are telling us.

Tracking Neighborhood Characteristics in the Digital Age

One opportunity that modern digital data offer urban science is an enhanced ability to track events and conditions across the urban landscape. This is reflected in the colloquial understanding of 311 as the "eyes and ears of the city" but is equally applicable to many other types of administrative records, social media posts, and sensor readings that document the patterns of the urban landscape. Such measures of the physical and social characteristics of a space are known as *ecometrics*. Ecometrics have their intellectual basis in the earliest studies of the city, which focused on inequities across neighborhoods in various outcomes, from delinquency and crime to physical and mental health.[7] They lacked a standardized methodological approach, however, until the mid-1990s,[8] when Robert Sampson and Stephen Raudenbush and their colleagues at the Project on Human Development in Chicago Neighborhoods developed two protocols, one using resident surveys and the other using neighborhood audits (known as systematic social observation, or SSO).[9] They also coined the term "ecometrics" to describe their application of tools from the field of psychometrics, which is concerned with the quantitative description of behavior, to the study of spaces, in this case neighborhoods. One of the main test cases for demonstrating their ecometric methodology was to measure physical and social disorder, or "broken windows," as these features are sometimes called. Since then, studies have replicated and extended these protocols in a variety of cities and across disciplines, including sociology, criminology, public health, community psychology, social work, child development, and others.[10]

Ecometrics might be seen as the precursor to the composite approach to measuring the urban landscape I described in Chapter 1. Where modern data systems and sensors compile information from many different sources, ecometrics combine multiple observations of a neighborhood to robustly assess local conditions. Given this consonance between them, modern digital data have the potential to overcome some of the weaknesses that exist in current ecometric protocols. First, existing methods require an immense amount of effort and resources. For example, Sampson and Raudenbush's neighborhood audits entailed driving a van equipped with cameras up and down more than 20,000 streets at 5 mph, followed by extensive coding of the videos. Second, the variety of measures has been relatively limited, concentrating on observations of disorder and surveys of physical conditions and social dynamics, the latter largely centered on social cohesion between neighbors and the collective ability to enforce social norms. Because modern digital data are naturally occurring, the effort required to create new ecometrics from them is likely less than for a whole-city survey or audit. Additionally, their variety and detail have the potential to support many neighborhood descriptors that have not previously been available.

As noted in the discussion of "big data," however, naturally occurring data may lack some of the elements required for the creation of rigorous ecometrics. Three problems in particular stand out. First, the substantive content of these data is noisy, and it is not immediately apparent what they can measure or how they do so. Second, there may be some aspect of data collection that creates systematic biases in measurement. Third, there is no information about what scale of geographical analysis the data can support—for example, census block groups (CBGs) or tracts—or over what time spans. This chapter puts forward a set of guidelines for ecometrics using modern digital data that attends to each of the three main issues: (1) *extract constructs* of interest and isolate them from irrelevant information; (2) address *validity* by identifying and adjusting for any sources of bias; and (3) establish criteria for *reliability* and the most appropriate spatial and temporal windows for their measurement.

Not coincidentally, I originally undertook this work with Robert Sampson and our colleague Christopher Winship, in addition to the city representatives mentioned at the beginning of this chapter. Like Sampson and Raudenbush, we illustrated our methodology by measuring physical disorder, this time based on 311 reports, which I again do here, as it is a useful and accessible case.[11] The proceeding sections walk through the three guidelines one-by-one. Though the explicit focus is on ecometrics, it is important to keep in mind that the guidelines are applicable to any similar work with modern digital data. Each of the three sections begins with the conceptual problem and proposed methodological solution and ends with a general summary. The empirical demonstration of methodology is sandwiched in between. These parts are clearly delineated, enabling readers to access all of the chapter's main points, regardless of the level at which they choose to engage with the methodology. For those who want to go further and analyze the data used in this chapter themselves, they are available through BARI's Boston Data Portal.[12]

Content: Capturing the Construct of Interest

The diverse content that distinguishes modern digital data is also one of its greatest challenges. On the one hand, it means that many aspects of society might be measured with precision and detail. On the other hand, the data come with no guidelines detailing what the data actually *can* measure or how to isolate them from other threads of information contained within the data set. Traditionally, research measures are derived from protocols designed to access an underlying construct. Administrative data are not endowed with an a priori theoretical organization of this sort. Records of 311 cases, for example, are a by-product of a system intended to transmit the needs of constituents to the appropriate government agencies, and their organization reflects this function rather than a deliberate intent to measure neighborhood characteristics. Consequently, we do not entirely know what the "eyes and ears of the city" are actually seeing, hearing, and communicating about the urban landscape. Furthermore, whatever these measures happen to be, are they of any interest to researchers, policymakers, and practitioners?

The Boston system handles ~175,000 cases annually, covering 225 case types, ranging from reports of graffiti, to tree emergencies, to requests for bulk item pickups, to complaints about malfunctioning traffic signals, to questions about parking schedules. This range of information would suggest that 311 requests could effectively describe variation across neighborhoods on multiple dimensions, but this would require methodologies that can separate these dimensions from each other. One particular aspect of urban neighborhoods captured by 311 records is physical disorder, or deterioration and denigration of spaces and structures, including loose garbage, graffiti, and dilapidation. Thanks to the popularity of broken windows theory over the past 30 years, physical disorder is regularly examined and referenced in criminology, sociology, and public health studies. A notable proportion of 311 reports reference issues that reflect physical disorder (e.g., graffiti), though many others do not (e.g., bulk item pickups), meaning it will be necessary to distinguish between them. Physical disorder also makes a worthwhile proof of concept for extracting ecometrics from modern digital data, because the resultant measures will be relevant to researchers and practitioners alike.

The Importance of Broken Windows

Why measure physical disorder in the first place? Physical disorder is one component of the more broadly defined construct of neighborhood disorder, which encompasses any visual cues that reflect a "breakdown of the local social order."[13] These visual cues can be the behaviors that embody such breakdowns (e.g., public drunkenness, loitering, and panhandling), known as social disorder, or, in the case of physical disorder, artifacts of such behavior that have left a mark on the space, including empty beer cans, dilapidated housing, or graffiti. Though disorder has entered popular consciousness through the evocative "broken windows" theory (BWT), it has a long history as an indicator of neighborhood quality. From Charles Booth's maps of the conditions of nineteenth-century London, to the early Chicago School of Sociology's writings on urban contexts in the 1920s and '30s, to Jane Jacobs's descriptions of New York City in the 1960s, urban scholars have often used disorder as a proxy for less-visible maladies and the overall well-being of the community.

BWT is distinctive in that it attributed a causal mechanism to disorder, arguing that these visual cues lead to increases in crime in a neighborhood.[14] More recent work building off of this premise has extended the hypothesis to suggest that disorder might also cause elevated stress and related health outcomes,[15] higher levels of risky behavior,[16] and juvenile delinquency.[17] There have been extensive debates regarding BWT and the extent to which disorder actually has each of these impacts on communities and the residents who live there. One of the main critiques is that disorder is strongly correlated with all of these outcomes, particularly crime, because it is just one of a vast array of products influenced by a neighborhood's capacity to regulate behavior and spaces, known as *collective efficacy*. This argument was borne out by Sampson and Raudenbush, who used ecometrics to show that disorder and crime are actually just cosymptoms of a community with weak collective efficacy.[18]

Though BWT is often treated as an ecological theory that describes disorder's role in accelerating urban decline, at its heart it is a theory of how disorder impacts individuals. In terms of crime, it posits that disorder signals a space that harbors uncivil or delinquent behavior, causing individuals to either (a) feel liberated to engage in such behavior as well, thereby contributing to disorder and crime, or (b) retreat socially out of fear of potential danger, undermining the natural capacity of the neighborhood to discourage crime. The biosocial perspective argues that the stress associated with this second effect is also responsible for any health consequences of disorder.[19] My colleagues Chelsea Farrell and Brandon Welsh and I recently undertook a meta-analysis of studies that tested the effects of disorder on individual-level behaviors and outcomes. We found that, when controlling for important correlates such as median income and collective efficacy, disorder had a limited, practically negligible effect on residents' aggression and criminality as well as on their attitudes toward the neighborhood. It did have a consistent effect on medical outcomes related to stress and mental health, though not physical health. Whereas previous critiques cast doubt on disorder's importance for neighborhood-level outcomes, this newer work does the same for individual-level outcomes, except in terms of mental health.

The mixed evidence for BWT does not mean disorder is no longer of interest. First, disorder does appear to have a salient effect on mental health in residents, if not on aggression and neighborhood attitudes. There is also a second value of measuring disorder embedded in theory surrounding collective efficacy. How a neighborhood staves off or succumbs to disorder acts as a model test case for understanding the social machinery of a neighborhood. Early urban theorists were drawn to disorder (or its absence) for this very reason, long before BWT attributed a causal role to disorder, and it is in this same spirit that it remains a pertinent aspect of a neighborhood's scenery.

Isolating Physical Disorder from 311 Reports

One of the major contributions of Raudenbush and Sampson's ecometric approach was the introduction of the *item-response model*, a tool commonly used in psychometrics and probably most recognizable in the context of standardized testing. A student who takes the Scholastic Assessment Test (SAT), for example, completes many questions (i.e., items) of varying difficulty that are then used to collectively assess a single underlying capacity (i.e., scholastic aptitude). In the case of disorder, a neighborhood audit or survey treats various aspects of disorder—graffiti, dilapidation, loose garbage—as distinct items and combines them to create a comprehensive measure. The item-response model translates well to administrative data, especially when cases are categorized by content, as they are in 311. There are two steps when constructing a measure based on an item-response model. The first is to define the construct of interest and use it to select appropriate items. The second is to use correlations between items to determine whether they reflect a single construct or instead actually capture multiple constructs.

Selecting Items

There have historically been two definitions of physical disorder. Raudenbush and Sampson's measure focused on the publicly visible artifacts of social incivilities, such as graffiti and forms of litter arising from illegal or problematic behavior (e.g., used condoms, empty beer bottles, hypodermic needles).[20] Other researchers have since expanded this definition to include any evidence that "spaces are not being kept or used properly."[21] This has led to a variety of protocols that also include items that, while not the result of flagrant incivilities, reflect an overall pattern of neglect, including deteriorating or abandoned housing, unkempt lawns or vegetation, and litter of all kinds.[22] One important consequence of this approach is that it extends measurement to elements of the neighborhood that are technically private but whose appearance and use are a visible part of the local scenery, such as front porches, lawns, and the facades of houses. Because this is the current convention, it is the basis for the work presented here.

When we originally completed this study in 2012, Boston's 311 system had received 334,874 requests for service via its three channels (hotline calls, internet self-service portal, and smartphone application), covering 178 case types,[23] of which 33 might be evidence of either denigration or neglect to spaces and structures (reported in Table 2.1). These data have since been published on BARI's Boston Data Portal.[24] Importantly, we did not include instances of natural deterioration, such as potholes or

TABLE 2.1 Case types that reflect human neglect or denigration of the neighborhood, including their frequency, categorization by factor analysis, and factor loadings

Case type	Count	Factor loading
Housing issues		
Bedbugs	871	.49
Breathe easy	590	.53
Chronic dampness/mold	442	.44
Heat—excessive, insufficient	2,175	.62
Maintenance complaint—residential	687	.54
Mice infestation—residential	796	.59
Pest infestation—residential	330	.52
Poor ventilation[a]	26	—
Squalid living conditions[a]	128	—
Unsatisfactory living conditions	8,948	.85
Unsatisfactory utilities—electrical, plumbing	174	.41
Uncivil use of space		
Abandoned building	238	.36
Illegal occupancy	642	.42
Illegal rooming house	471	.47
Maintenance—homeowner	180	.41
Parking on front/back yards (illegal parking)	336	.42
Poor condition of property	2,438	.80
Trash on vacant lot	432	.57
Big buildings		
Big buildings enforcement	236	.68
Big buildings online request	274	.72
Big buildings resident complaint	209	.60
Graffiti		
Graffiti removal	8,826	.83
PWD graffiti	847	.50
Trash		
Abandoned bicycle	144	.45
Empty litter basket[b]	802	.30
Illegal dumping	2,292	.87
Improper storage of trash (barrels)	4,756	.91
Rodent activity	3,287	.40
No factor (discarded)		
Illegal auto body shop	105	—
Illegal posting of signs	236	—
Illegal use	137	—
Overflowing or unkempt dumpster[a]	526	—
Pigeon infestation	82	—

Note: For factor analysis, $N = 544$ census block groups. An iterated principal factors estimation was used with a promax rotation.

a. Items did not load upon initial factor analysis but were added based on content similar to factor or one or more of its constituent items.

b. Item loaded at >.3 on both the trash and graffiti factors. It was maintained on the trash factor for reasons of content.

streetlight outages. Many of the selected case types are usual suspects, such as graffiti and abandoned buildings. Others are similar in content but rarer given their intensity, such as "squalid living conditions." Still others are unfamiliar but seemingly relevant, such as cars illegally parked on a lawn. Possibly most notable are those that are novel because they are more often experienced in private spaces, such as failing utilities or rodent infestations. Such cases highlight 311's ability to "see" the conditions inside houses, adding a new dimension of disorder that is not accessible to sidewalk-based audits. Though the array of case types capturing disorder is impressive, it is important to point out that just over 80 percent of case types were deemed irrelevant. To be fair, the 33 case types of interest accounted for a disproportionate 50 percent of all reports, but even that means that we discarded over half of the database in order to isolate our desired construct.

Factor Analysis

The item-response model assumes that the selected items actually reflect a shared underlying process or related set of processes. To evaluate whether this is the case, we use factor analysis to examine the correlations between items across neighborhoods over the 2.5-year period of data (approximated using census block groups). If they are sufficiently strong, there is reason to believe they reflect a single construct, or "factor." If not, one or more items might be omitted from the final measure. More interesting is that the items may actually capture multiple constructs. This would stand in contrast to existing measures of disorder, nearly all of which consist of a single factor. The only exception is Ross and Mirowsky's survey measure, which includes two components, "disorder" and "decay," that approximate the dichotomy between physical conditions arising from social disorder and others arising from neglect.[25]

Our factor analysis organized 28 of our 33 case types into five dimensions of disorder; five were discarded because they did not load on any factor, indicating that they were not part of the construct.[26] The items included in each are reported in Table 2.1, but in general terms they might be described as follows:

- *Housing issues,* including poor maintenance by property owners (e.g., poor heating, chronic dampness) and the presence of pests (e.g., bedbugs).

- *"Uncivil" use of space,* or private actions that negatively impact the public sphere (e.g., illegal rooming house, poor conditions of property, and abandoned building).
- *Big buildings complaints,* regarding the upkeep of large apartment, condo, and office buildings and the like.
- *Graffiti,* as reported by both constituents and public works employees.
- *Trash,* including the inappropriate disposal of trash, such as illegal dumping, improper storage of trash barrels, and abandoned bicycles. This construct also included rodent activity, which, though not an incivility itself, is often a consequence of poor trash storage.

Because nearly all previous measures of physical disorder had only one dimension, we examined whether these five factors might themselves reduce to a set of higher-order measures of disorder. Rather than combine into a single superordinate measure, they instead broke out into two separate dimensions of physical disorder, as illustrated in Figure 2.1: *denigration of the public space,* comprised of trash and graffiti; and poor care or *negligence for private space,* comprised of big buildings, housing, and uncivil use. For brevity, we refer to these two dimensions as *public denigration* and *private neglect.* These relationships are illustrated in Figure 2.1.[27]

Summary: Private and Public Spheres of Disorder

The first task of developing a measure of physical disorder from 311 records was to isolate the relevant content and organize it into interpretable measures. Already, we see some of the potential advantages that administrative data have over previous ecometric methodologies. First, the case types handled by the system are sufficiently diverse to capture two distinct but related aspects of physical disorder: *private neglect* and *public denigration.* These further break down into five lower-level categories that are more specific: *housing, uncivil use of space,* and *big buildings* for private neglect; and *graffiti* and *trash* for public denigration. This multidimensionality not only reflects a more nuanced measurement of physical disorder but also opens up access to a previously unavailable component of physical disorder. Whereas existing protocols, especially those utilizing neighborhood audits, were limited to those elements of disorder that could be observed from the street, 311 reports include problems

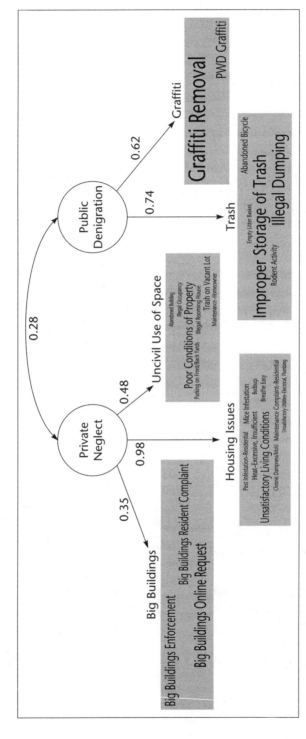

FIGURE 2.1 A two-dimensional measure of physical disorder, based on five categories of 311 case types. Word clouds contain all items included in each category, with size of the words reflecting the relative proportion of reports with that case type.

Note: Standardized parameters from the best-fitting model are reported. CFI = .95; SRMR = .05; *N* = 543 census block groups. All parameters are significant at *p* < .001.

occurring inside buildings. In this manner, the "eyes and ears of the city" are able to see conditions in both public and private spaces, providing a comprehensive view of deterioration and denigration in a neighborhood. For the sake of brevity, the foregoing analyses focus specifically on these two higher-order measures.

Validity: Aligning Data with Reality

It is tempting to treat administrative records, social media posts, and the like as a faithful representation of the pulse of the city. Once one isolates the content that reflects a particular construct of interest, a new dimension of the urban landscape should be laid bare. The difficulty with this logic is that the data were not collected systematically with the goal of capturing objective information in an unbiased fashion. Instead, aspects of the data-generation process may imbue the data with inherent biases, confounding any measures based on them.

The phrase "inherent biases" would suggest that naturally occurring data are a dead end for rigorous research and largely useless for policy and practice. This is not necessarily the case. If we can identify the sources of bias and correct for them, we will be able to access the information we actually want. Bias is nothing new to social science, and there are tools for addressing it, but the nature of bias in these data is a bit different from what we are accustomed to. Survey researchers have long recognized the biases that can be created when the sample of participants is not representative of the broader population. For example, many studies see an underrepresentation of disadvantaged or undereducated populations. In such cases, a weighted model will magnify the importance of individuals with lower incomes in order to create greater balance. The bias of naturally occurring data, however, arises because the actions that generate the information of interest (e.g., reports of physical disorder) are not systematic but instead are driven by some other process. This case is novel because it arises from a lack of control over data collection and creates a need for new methodological solutions. For example, Derek Ruths and his team have conducted a number of studies attempting to impart validity to social media data, including one study that used frequency and content of posts to distinguish individuals from organizations.[28] In some cases, this form of bias not only presents a new challenge but can also inspire further research, as the source of bias is itself a phenomenon of interest. This, as we will see later in this chapter, is true for the case of 311.

To illustrate the potential for bias in 311 data, one will note that each report is in fact the coincidence of two events: the issue itself and the decision of a resident or passerby to report it. Consequently, the distribution of reports depends not only on the density of issues across space but also on the probability that they will be reported in a given area. If this second value varied across neighborhoods, it would create systematic biases in any measure based on 311 data. In regions where residents are not inclined to make such calls, an issue might sit unnoted for a lengthy period, or even indefinitely, creating a gap (i.e., false negative) in the database. Conversely, there might be neighborhoods in which residents are quite vigilant, even generating multiple reports for a single issue, which would in turn create false positives and exaggerate the prevalence of disorder. The resultant variation in reporting might be referred to as the *civic response rate*, and is something for which any valid 311-based measure of neighborhood conditions will need to account.

This section describes the four methodological steps my colleagues and I took to establish a set of validated, 311-based measures of physical disorder that account for the bias introduced by the civic response rate. First, we used two neighborhood audits—identifying streetlight outages and broken sidewalk panels—to assay the propensity of a neighborhood's residents or visitors to report an issue. This in turn acts as an independent measure of civic response rate. Second, we created and evaluated a measure estimating the civic response rate based on the content of the 311 database. This was critical because if the measurement of civic response rate depended on neighborhood audits, our "novel" methodology would require just as much work as traditional protocols. In contrast, an automated estimate of the civic response rate would allow the continual production of an "adjustment factor" that accounts for bias in the raw measures of disorder. Third, we had to calibrate our adjustment factor against objective measures of physical disorder, determining how heavy its influence should be. This was done using observations from an additional neighborhood audit that assessed loose litter on streets and sidewalks.

The first three steps constitute a complete methodology for translating a raw database of 311 requests into a measure of physical disorder across a city, but we could not stop there. As the fourth and concluding step, we had to establish construct validity for our new measures, meaning we had to determine their substantive interpretation based on relationships with established variables.[29] In other words, did our adjusted measures of disorder correlate with those characteristics that they logically should? To examine this question, we compared our new adjusted measures with a series of demographic, economic, and social indicators traditionally associated with disorder.

Step 1: Assaying the Civic Response Rate

In summer 2011, I recruited a team of students at the University of Massachusetts Boston, where I was teaching classes, to conduct neighborhood audits that would estimate the civic response rate. Over the course of the study, we visited a demographically and socioeconomically representative sample of approximately half of Boston's census tracts. In each census tract, a pair of team members recorded for both sides of every street segment[30] (1) whether there were any streetlight outages and (2) the level of loose garbage on the street and sidewalk. In total, we assessed 4,239 street segments and identified 244 streetlight outages. For now, I focus on the streetlight outages, as they were central to estimating the civic response rate, but we will return to the garbage ratings later in this section. In a second audit, a consulting group hired by the city of Boston's Public Works Department assessed all of the city's sidewalks between November 2009 and April 2012. For each sidewalk, the assessors noted the proportion of panels that required replacement (i.e., cracked, broken) and subtracted this from the total, creating a measure of sidewalk quality. More details on the audits are available in Appendix A.

Each of the two audits produced a map that reflected the distribution of a particular type of public issue across the city. By cross-referencing these maps with the 311 database, we were able to identify when and where these issues were reported. As might be assumed, the probability of a streetlight outage being reported increased at a decreasing rate over time. Nine percent of outages were reported by constituents within a week of the audit and 22 percent by the end of the first month. After five months, 67 percent of streetlight outages had been reported by a constituent. For sidewalks, only 4 percent elicited requests for repair, though the majority of these (62 percent) elicited more than one, and some had many reports associated with them (*max* = 19). Unsurprisingly, those with calls also had more broken panels ($t_{df=27,386}$ = 3.79, $p < .001$). If we compare these same metrics across tracts—measuring for each how quickly people report a streetlight outage and how likely a broken sidewalk is to elicit repair requests—we can then estimate the propensity of each neighborhood to report problems; that is, its civic response rate.[31]

There was indeed considerable variation in civic response rates across the city. For streetlight outages, this was most apparent when estimating whether a neighborhood reported a streetlight outage within two months, ranging from a probability of 19 percent to as high as 72 percent across neighborhoods.[32] Tracts also varied in their likelihood of reporting a broken sidewalk; reporting for the average sidewalk, which had about one-third of its panels broken, ranged from 2 percent at the lowest to 11 percent at the highest.[33] This substantial range in the propensity to report an issue indicates that the civic response rate could in fact create meaningful bias in any measure of neighborhood conditions based on 311 records.

Step 2: Estimating Civic Response Rate from 311 Reports

Given that the civic response rate varies across neighborhoods, we will need to account for it if we want to create valid measures of neighborhood conditions based on 311 reports. Doing so poses its own measurement challenge. Whereas the preceding subsection measured the civic response rate directly, the broader goal is to estimate it indirectly through the 311 database. We could, of course, use the audit-based measures of civic response rate to adjust our measures of physical disorder, but this would be a temporary solution that might work for one or two years. Eventually, variation in the civic response rate will shift, with some places becoming more responsive and others less so. As a result, the continued measurement of physical disorder would require repeated neighborhood audits assessing the civic response rate. Instead, if the civic response rate could be estimated through the 311 database, it might be measured as often as desired (within reason, as we will explore further in the next section, on reliability), thereby enabling automated, repeatable measures of neighborhood conditions based on 311 that account for the civic response rate at that time. In order to do so, we must again isolate relevant content from the database, this time reflecting the civic response rate, and then coordinate it with the audit-based measures.

Defining Civic Response Rate

In order to estimate the civic response rate from the 311 database, it is first necessary to determine what elements constitute it. My colleagues and I proposed two. First is *engagement*, or knowledge of 311 and the willingness to use it. A large part of the battle for any public service agency is informing residents of available services and convincing them to use them. This can be particularly difficult when communicating with disadvantaged or immigrant groups that either prefer not to interact with the government or do not expect it to be responsive.[34] The second is *custodianship*. Knowing of and being willing to use 311 is a necessary condition for reporting a public issue, but it is not a sufficient one. When calling in a report about something like graffiti or illegal dumping, one is taking responsibility for the public space, requiring a different set of motivations than a request addressing one's personal needs (e.g., a request for a bulk item pickup).

To develop indicators of engagement and custodianship from the 311 database, we again used case types to limit our attention to reporting on particular situations of interest. In addition, we leveraged the user accounts maintained by the city to map reporters across the city. This was based on the logic that the density of reporters is most reflective of whether any person will bring a particular issue to the government's attention. We see the value of each of these techniques for measuring both engagement and custodianship. First, the most direct indicator of engagement would be to tabulate the number of individuals who do and do not know about 311, which can be approximated as the proportion of neighborhood residents who have an account. A less direct approach would be to identify case types whose need is likely to be even across the city. For example, one might expect residents of all neighborhoods to have a similar need for sanitation services to pick up bulk items. Another example of an evenly distributed need is for snowplows during a snowstorm, controlling for certain infrastructural characteristics.[35] In these cases, the geographic distribution of reports reflects the likelihood of utilizing the system.

Measuring custodianship requires a particular focus on reports that document a case of public deterioration and, in turn, a constituent's decision to take action regarding it. For this reason, we identified a subset of 59 case types that reflect issues in the public domain, including many (but not all) of the case types regarding physical disorder, and also including instances of natural deterioration, such as streetlight outages.[36]

Unfortunately, it is not possible to treat any one of these types as a benchmark, as is done with bulk item pickups and snowplow requests for engagement, because the very issue at hand is whether public issues are uniformly distributed across the city. Instead, we focused on reporters and their activities, limiting our attention to those who have acted as custodians (i.e., reporting one or more public issues). In 2011, for example, only 46 percent of registered users who made a report acted as custodians, indicating that this is a distinct way of using the system. Going further, whereas most custodians report public issues only on rare occasions—in 2011, 87 percent of custodians made two or fewer such reports—there are those who are considerably more active (18 reporters made over 100 reports). Given their zeal for neighborhood maintenance, we refer to individuals who make three or more reports in a year as "exemplars." More important for our purposes here, though, is their greater reliability in making custodial reports. These two groups, typical and exemplar custodians, represent resources for custodianship, and neighborhoods with a greater number of one or the other would be expected to report public issues more often and more quickly.

Coordinating Direct and Indirect Measures of the Civic Response Rate

To recap, we have three indicators for measuring a neighborhood's engagement (*total registered users, bulk item pickups,* and *snowplow requests*)[37] and two for measuring custodianship (*typical custodians* and *exemplars*). Before analysis, however, we removed the measure of all users from engagement, as it was so strongly correlated with typical custodians that they were deemed to be the same measure ($r = .93$). The analysis that follows aligns these indicators with the measures from the neighborhood audits in order to construct a final algorithm for estimating the civic response rate from the 311 database.[38] For user accounts, as elsewhere in this book, the home address is used whenever it is on record (~45 percent of registered users), and for others it is estimated as the census geography within which the individual person makes the most reports (accurate for 98 percent of custodians for census tracts).

A technique called structural equation modeling made it possible to evaluate our approach to estimating the civic response rate. This enabled us to do two things. First, we were able to treat engagement and custodianship as "latent" or conceptual constructs that were manifest through one or more measured variables, which is how we theorized them. We could also test the extent to which the measures from the neighborhood audits related to these two constructs. As illustrated in Figure 2.2, the final best-fitting model strongly supported our proposed strategy for measuring civic response rate.[39] Bulk item pickups ($\beta = .84$, $p < .001$) and snowplow requests ($\beta = .58$, $p < .001$) acted as indicators of engagement, and typical and exemplar custodians acted as indicators of custodianship (typical custodians: $\beta = .52$, $p < .001$; exemplars: $\beta = .74$, $p < .001$). With the removal of the measure of all users, it was also necessary to have typical reporters of public issues act as an indicator of engagement ($\beta = .50$, $p < .001$). All of this accounted for the tendency of neighborhoods with greater total population to have more typical and exemplar custodians (typical custodians: $\beta = .13$, $p < .05$; exemplars $\beta = .16$, $p < .01$).

The most notable result from this model was that the two objective measures of civic response rate were only related to the latent construct of custodianship (sidewalks: $\beta = .34$, $p < .001$; streetlight outages: $\beta = .18$, $p < .05$) and not to engagement. This reflects the fact that engagement

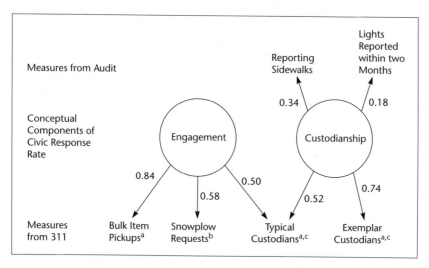

FIGURE 2.2 Building a 311-derived measure of the civic response rate based on relationships with objective measures from neighborhood audits.

Note: CFI = .95, SRMR = .06; N = 195 census block groups with measures on all variables. All parameters are significant at $p < .05$.

a. Log-transformed before analysis.

b. Controlled for total population, total street length, and dead-end length before analysis.

c. Controlled for total population.

might be necessary for reporting public issues—indeed, one would need to know of and be willing to use 311 to be a custodian as defined here—but is not sufficient for doing so. Instead, the key factor in determining the civic response rate of a neighborhood was the density of custodians, or the people who would invest the effort to address a streetlight outage, broken sidewalk, or other instance of deterioration in the urban commons. It also means that custodianship is the critical quality that makes the "eyes and ears of the city" stronger in some areas than in others and thereby introduces bias into any 311-based measure of neighborhood conditions.

Step 3: Calibrating the Adjustment Factor

We can now use our measure of the civic response rate, which it turns out depends primarily on custodianship, to adjust the raw measures of physical disorder to better reflect objective conditions. This process might be thought of as being similar to a volume knob that balances out regional differences in custodianship. Where custodianship is lower, we might "turn up the volume" on the raw number of reports of physical disorder, assuming that some issues are going unreported. Where custodianship is higher, we need to turn down the volume in order to temper outstanding vigilance. It is not immediately clear, though, how much influence this adjustment factor should have, meaning we will need to calibrate it against objective measures of disorder. For this purpose, we again utilize the neighborhood audits. Recall that the student team that recorded streetlight outages also rated street litter, a feature that is traditionally at the center of measures of physical disorder. From these ratings, we created neighborhood-level measures of litter.[40]

Calibrating the adjustment factor occurred in two parts. First, we ran regressions to examine the relationship between raw counts of case types in the two dimensions of disorder[41] and our objective measure of litter. This analysis was limited to residential neighborhoods (excluding regions dominated by institutions, parks, or downtown areas), as the predictive relationship between local behavior and loose litter would be most clear in these areas; in others, litter would be subject to dynamics that would not necessarily influence the other components of physical disorder (e.g., graffiti) in the same way, such as high pedestrian traffic.[42] The association with litter levels was strong for raw counts of cases of private neglect

(β = .63, p < .001) but more moderate for public denigration (β = .18, p < .05), indicating a potential need to adjust at least the latter measure to better reflect objective conditions.

Second, we created a composite measure of custodianship for each neighborhood using the parameter estimates from Figure 2.2, which would act as the basis for our adjustment factor. Importantly, the effect of a volume knob is always subject to the amount of noise it is amplifying and dampening. For this reason, we created an interaction effect that made the influence of custodianship proportional to the quantity of reports.[43] By adding this adjustment factor to each of the previous regressions, the final parameter estimates determined the amount of influence it should have to best align with objective levels of disorder. As hoped, the adjustment factor strengthened the relationship between each of the 311-based measures of disorder with levels of litter. This was particularly true for public denigration (Δ R^2 =.06, p < .01), doubling its overall relationship with levels of street garbage. The impact of the adjustment factor was less dramatic for private neglect (Δ R^2 =.01, p < .05), though this is unsurprising given the strong correlation it already had with street garbage before adjustment. This verifies the calibration and suggests that the final, adjusted measure in fact reflects objective levels of disorder, accounting for the civic response rate.

Step 4: Establishing Construct Validity

The fourth and final step of establishing validity for 311-derived measures of physical disorder was to evaluate construct validity. In order to confirm whether the adjustment factor in fact created measures that faithfully reflect neighborhood conditions, we examined their relationships with other neighborhood indicators associated with blight. These included median income, home ownership, and density of minority ethnicities from the U.S. Census Bureau's American Community Survey (ACS; 2005–2009); measures of perceived physical disorder and collective efficacy (i.e., social cohesion and social control between neighbors) from a resident survey (the Boston Neighborhood Survey); and reports of gun-related incidents from Boston's 911 call record (2011). We again limit our analysis to residential neighborhoods, but for better comparability with previous studies examining such correlations, we transition from census block groups to census tracts as the unit of analysis.[44]

TABLE 2.2 Establishing construct validity for measures of physical disorder from 311 reports by correlating them with other neighborhood characteristics typically associated with blight

	Private neglect	Public denigration
Median income	−.59***	−.39***
Home ownership	−.36***	−.49***
% Black	.61***	−.05
% Hispanic	.27***	.41***
Collective efficacy	−.38***	−.48***
Perceived physical disorder	.44***	.48***
Gun-related incidents	.68***	.27***

Note: N = 428 residential census tracts.
*** $p < .001$.

The measures of private neglect and public denigration had many of the anticipated relationships, as shown in Table 2.2. They were lower where there was higher median income, home ownership, and collective efficacy, and greater where there were more gun-related incidents, higher resident perceptions of disorder, and a higher density of Hispanic residents. The one unexpected finding was that the density of black residents, while strongly correlated with private neglect, held no correlation with public denigration. These correlations are largely consistent with the relationships previous measures of disorder have held with indicators of blight. For example, the correlation between private neglect and income in Boston is −.59, whereas Raudenbush and Sampson found that disorder and poverty correlate at .64 in Chicago.[45] Though the correlations of our adjusted measures and perceived disorder might seem low, they are similar to previous comparisons between these two constructs, reflecting the consistent finding that neighborhood conditions and resident perceptions of them are not always equivalent.[46]

Summary: Adjusting for the Civic Response Rate

This section has walked through a process that translated raw counts of 311 reports of physical disorder, beset by bias from a "civic response rate," into a set of adjusted measures that better reflect objective conditions. This entailed (1) quantifying differences in the civic response rate across neighborhoods through independent audits; (2) the conceptual and empirical development of 311-based measures of civic response rate, which turned out to depend on custodianship; (3) calibration of an adjustment factor that accounted for varying levels of custodianship; and (4) evaluation of construct validity by examining correlations between the final adjusted measures and demographic and social indicators known to be associated with disorder. Apart from their practical value, the resultant measures act as a proof of concept, demonstrating that it is possible to adjust for inherent biases in naturally occurring data and create validated measures. Further, the discovery of custodianship as the critical factor underlying the civic response rate revealed that the source of bias itself might be interesting if subjected to the same rigorous theoretical considerations required to extract a meaningful, interpretable measure.

Reliability: Criteria for Spatiotemporal Scales

Having solved the challenges of content and validity, we now have a methodology for measuring physical disorder using the 311 system. However, it still lacks guidelines for how such measures should be bounded in space and time. The previous methodological steps were conducted with a period of more than two years, but is it possible to measure neighborhood conditions more regularly, say every year or even every few months? This brings us to the third feature of research-quality data that is missing from naturally occurring data: criteria for reliability, or how often and at what scale a measure should be calculated in order to be robust to stochastic processes. The interests here are twofold. The first regards the "optimal" time window for cross-sectional measurement at a given geographic resolution (e.g., census block groups or census tracts). Because we will presumably have measures across multiple time windows, our second interest is to assess the ability to track longitudinal trajectories of neighborhoods relative to each other. In each case, the goal is a time interval that is as small as possible, thereby maximizing precision and frequency of measurement, but not so small as to be vulnerable to random events.

This third guideline is largely a technical exercise based on an existing technique for ecometrics and thus offers little in terms of conceptual or methodological advancement. That said, it is still important when considering how to properly construct and utilize administrative records in this way. For this reason, I include it, but do so only in brief. Those looking for more details should visit the article in which we presented the work in greater depth.[47]

Analysis

The measures of physical disorder are not unitary measures but are actually composites that combine counts of reports of elements of disorder with the prevalence of the two groups of custodians. For this reason, the establishment of criteria for reliability for our final measures of physical disorder requires that we first identify the appropriate time interval for each of the component measures. This could then be tested for the composite measure. We compared reliabilities for eight different temporal windows for both census block groups and tracts: one, two, and three weeks, and one, two, three, four, and six months. One will note, however, that establishing reliability in this way is not possible for the measure of exemplar reporters, because exemplars are identified by their behavior over the course of a complete year. For this reason, we did not calculate their reliability but introduce them only for the composite measures.[48]

We leveraged multilevel models (or hierarchical linear models, or HLMs, which we also did in the previous analyses; see note 31), this time to assess the consistency of the multiple measures taken from a single neighborhood over time and how well they enable us to statistically distinguish between neighborhoods. In doing so, we sought time windows for which the measures within a neighborhood correlated with each other at a level of .7 or higher (based on the intraclass correlation coefficient, or ICC). Reliabilities attained even this relatively stringent criterion for rather short time intervals (full results are available in Appendix B). For CBGs, either private neglect or public denigration could be measured reliably every six months. For census tracts, the same value was two months. Interestingly, counts of public reporters, though far fewer in number than actual calls, featured greater consistency within a region than either measure of physical disorder, reaching sufficient reliability for three-month windows for CBGs and one-month windows for census tracts. The multilevel models were also capable of discerning longitudinal trends in disorder for these time windows based on the significant variation in slopes. To conclude, we examined whether these same properties also held for the adjusted measures,[49] which are a composite of counts of cases and the interaction with custodianship. For both measures of disorder, the ICC was lower for the composite measures, but not alarmingly so. This was true for two-month intervals for tracts (public denigration: ICC = .44; private neglect: ICC = .65) and six-month intervals for block groups (public denigration: ICC = .51; private neglect: ICC = .68).

Summary: How Often to Measure Disorder

I have moved through the establishment of reliability quickly for two reasons. Not only is it largely a technical exercise, but it is also the least novel methodologically of the three steps presented here, meaning its stand-alone contribution is limited. That said, the results of this analysis do highlight some of the advantages that arise from the size of modern digital data. ICCs of this level are highly coveted in survey and observational measurement in the social and behavioral sciences, and here they were achieved for measures of two to six months—far more frequent than any existing ecometric protocol could accomplish. Furthermore, this level of reliability was maintained while also supporting longitudinal tracking. This is highly distinctive and opens up the possibility for complex research designs examining long-term trends in disorder.

The Opportunity of Naturally Occurring Data

Depending on one's perspective, naturally occurring data either promise to be transformative for the social sciences, including the study of cities, or are fraught with too many biases and assumptions to be worthwhile. As with nearly all scientific debates, the answer is somewhere in between these extremes. This chapter presented a set of methodological guidelines for walking this middle road, addressing the three main interpretive challenges and deficiencies of these novel resources:

1. *Extract constructs* that reflect the theoretical concept of interest by isolating relevant content from the noise surrounding it. This is often facilitated by an item-response model and factor analysis, as in our identification of 28 case types that constituted two higher-order and five lower-order categories of deterioration and denigration within a neighborhood. Even when measuring engagement and custodianship, which required more flexible use of the database,

we still developed multiple indicators and assessed their statistical relationships to create final constructs.

2. *Validate the measure* by identifying and adjusting for any bias that might be introduced by the data-generating process. Because 311 records are the product of constituent reports, we needed to measure, describe, and then account for variation in civic response rates across neighborhoods.

3. *Establish criteria for reliability* in the measure's ability to track information across space and time. We saw that we could track our two measures of physical disorder every two to six months (for census tracts and block groups, respectively).

The work here provides a proof of concept, realizing 311's purported role as "eyes and ears" that crowdsource neighborhood conditions in real time. The measures hold a number of advantages over ecometrics based on surveys and neighborhood audits. First, they generate a distinctively multidimensional view of physical disorder, in part thanks to 311's ability to see disorder both in public *and* in private spaces. Second, their continuity across space and time enables repeated measurement every two to six months, whereas no previous protocol had been conducted for an entire city more than twice in a decade. Finally, repeat measures are nearly costless. If done manually, they require only a few hours of a research assistant's time to access new data and rerun the code; recent technological advances in the automation of data transfer and processing have cut back on this time investment even further. In contrast, whole-city assessments using surveys and audits cost upward of $100,000. Some readers will note that the development of the methodology entailed considerable work, including two independent data collections and a lengthy set of analyses. Nonetheless, that investment of cost and effort would be necessary for any traditional protocol for measuring disorder and in our case laid the groundwork for a methodology that can be reproduced within Boston and can also be applied to other cities with their own 311 systems. In addition, many cities frequently conduct audit studies, so it is reasonable to assume that there will be additional opportunities to create validation measures.

Of course, the specific methodology and indicators presented here are an initial step, and there is more work to be done to refine them. First, we operated on the assumption that the civic response rate is consistent across case types, but this may not be true. Even in our own data, reporting rates for streetlight outages and broken sidewalks were only moderately correlated. Furthermore, the relationship between public denigration and street garbage was weaker than might be expected. It could be that a neighborhood's tendency to report man-made incivilities is not fully captured in its efficacy in reporting instances of natural deterioration such as streetlight outages and sidewalk cracks. Put another way, not all issues in the public domain are equivalent. Future validation efforts for 311 and related data sets will need to carefully evaluate the most effective measures both for objective comparison and internal adjustment, as these might differ depending on the particular set of conditions that are intended to be the focus.

A second pitfall is that of feedback loops between the use of data and its generation. This was a major concern of Lazer et al.'s critique of Google Flu, in that search engine usage might have shifted based on the information Google Flu was providing, thereby changing the very content the algorithm was using to predict flu cases.[50] Extending this concern to the current example, if the city of Boston uses the distribution of custodianship to guide outreach, it might change how those neighborhoods utilize the system. The methodology could be robust to such shifts, as custodianship is remeasured regularly based on the current number of typical and exemplar custodians in a region. But what if changes in use of 311 make these measures less effective as indicators of custodianship and the civic response rate? Certain types of messaging might cause individuals to report issues farther from their home neighborhood, making counts of resident custodians less informative. Assurances that users can make reports anonymously could lead to a rise in actual custodianship that is not captured by the density of registered users. In these or similar cases, the definition of the adjustment factor and its calibration would need to be revisited. As we have learned from the parable of Google Flu, close attention to feedback loops is critical when one uses data to drive a public service.

The Generalized Ecometric Approach

Given the diverse array of novel data describing the city, the guidelines proposed here promise to greatly expand the characteristics of the urban landscape that we can measure and track. We might call this a *generalized ecometric approach,* applicable to any data source, and, in theory, to any level of geography, including streets or even individual addresses. BARI has already undertaken this broader mission in conjunction with the city of Boston, using administrative records to build an extended library of ecometrics that visitors can visualize and download through our Boston Data Portal, including indicators of social disorder, crime, and medical emergencies derived from 911 dispatches;[51] two forms of investment and growth, one based on local investment and the other on major developments, drawn from building permits;[52] and building ages and trends in assessed value, obtained from tax assessments. Much of this work is driven by student projects in Northeastern University's urban informatics program or supported by BARI research seed grants.

There have been numerous creative efforts beyond Boston to leverage novel digital data to measure neighborhood characteristics. Legewie and Schaeffer used 311 reports in New York City, for example, to measure conflict between neighbors, using reports of noise complaints and other semisubjective nuisances.[53] For social media, Daniela Quercia's team has used Twitter "tweets" to track the experiential landscape of the city, including smells and sounds,[54] while others have demonstrated the use of Instagram to measure social segregation.[55] The University of Chicago's Array of Things sensor system, mentioned in Chapter 1, tracks ambient (e.g., heat, sunlight, rainfall), atmospheric (e.g., pollutant concentrations), and activity (e.g., pedestrian volume) metrics at highly localized resolutions. And some opportunities are only now being pursued, such as the use of communication patterns through various electronic platforms to measure social organization, one of the oldest concepts in urban science. Overall, the confluence of these various lines of work is an extended set of methodologies for measuring and tracking the social and physical ecology of neighborhoods, sometimes with updated versions of traditional measures and other times capturing aspects of the urban landscape that were not previously accessible.

An extended library of ecometrics has broad-based value. When incorporated into dashboards, it can help policymakers and practitioners improve their responsiveness to on-the-ground conditions. If such dashboards are made public and interpretable, the contents can help local organizations and residents better understand and advocate for their communities. For researchers, however, measurement is just an early stage of the scientific enterprise, and the real excitement is around the kinds of questions that we might ask with these metrics. Let us consider four such opportunities. First, we can combine these novel metrics with traditional methodologies, such as surveys and audits, to gain a more comprehensive view of neighborhoods. This is particularly important because it would be foolish to think that naturally occurring data could completely replace existing protocols; moreover, they will complement them in the deeper study of the city. Second, as noted, the generalized ecometric approach can accommodate the finer geographic resolutions of streets and even addresses, provided measures are properly constructed. The ecometric approach offers an interpretive frame for understanding these features of what one might call microplaces and how they contribute to the ecology of a neighborhood. Third, the longitudinal nature of the indicators can support studies of cross-time dynamics. These might assess the persistence of particular characteristics and also test their tendency to encourage or inhibit other events or conditions in the future. Finally, because the data are collected continuously, they facilitate the evaluation of experiments and interventions; the "before" data already exist and can be compared with the "after" data that are forthcoming. These four opportunities support a wide range of research questions, in turn imparting even more practical value to the data themselves. Each will appear at different points during the studies in this book.

Conclusion

In demonstrating how modern digital data can reconfigure ecometrics, this chapter has offered lessons that are applicable to urban informatics more broadly and to the computational social sciences writ large. When translating records into measurement, there is always a need to extract the desired constructs, validate their real-world interpretation, and establish criteria for reliability. This is true whether the unit of analysis is a geographic region, a person, a school, a train line, a company, or any other population of items that a researcher wants to examine.

My hope is that the guidelines presented here are also sufficiently flexible to support an approach to urban informatics that balances data and theory. Essentially, the ongoing tension regarding which of these two should lead inquiry is the newest iteration in the age-old debate between deductive and inductive reasoning. The social sciences have long preferred deductive approaches, lest we fall into the trap of overfitting models and creating new "knowledge" out of artifactual results. This is reflected here in the decision to illustrate the ecometric approach to "big data" with a modified version of one of urban science's most classical measures, capitalizing on existing theory to guide our process. Nonetheless, in the words of Sherlock Holmes, it is a capital mistake to theorize in the absence of data. Many of our current theories were built to explain observations made through traditional data sources, and consequently they are not always well suited to the new content and complexities presented by novel digital data. As Lazer et al. wondered, how much can current theory really tell us about the structure and processes of the complete social network of a city of a million people?[56] It is thus necessary for us, at least at times, to learn inductively from the data. These insights will in turn be subject to the same rigorous evaluation required of any new theory, creating a "checks-and-balances" approach to urban informatics.

In this chapter, we have already seen a valuable example of the ability of data to lead us to new ideas. In seeking to identify the source of bias in the 311 database's representation of neighborhood conditions, we developed the concept of custodianship—the intentional effort to take care of the public spaces and infrastructure of a neighborhood—and discovered that it was statistically distinct from simply engaging with a government service. Furthermore, it ended up being the foundation of the civic response rate, giving it both practical and theoretical salience. As one might recall from the beginning of this chapter, this was the second question that our initial meeting at City Hall identified as the major opportunity of 311 data: a direct window into the utilization of government services. In addition, custodianship harkens back to the inspiration that the earliest urban scholars saw in disorder. To them, disorder was not so much the causal engine of decline depicted in broken windows theory but instead an indicator of a neighborhood's ability to manage itself and its spaces. The further probing of custodianship through 311 would presumably be able to answer questions about neighborhood functioning that have long been of interest but have not yet been accessible. Consequently, what started out as unwanted bias becomes a truly original contribution of the 311 data set: the opportunity to pursue a wide range of unanswered questions about how individuals contribute to the upkeep of public spaces and infrastructure—or the urban commons. Going further, we can examine the consequences of these behaviors for the broader community, and the lessons they teach us for "civic tech" and other programs that incorporate the public into governance. This opportunity is the inspiration for Parts II and III of this book.

PART II

Maintenance of the Urban Commons

CHAPTER 3

Caring for One's Territory

ALL SOCIETIES HAVE A "COMMON." Whether it be grazing space for live-stock, waters for fishing, or even the sidewalks, streets, and parks of a neighborhood, these collectively held spaces or resources generate both value and responsibility for all who use them. A 311 system provides a novel mechanism by which the residents of urban neighborhoods can con-tribute to the maintenance of their commons, allowing them to channel *custodianship*, or efforts to prevent or counteract physical disorder, through government services. In turn, this makes them a part of activities they would not otherwise have the expertise, equipment, or authority to address—replacing a streetlight, painting over graffiti, or paving a pothole, for example. That Boston has become a leader in this collaborative ap-proach to urban commons only extends its legacy as a city at the forefront of innovations in the management of the urban environment. As Michael Rawson details in his book *Eden on the Charles*, Boston constructed the first public water system, practically "invented" the pastoral suburbs, and built a municipal park system of unprecedented scope, referred to as the Emerald Necklace.[1] All were pioneering efforts to preserve the natural re-sources and spaces on which the community depends.

One prominent environmental reform in Boston history remains enshrined as one of its most famous (and beautiful) landmarks. It is also a namesake for this book: Boston Common. As its name would indicate, Boston Common was originally constructed according to the British tradition of maintaining common lands for the grazing of cattle, which is how it was utilized for many decades. It was not until the mid-nineteenth century that it became the bucolic park that we know today, enjoyed by tourist and local alike for strolling, sunbathing, and the occasional swan boat ride. How this came to be, however, is not necessarily as communitarian as the creation of a "public park" might suggest. Over the years, the Common's central location placed it adjacent to important civic and business centers, and therefore the sorts of neighborhoods in which the most well-to-do (and influential) Bostonians lived and worked. As Rawson explains, this localized demographic shift, along with a broader societal trend away from husbandry, meant that very few of the Common's newest neighbors had cattle to graze. They thus had a different vision of its value as a public resource.

Boston's wealthier residents viewed the Common as an attractive piece of open green space where one might escape the density, bustle, and grime of the rest of the city. This ideal was only fully realized, however, if you could also remove the cattle that were little more than dirty, noisy, potentially dangerous nuisances. As such, "enclosure" of the Common (i.e., enclosed to grazing) gradually gained popularity, though not without resistance from those in the lower classes who still kept livestock there and their proponents. In 1830, after decades of argument and debate, the Boston City Council finally set aside the Common for the exclusive use of human recreation, placing it off-limits to grazing (to be fair, only a few hundred people still grazed cattle there). In doing so, they created the first public park in America that was dedicated entirely to recreation.

The case of 311 does not involve a battle between the upper and lower classes, but there are some notable parallels with the enclosure of Boston Common. Both initiatives center on the management of public spaces, specifically the implementation of social norms surrounding their use and treatment. In each, the motivating force appears to be a care for these common spaces and a desire to enjoy them. Part II of this book attempts to better understand these motivations, the pursuant actions of individual community members, and the way they contribute to the collective maintenance of the commons. Research to date has largely focused on the institutional structures that manage the commons, and allied work on collective efficacy in urban neighborhoods has similarly studied the contextual factors that predict the ability to complete shared tasks. Much less is known, however, about the discrete behaviors that determine the conditions of the commons—or what we might call the behavioral dynamics of the commons. The 311 database offers a unique opportunity to access individual differences in custodianship and how these variations influence collective outcomes, something that has not been possible through existing methodologies. This chapter focuses on where, how often, and, most importantly, *why* individuals choose to take action surrounding the commons. Chapter 4 then follows by bridging these individual-level patterns to a community's overall efficacy in maintaining its commons.

The motivations for maintaining the commons have vexed scholars for some time. The commons benefit everyone, but there are no clear incentives for a given individual to invest the time and effort to maintain them, raising the question of how they are sustained over time. I propose that such action is motivated by the innate human capacity for territoriality, or the tendency to identify with and claim objects and spaces. Whereas the patricians of nineteenth-century Boston sought to claim the Common for their own preferred uses and to exclude those uses they found discomfiting, modern Bostonians utilize 311 to counteract unwanted deterioration and denigration throughout the neighborhoods of the city. A similar logic might be applied to other types of commons the world over.

I assess this *territoriality thesis* by examining how and why individual Bostonians use 311 to contribute to the maintenance of their own local urban commons. The analysis that follows embodies the twofold value of urban informatics articulated in Part I by providing a theoretical foundation for understanding the behavioral dynamics of the commons, a foundation that can then be translated into practical lessons for the programs and policies that seek to support communities in their maintenance of the commons. These insights are of course immediately relevant to the 311 system in Boston but are also extensible to other 311 systems and even to commons of other types. Part II takes the first step in this process, developing this theoretical foundation in anticipation of its subsequent relevance. As it does so, the analytic tests of the territoriality thesis are light relative to some other chapters in this volume and therefore are well integrated with the conceptual narrative. Nonetheless, all sections conclude with a nontechnical summary.

Why Care for the Commons?

The Problem of the Commons

Commons hold generalized value for the members of a society, and in many cases they are vital to the livelihood of a sizable proportion of the population. Because they are held collectively, however, they are vulnerable to the self-oriented motives of individual community members. This is most often described in cases of depletable resources, such as food or timber, in which individuals might take more than their fair share, thereby hindering the current and future access of others. Similarly, when the "resource" in question is the use and experience of a space, as in the urban commons, there is no inherent incentive for individuals to engage in what I refer to as *custodianship;* that is, to address instances of deterioration or denigration. Such issues are everyone's problem but no one's formal responsibility, and it is thus in each individual's best interest to save their own time and energy by waiting for others to take action. This tension between individual- and group-level interests was described by Garrett Hardin as leading to the "tragedy of the commons."[2]

Despite the apparent inevitability of the tragedy of the commons, societies around the world have successfully sustained shared resources and spaces over many years and even centuries. In trying to understand this paradox, research on the commons has sought to illuminate the practices and institutions that societies put into place to achieve this goal. The empirical targets of such work have been diverse, including fisheries from Canada, to Mexico, to Turkey,[3] groundwater in California,[4] crimes against wildlife,[5] and even the "virtual commons" of intellectual property in the modern context of public, online, and open-source resources.[6] Traditional perspectives on the management of the commons debated the relative merits of privatization and regulation. The former grants each individual a particular portion of the commons, thereby providing a material incentive for sustainment.[7] In the latter, government is directly responsible for raising the funds for and administering any activities necessary for monitoring usage and attending to problems.[8]

Over the past two decades, another paradigm has emerged, based on the work of Nobel laureate Elinor Ostrom and her colleagues. They have argued that in many situations local groups develop informal institutions and practices that are uniquely tailored to the commons in question.[9] Consequently, they often outperform the more generalized, formal interventions of privatization or regulation. For example, in her book *Governing the Commons,* Ostrom compares multiple communities that face the same challenge of sharing scant or unpredictable sources of freshwater.[10] In California, multiple regional consortia have protected low water tables through legally enforced limitations on water extraction. In dry regions of Spain, communal irrigation channels (*huertas*) have been managed through turn-taking systems for over a millennium. In the Philippines, where water is so abundant as to be dangerous during the rainy season, permission to use the public irrigation systems (*zanjeras*) depends instead on the contribution of effort and materials to annual maintenance. In each case, the local community has succeeded in developing a locally specific set of rules and regulations for water consumption that leverages the particularities of the local ecology and social organization. Following this literature, the process by which a community sustains its commons depends on local context. Let us then take a closer look at the nature of the urban commons.

The Urban Commons

City dwellers live in a continuous commons, with private residences and businesses nestled in a matrix of shared streets and sidewalks. Dotted throughout are public planters for trees and flowers, and various green spaces where people relax and play. The residents of a neighborhood do not typically share any harvestable resources, but they do share the experience of these spaces, all of which might fall into disrepair. Streets and sidewalks can crack and crumble. The foliage of parks and public planters might similarly become unkempt, and furniture and playground equipment can rust and break. Thanks to high population density and small lots, the facades and lawns of private residences are a component of the public scenery, making their dilapidation a collective concern. This fuzzy line between private and public is reflected in building maintenance codes in cities around the world. Of course, throughout the urban commons there is also the risk of accumulating litter. All of these examples of physical disorder say nothing of the social disorder, such as public drunkenness, rowdy teenagers, and panhandling, that can also beset these spaces.

Given the diverse array of elements and activities that might be present in the urban commons, custodianship for it can manifest in a number of different ways. Residents sweep trash or leaves from the sidewalk or edge of the street. During snowstorms, people work together to dig out walkways, parking spaces, and fire hydrants. Community members or businesses adopt planters for trees or other foliage, committing to watering and pruning them. A related, more complex example is that of the community garden, where multiple tenants work together to manage a shared space for growing flowers and food in an urban context. Adults can intervene when teenagers are creating a nuisance. In addition to all of these direct actions, the residents of a neighborhood can contact authorities when they need their assistance in addressing some issue, be it physical deterioration, such as a pothole or graffiti, or unwanted social behavior. Though the impact of the community member's actions are indirect in such cases, this is still a form of custodianship, as the effort and intention is the same: to maintain and defend the public spaces of the neighborhood from deterioration and degradation. Presumably, the motivations also remain consistent.

As discussed in Chapter 2, the study of the maintenance of the urban commons has centered on levels of physical and social disorder in a neighborhood, driven largely by interest in broken windows theory and collective efficacy. The latter relates strongly to the question here, as Robert Sampson and his colleagues have shown that the prevention and elimination of disorder is a key manifestation of a community's ability to pursue and achieve shared goals.[11] Efforts to understand the emergence of collective efficacy have generally focused on how demographic characteristics that inhibit the construction of social relationships within a neighborhood, including concentrated disadvantage, residential instability, and ethnic heterogeneity, predict resident reports of collective efficacy.[12] There are three weaknesses to this methodological approach. First, though a neighborhood might have an overarching capacity for achieving shared goals, collective efficacy is most accurately described in terms of the specific task at hand.[13] This stands to reason, as a community might be more effective at taking action in the face of some challenges than in others. Second, surveys on collective efficacy are actually hypothetical measures of what residents think would happen in certain situations rather than direct assessments of a community's response to a challenge. Third, work on collective efficacy has taken an approach similar to that of Ostrom and her colleagues, emphasizing the role of community-level characteristics in determining the appearance and use of public resources, paying less attention to the behaviors that directly contribute to these outcomes. The work here attempts to move beyond each of these three limitations by focusing on a neighborhood's demonstrated collective efficacy in maintaining the urban commons and on the behaviors responsible for doing so.

From Institutional Processes to Behavioral Dynamics

Research on both the commons and collective efficacy has focused on the role of group-level characteristics in the maintenance of shared resources and spaces. These insights are critical, but the fact remains that maintenance must be perpetuated by the custodianship of individual community members, the very behaviors that local institutions and relationships must manage.[14] We have very little knowledge about these behaviors, their motivations, and the dynamics by which they do or do not sustain the commons. Who is taking such action? When and why do they do so? Is a small subset of individuals largely responsible, or is custodianship evenly distributed across the community's members? Put another way, we may be able to predict *whether* a neighborhood is able to maintain local spaces, based on its group-level characteristics, but far less about *how* this maintenance actually occurs.

The 311 system offers a unique opportunity to pursue research on the behavioral dynamics of the commons, which otherwise faces a major challenge of measurement. Examining the maintenance of a given commons would take hours upon hours of observation. Doing so in a way that reveals individual differences in maintenance, which would be necessary to understand the behaviors themselves, would be even more arduous. Comparing these results across multiple commons, in order to understand how they contribute to collective outcomes, would be virtually impossible with traditional methods. By documenting tens of thousands of requests for government services, 311 inadvertently conducts the long-term "observation" of neighborhood maintenance, which would be untenable for an in-person research protocol. Because the database distinguishes between 311 users, we can compare individual patterns of behavior both within and between neighborhoods, revealing not only which communities are successfully maintaining the commons but how they are doing so. We begin with the question of motivation: Why do people take action on issues in the urban commons even when there is no formal requirement or incentive for doing so?

Territoriality and the Commons

There are few empirical studies of the behavioral dynamics of real-world commons as I define the term here—that is, the individual-level motivations and actions that impact the conditions of public spaces and resources. Without this detailed knowledge, most work has instead made simplifying assumptions as to how people do or do not contribute to the commons. The most prominent such assumption is readily visible in a large body of literature that simulates how population composition determines local sustainability. This work typically divides the world into two types of actors: cooperators, who act in the best interests of the commons, and noncooperators, or free riders, who avail themselves of the commons in ways that either denigrate or neglect their long-term maintenance.[15] Simple assumptions of this sort make social dilemmas tractable for simulation models and have helped to articulate the viability of commons under a variety of contexts. That said, when such assumptions are taken as a faithful representation of reality, they leave a gap in our understanding of the motivations that make an individual a "cooperator" or not, knowledge that is necessary for empirical studies of when and where individuals will act for the benefit of the commons.

Work using the cooperator–free-rider model tends to make one of two assumptions about the behavioral motivations surrounding the commons. One is rooted in the rational actor model, which posits that human behavior is motivated solely by the perceived costs and benefits of an act. This provides the logic behind the "tragedy of the commons" and calls for attention to contexts and institutions that can incentivize action. A major weakness of this approach, though, is that it collapses the diverse array of motivations into a single cost-benefit heuristic, thereby losing the richness of human psychology. While the calculus of the rational actor model may be correct for modeling purposes, it loses how humans enter into each specific activity. It in turn overemphasizes material outcomes (i.e., utility, as rational actor theorists call it), losing sight of any contextual factors that stimulate action without directly affecting objective costs and benefits.

When commons researchers do consider motivations that are "domain-specific," being associated with a particular context and goals, they turn to prosociality, or positive social behavior. This is based on the alternative assumption that, because of the impact the maintenance of the commons has on the public good, it should be classed with other forms of prosociality, such as sharing, empathy, and helpfulness. However, this logic focuses on the consequences of the behavior, which is at best an indirect way of understanding its origins, and can often be misleading.[16] If instead we compare the behaviors associated with prosociality to those involved in the maintenance of the commons, it becomes apparent that the underlying motivations might be quite different. Whereas sharing and helpfulness entail direct social interactions and exchanges, the decision to either care for or neglect the commons is an interaction with space, and the benefits for others are only in the abstract. Put another way, just as interpersonal prosociality is motivated by concern for other people, custodianship is motivated by concern for the space, something also known as *territoriality*.

The term territoriality grows out of, and is thus most often associated with, work by biologists on how animals claim and defend spaces.[17] Given these origins, it typically conjures up images of lions and hyenas battling over a recent kill, bears marking trees in the forest, and the like. Social and environmental psychologists, however, have noted that humans exhibit their own particular form of territoriality in myriad contexts, from the way teenagers decorate their rooms to how an office worker does the same for her cubicle, "making it her own."[18] One of my favorite expressions of territoriality is on display in my classroom every semester. Each student chooses a seat the first week and proceeds to keep it, rarely if ever sitting elsewhere.[19] As these examples illustrate, human territoriality still serves the purpose of managing social roles around objects and spaces, but it does so in a way that goes beyond defense and exclusion and also encompasses upkeep and personalization. This has led to an expanded definition of territoriality, spanning all attitudes, cognitions, and behaviors that arise from a sense of ownership of an object or space.[20] Key to this definition is an emphasis on psychological ownership, rather than the traditional legal definition of ownership, meaning that territoriality is motivated by a "feeling of possessiveness and of being psychologically tied to an object."[21]

A considerable amount of research has examined the expression of territoriality in urban neighborhoods, largely focusing on physical artifacts that are seen as manifestations of such motivations. For example, Barbara Brown and her colleagues treated house decorations during the holidays as a manifestation of territoriality.[22] Others have done the same for fences and "NO TRESPASSING" signs.[23] This work highlights two major implications for the application of the modern, expanded definition of territoriality to the maintenance of the commons. First, human territoriality is divided into two components, each of which is visible in neighborhoods: caretaking, or the general maintenance and personalization associated with owning something, reflected in basic upkeep or holiday decorations; and defense from intrusion or violation by others, as reflected in fences and "NO TRESPASSING" signs.[24] Second, the distinction between psychological and legal ownership permits territoriality to extend geographically from private items to shared ones, the latter driven by collective psychological ownership.[25] We see evidence for this in that territoriality predicts the maintenance not only of houses but also of entire neighborhoods. For this reason, theorists have separated territoriality in urban neighborhoods across two geographic levels:[26] the primary territory, or the home and directly abutting spaces, and the secondary territory, or shared spaces perceived as being collectively owned.

A major weakness of the work on territoriality in urban neighborhoods is its limited success in demonstrating a relationship between physical artifacts and territorial motivations. A handful of studies have shown that houses and neighborhoods whose residents express a more territorial connection with the space are better maintained,[27] which is consistent with the territorial thesis presented here, but most other work has logically equated territorial motivations with physical artifacts defined as "territoriality" without validating the assumption that the one in fact leads to the other. This again is attributable to the methodological challenge described in the previous subsection; with current protocols, it is very difficult to assess individual differences in custodianship and, in turn, to evaluate the associated motivations.

The Territoriality Thesis of the Commons

Based on the existing work on territoriality in urban neighborhoods, I propose the *territoriality thesis* of the commons: that custodianship, and therefore the maintenance of the urban commons, is rooted in the innate human capacity for territoriality. Though this hypothesis is based largely on work in urban neighborhoods, it would seem extensible to any situation in which individuals share resources or space. The remainder of this chapter tests this proposition by using 311 reports, which, returning to Chapter 2's lessons about the usage of administrative data, entails two major challenges. First, I isolate the content relevant to custodianship from other information within the 311 database and develop methodologies for its measurement. Second, I establish construct validity through two separate tests. The first is a relatively simple examination of whether the geographic distribution of reporting is consistent with what would be expected of a territorial behavior. Because territoriality is driven by psychological ownership, it would follow that custodianship, and therefore 311 reporting, would be anchored by the home. Going further, I present a more direct test, marrying the "big data" of the 311 database to the "small data" of a survey of 311 reporters to evaluate whether custodianship is related to self-reported territorial motivations. Moving beyond these challenges of measurement and validation, the third section combines these methodologies to further investigate the differences between behaviors that reflect the two components of territoriality: those that are merely beneficent and those that actively defend the space against the improprieties of others.

Before I embark on this analysis, it is important to address the strengths and limitations of the data set and their implications for the inferences we can make. As the reader will see, the sample is quite large for social science research, with tens of thousands of individuals. A large sample and a representative sample, however, are two different things. Chapter 2 demonstrated that the tendency to make reports varies across neighborhoods, and this is almost certainly correlated with racial and socioeconomic characteristics. Though this question is examined more closely in Chapter 4, it would seem likely that disadvantaged groups, especially those that do not speak English as a first language, are less likely to report public issues through 311. Another concern is that the data only contain reports under the jurisdiction of the city of Boston. This is an administrative distinction, meaning no reports reference issues in surrounding municipalities or even in locations within the city that pertain to state agencies, such as subway stations. These limitations in the data are important and must be kept in mind moving forward. At the same time, they do not appear to undermine any evidence found for the territoriality thesis. First, for this to be the case, disadvantaged populations would have to express custodianship at a broader geographical scale than those with higher socioeconomic status, in which case their exclusion would overstate the support for the territoriality thesis, or that these groups take action on the commons based on a set of motivations completely distinct from those of their more affluent counterparts. There is little reason to believe that either of these would be the case. Similarly, although the data set is subject to artificial geographic boundaries, Boston is not a small space. Consequently, this constraint will probably only affect our ability to comprehensively observe the reporting of a few individuals living near the borders of the city. There is also no reason to believe that Bostonians themselves will express custodianship in a manner different from that of other communities. Thus, the insights that follow are likely extensible to populations not well represented in the data. Also, as in Chapter 2, those interested in analyzing the data themselves can access them through the Boston Data Portal.[28]

Test #1: The Geographical Distribution of Custodianship

Measuring Custodianship

The first step for testing the territoriality thesis is to isolate the content from the 311 database that reflects custodianship and to organize it for analysis. We have already seen the basis for this in Chapter 2, in which I presented a measure of custodianship at the neighborhood level.[29] The 311 user accounts make it possible to map registered individuals across the city and to characterize how each has utilized the system. For example, we identified a subset of 77 case types (of 225 handled by the system) that reflected issues in the public domain, such as streetlight outages and graffiti removal, rather than personal needs, such as requests for bulk item pickups. These case types and their frequencies are reported in Table 3.1. This made it possible to distinguish custodians, who had used the system to report one or more public issues, from those who did not. We can extend this same logic of using case records to describe how individuals utilize 311, including examinations of when, where, and how often an individual reported public issues. Additionally, the account is often accompanied by contact information provided by the user, including home address and e-mail. Altogether, this information supports a variety of research designs and measurement techniques, as we will see.

Between March 1, 2010, and December 31, 2015, there were 170,886 registered accounts that made at least one request for services via 311 in Boston (excluding accounts pertaining to city employees).[30] Of these, 79,073 (46 percent) qualified as custodians by making at least one report

TABLE 3.1 311 case types referencing issues in the public space and their frequencies in the time period analyzed

Case type	Count	Case type	Count
Abandoned bicycle	1,173	Overflowing or unkempt dumpster	1,522
Abandoned building	700	Park improvement requests	135
Abandoned vehicles	11,846	Park maintenance requests	317
Abandoned vehicles—private tow	12	Park safety notifications	4
Bridge maintenance	123	Parking enforcement	13,003
Building inspection request	9,316	Parking meter repairs	642
Bus stop issues	165	Parking on front/back yards (illegal parking)	1,076
BWSC pothole	129		
Catch basin	2,095	Parks general request	1,051
City/state snow issues	705	Parks lighting issues	11
Construction debris	679	Parks lighting/electrical issues	323
Corporate or community group service day cleanup	8	Pavement marking inspection	142
		Pavement marking maintenance/inspection	1,518
Downed wire	392		
Empty litter basket	5,991	Pick up dead animal	11,224
Exceeding terms of permit	538	Pigeon infestation	188
Fire hydrant	1,066	PWD graffiti	4,305
General lighting request	5,282	Request for litter basket installation	730
Graffiti removal	23,730	Request for pothole repair	36,112
Highway maintenance	9,444	Request for snow plowing	61,843
Illegal auto body shop	402	Requests for street cleaning	44,964
Illegal dumping	6,260	Requests for traffic signal studies or reviews	1,758
Illegal occupancy	1,712		
Illegal posting of signs	606	Roadway repair	1,593
Illegal rooming house	1,044	Rodent activity	10,351
Illegal use	159	Sidewalk cover/manhole	1,559
Illegal vending	272	Sidewalk repair	10,237
Improper storage of trash (barrels)	15,983	Sidewalk repair (make safe)	18,709
Install new lighting	293	Sign repair	12,741
Knockdown replacement	983	Snow removal	23,051
Late bus issues	234	Streetlight knockdowns	3,285
Litter basket maintenance	470	Streetlight outages	41,032
Misc. snow complaint	3,094	Traffic signal inspection	2,282
Missed trash/recycling/yard waste/bulk item	47,239	Traffic signal repair/inspection	15,906
		Trash on vacant lot	1,245
Missing sign	4,328	Tree emergencies	8,539
Needle pickup	819	Tree in park	139
New sign, crosswalk, or pavement marking	4,275	Tree maintenance requests	21,818
New sign, crosswalk, or pavement marking	2,411	Unshoveled sidewalk	48
New tree requests	6,530	Upgrade existing lighting	278
News boxes	1,139	Utility casting repair	592

Note: Includes only cases that remained after removing those that could not be mapped.

referencing an issue in the public space. This amounts to approximately 10 percent of Boston's population. As in Chapter 2's analysis of 2011, we find that reporting was a relatively rare behavior for most individuals, even with the longer time span. The majority of custodians reported one public issue (65 percent), and 89 percent of users made three or fewer reports over the nearly six-year period. Nonetheless, there were some noteworthy outliers: 77 individuals reported 100 or more public issues, and two even reported over 1,000!

The Geographic Distribution of Custodianship

A key component of the territoriality thesis is that reporting is anchored by the home, a hypothesis that can be tested only if we know the distance of 311 requests from the home of the reporter. Such a calculation is in fact possible for the 49,707 custodians (50 percent) who had a home address on file, but before doing so it is worth considering what would qualify as evidence for this proposition. Previous research has found that urban residents predominantly describe "their neighborhood" as covering a space within a half mile (or ~800 m) of their home, though many describe something somewhat smaller.[31] This is further reflected in people's walking range, which is typically limited to around three-quarters of a mile from home.[32] The narrow definition of neighborhood is not simply an artifact of constrained physical movement, however. Most city dwellers travel to other neighborhoods for work, recreation, shopping, and to visit friends and relatives.[33] For example, according to the U.S. Census Bureau's 2013 American Community Survey, 79 percent of Bostonians traveled to work in a motor vehicle and 83 percent had a commute longer than fifteen minutes, indicating that the vast majority of residents work at a location outside the home neighborhood. From this, it would appear that the average urbanite has the regular opportunity to report issues via 311 in a number of locations around the city. Despite this, the territorial thesis would predict that most users do not avail themselves of these opportunities and instead limit their reporting to issues within a half mile of their home. An even stricter test would be to examine the narrowest definition of "neighborhood"—the block of residence and the adjoining blocks (approximately 150 m in Boston)—to see just how localized custodianship might be.

An initial look at the reports provides strong initial support for the territoriality thesis: the median distance of an issue from a reporter's home was 0 m—literally at or in front of a person's front door—and 77 percent of reports fell within the narrowest definition of neighborhood. Analysis of individual reporters told a similar story. More than half of individuals (57 percent) reported issues only in the spaces directly in front of his or her house (i.e., a range of 0 m). Furthermore, 81 percent of individuals reported issues only within 150 m of home, and 89 percent did so exclusively within 800 m of home. Of course, just as a handful of individuals made a very large number of reports, there were those whose custodianship covered a broader geographical range: 9 percent of individuals made reports more than 1,600 m (~1 mile) from home, and 4 percent did so more than 5 km from home. Sixteen individuals even had a range greater than 15 km, spanning the city from tip to tip. Such cases, however, were not the norm.

A Flexible Definition of "Home" Neighborhood

Rigid thresholds for the "home neighborhood," such as 150 m or 800 m, can be useful for illustration, but they do not account for the fact, noted previously, that individuals vary considerably when defining the geographic extent of their neighborhood. How an individual perceives these boundaries might reflect the range over which that person feels a sense of ownership, and, in turn, is most likely to act as a custodian. An ideal approach, then, would be to define each individual's home neighborhood as the contiguous region around the home with reports. This is possible using an algorithm that identifies clusters of reports that fall within a certain distance of each other,[34] thereby approximating contiguous regions of activity. Here I will continue to use the most stringent definition of a neighborhood, defining a home cluster as one containing at least one report within 150 m of the reporter's home and a nonhome cluster as containing no reports within 150 m of the reporter's home.[35] Figure 3.1 illustrates these clusters for select respondents from our survey of 311 users (see the next section for more on the survey).

The clustering procedure found that 91 percent of custodians reported within their home neighborhood and that only 17 percent had one or more nonhome clusters. This methodology, however, also offers a distinctive window into the variability in home ranges. Consistent with the

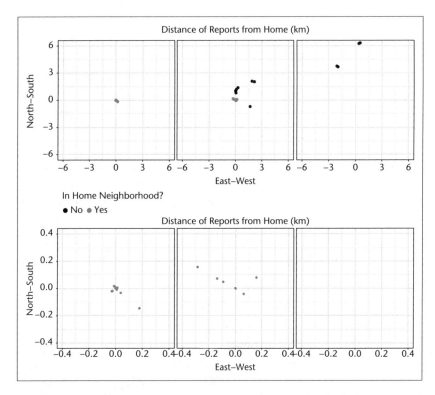

FIGURE 3.1 Map of reports relative to home address for individuals illustrating three groups, classified by their geographic clusters of reporting (see the text for the procedure): those who made reports only in the home neighborhood (90 percent of custodians; left panel), those who made reports both in and outside the home neighborhood (6 percent of custodians; center panel), and those who made reports only outside the home neighborhood (4 percent of custodians). The top panel includes all reports made, and the bottom panel zooms into the home neighborhood.

findings from the previous section, 96 percent of the home clusters were *entirely contained within 150 m of the custodian's home*. On the other end of the spectrum, 24 custodians (<0.1 percent) had a contiguous range of 800 m or more from their home. Even if one allows that the methodology used here sets an arbitrarily low threshold for perceived contiguity with the home address, it is noteworthy just how few people exhibited custodianship over a range often used as the definition of "neighborhood."

In parallel, we see a similar range in the number of reports both within and outside the home neighborhood. Sixty-two percent of custodians with a home cluster had only one report in that area, and 89 percent had three or fewer reports. There were again those that were far more active, including 619 custodians (2 percent) who reported 10 or more issues in their home range. Almost perfectly in parallel, of the 17 percent of custodians who had a region of reporting away from the home neighborhood, 68 percent made only one such report, and 91 percent made three or fewer.

Summary: Custodianship, Anchored by the Home

This section presented a methodology for describing an individual's usage of the 311 system, including measures for when, where, and how often he or she acts as a custodian. The distribution of these measures was striking. The vast majority of custodians only reported public issues on rare occasions (89 percent made fewer than three reports in six-plus years) and in areas near their homes (81 percent made no reports more than 150 m from their home). The latter finding provides immediate evidence for the territorial thesis, as custodianship appears to be constrained to areas near the house, even though nearly all Bostonians interact with, and therefore have likely had the opportunity to report issues in, places much farther afield. When we identified geographic clusters of reports for each user, 91 percent had a "home cluster" that included reports within 150 m of their home, and only 17 percent had clusters that were located elsewhere in the city. Although we do see remarkable consistency in the nature of custodianship from these numbers, there was substantial variation, with certain individuals reporting more than 100 issues and over ranges of a half mile or more. These large variations in both quantity and range persist when we constrain the analysis to home clusters. This demonstrates that urbanites vary widely not only in the range over which they express custodianship but also in how strongly they express it both within and beyond the regions contiguous to their home.

Test #2: Verifying Territorial Motivations

Showing that the geographic distribution of custodianship is centered on the home is consistent with the territoriality thesis but provides only indirect evidence for it. A stronger approach to establishing validity would be to examine whether territorial motivations actually predict patterns of custodianship. As with the effort to validate measures of physical disorder in Chapter 2, this requires the alignment of the 311 database with external data sources. To this end, I conducted a survey of registered 311 users in collaboration with colleagues at the Engagement Lab at Emerson College (director Eric Gordon and then postdoc Jessica Baldwin-Philippi, now assistant professor at Fordham University). The survey asked about people's experiences with the system and their motives for using it. We then linked the responses to user account data. In this manner, we married "big data" with "small data," using the latter to impart a clearer interpretation to the former.[36]

The Survey

We invited all registered users of Boston's 311 system with an e-mail address on file who had made at least one request for service during 2012 to take a survey that asked about their usage of the system, as well as some other personal information (e.g., demographics). We merged the survey responses with the 311 database by e-mail address, enabling us to analyze the responses in conjunction with reporting patterns during 2012. The final sample used here consists of 674 respondents who could be merged with a particular user account and who had completed all items of interest.[37] Importantly, the survey included a mix of both custodians and noncustodians (64 percent custodians), providing a valuable opportunity to examine differences between the two groups. Because all survey participants knew of and used 311, we can evaluate the motivations for custodianship while controlling for any unmeasured factors that might influence a person's tendency to engage with the system in the first place.

The survey included two scales assessing territorial motivations for using the 311 system. *Benefiting the local community* was measured with two items: "[311 is important] because it improves my community" and "[It's helpful for] changing your neighborhood." *Enforcing norms* was measured with two items: "[It's important] because others do not follow laws and social norms of the community" and "[It's important] because it will make the neighborhood safer." The survey also asked about concerns about property values, an additional factor that might motivate individuals to maintain a neighborhood's public spaces. Anyone living in a neighborhood has something to gain or lose through its long-term trajectory,[38] and deterioration can lead to lower property values for all residences.[39] Thus, residents may be motivated to maintain the space not out of an interest in contributing to the community in defending the space from norm violations but because they are concerned about the neighborhood's economic fortunes. We assessed this with one survey item, "[It's important] because it's good for property values."

Another area of interest is the geographical distribution of an individual's custodianship. We have already seen how clustering algorithms can be used to describe reporting within the home neighborhood in an individualized fashion, but examining reporting beyond the home neighborhood is less straightforward. Despite the variety of information that 311 reports do contain, they do not come with labels like "place of work" or "home of friend," and it is not apparent how to infer these sorts of things from the information that is available. To overcome this challenge, the survey also asked participants about the neighborhoods in which they have used 311, including the neighborhoods in which they work, visit friends and family, and commute.

Finally, respondents reported their sex, race, age (in 10-year ranges), income, and highest education attained (many declined to report their income, so highest education was used as the main indicator of socioeconomic status). These are used as controls in the following analyses but also give us a fuller sense of our sample, which, it is important to note, was considerably more white, educated, and middle-aged than the overall population of Boston (see Table 3.2), though it is unclear how much the demographic composition of the survey sample differed from that of the population of 311 users. The activity levels of survey participants, on the other hand, were greater than expected, as they were more likely than the average 311 user to be custodians (64 percent vs. 47 percent). Additionally, those who were custodians made more total reports than expected (*mean* = 2.76 in 2012 in the sample; ~90 percent of custodians make two or fewer reports in a year). The results that follow need to be interpreted with the knowledge of this imbalance. One advantage of the inflated level of engagement with 311, though, is the access to greater variation for analysis.

Motivations for Using the CRM System

Respondents ranked benefiting the community as their greatest motivation for utilizing 311 ($M = 4.32$, $sd = 0.83$), followed by the opportunity

TABLE 3.2 Demographic composition of survey sample of 311 users

	Count (%)		Count (%)
Gender		*Ethnicity*	
Male	336 (50)	White	537 (80)
Female	338 (50)	Black	60 (9)
		Hispanic	17 (3)
		Asian	11 (2)
		Other	49 (7)
Education level		*Age*	
High school or less	36 (5)	18–24	10 (1)
Some college	90 (13)	25–34	116 (17)
Professional degree	17 (3)	35–44	160 (24)
Associate's degree	37 (5)	45–54	175 (26)
Bachelor's degree	226 (34)	55–64	125 (19)
Master's degree	219 (32)	65–74	76 (11)
Doctoral degree	49 (7)	>75	12 (2)

Note: Total N = 674.

to enforce local norms (M = 3.40, sd = 1.23). Notably, it appeared that the desire to maintain property values was not even seen as a meaningful part of the system's value, as its average ranking fell below the neutral rating on the Likert scale (M = 2.53, sd = 1.54).[40] When examining how these different motivations predicted variation in custodianship, we utilized multilevel models, as we did in Chapter 2. Of value here is that the models estimate regression parameters based on the differences between individuals in the same neighborhood (in this case, census tracts). This controls for localized conditions that might influence all residents' opportunity to report issues of various sorts and thereby create inherent similarities between neighbors.[41] The models that follow predicted whether an individual was a custodian and the extent to which he or she reported in different geographical contexts, including the number of reports and the geographical range of custodianship within the home neighborhood (based on the clustering technique described previously), as well as whether an individual stated on the survey that they had used 311 to make reports from neighborhoods other than their own. Because these outcome variables are either dichotomous (i.e., 0 / 1) or heavily skew (i.e., Poisson distributed, with a long tail of high values), the results here report odds ratios (O.R.) rather than the more familiar beta estimates.[42]

Whereas the latter can be either negative or positive, odds ratios describe the likelihood of an event, with values from 0 to 1 indicating lower likelihood (i.e., a negative effect) and values greater than one indicating a greater likelihood (i.e., a positive effect). All models used are reported in Appendix C, including the results of demographic predictors, which, for the sake of brevity, I give little attention here.

Custodians and noncustodians differed in their levels of territoriality, though only in their desire to benefit the community (O.R. = 1.32, $p < .05$). They did not differ in their desire to enforce norms or to maintain or raise property values (enforce: O.R. = 1.06, $p = ns$; property values: O.R. = 0.98, $p = ns$). Similarly, territorial motives were a strong predictor of custodianship within an individual's home neighborhood. Those who sought to benefit the community and to enforce local social norms not only reported more issues (benefit: O.R. = 1.26, $p < .001$; enforce: O.R. = 1.20, $p < .001$) but also reported over a greater geographical range surrounding the home (benefit: O.R. = 2.39, $p < .001$; enforce: O.R. = 1.36, $p < .001$). A desire to maintain local property values, however, was unrelated to reporting in either case (reports: O.R. = 0.95, $p = ns$; range: O.R. = 0.93, $p = ns$).

The story for spaces beyond the home neighborhood was less clear. These models tested nine relationships: whether each of the three motivations predicted the likelihood of reporting in an individual's neighborhood of work, on their commute, or when visiting friends or family. Of these nine, only one relationship was strong enough to be meaningful: those who expressed a greater desire to benefit the community were more likely to have reported issues on their commute (O.R. = 2.37, $p < .01$). Otherwise, neither of the two forms of territoriality nor the desire to maintain property values was associated with reporting in any of these three spaces.

Summary: Custodianship, Motivated by Territoriality

Here we see that motivations to both benefit and defend the community drive custodianship in the urban commons, but predominantly in areas near an individual's house. These results strongly support the territoriality thesis and its basis in the perceived ownership of a space. The implications are striking when one considers that over 80 percent of reports are made from an individual's home neighborhood, meaning that territoriality is a relevant factor for the vast majority of reporting. Importantly, these effects were independent of demographic factors as well as a desire to maintain property values, which in fact were not predictive of any form of 311 reporting.

Distinguishing between the Two Components of Territoriality

We have now seen two forms of evidence that 311 reports of public issues are indeed an expression of territoriality. With this knowledge in hand, we might go a step further. If human territoriality is divided into two components, caretaking and defense, can we observe expressions of each through the 311 database? If so, how else might they differ? Do they have different geographical profiles? Are they expressed by the same individuals? Answers to these questions will further elucidate the role of territoriality in urban neighborhoods.[43]

The motivations of caretaking and defense imply different types of action. Whereas the former refers to a general inclination toward maintenance, defense implies action against the incursions of other individuals. In the urban context, we might define the latter as "incivilities," or individual actions that constitute or contribute to disorder. To reflect this distinction, we can divide the 77 case types that indicate issues in the public domain into two groups: man-made incivilities (e.g., graffiti) and natural deterioration (e.g., streetlight outages). Twelve of the 77 case types had been previously classified in Chapter 2 as an instance of either public denigration or private neglect, making them man-made incivilities by definition. An additional nine case types also reflected man-made incivilities (e.g., overflowing dumpster, parking enforcement), even if they were not traditional forms of disorder. These 21 case types comprised 19 percent of all custodial calls, each capturing an instance in which a reporter took action to defend the public space from the negative effects that another person had on it. The 56 other case types were instances of natural deterioration, meaning the reporter was being proactive in the maintenance of the neighborhood, though not defending it against the violations of other individuals. As would be expected given the relative frequency of reports of natural deterioration and incivilities, 89 percent of custodians made reports about the latter, but only 20 percent made reports about the former (9 percent reported both).

To evaluate the extent to which these two types of custodial reporting actually reflect the two components of territoriality, we again turn to the

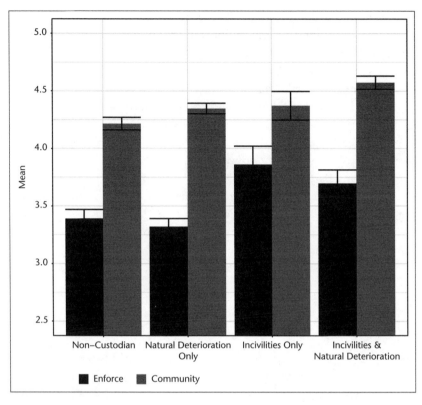

FIGURE 3.2 Differences in territoriality between noncustodians and custodians having reported issues arising from natural deterioration, incivilities, or both.

survey sample. During 2012, 43 percent of the survey participants made custodial reports only for issues of physical deterioration, 7 percent only for incivilities, and 14 percent made both types of custodial reports. As illustrated in Figure 3.2, these four groups appear to differ in their territorial motives, with the desire to benefit the community increasing as people participate in more types of reporting and the desire to enforce norms increasing for individuals who reported incivilities. I examined this relationship with an additional set of HLMs of the same form as those used earlier in the chapter. Because many individuals reported either zero incivilities or zero instances of natural deterioration, we examine two models for each, one predicting the likelihood of not having made any such reports (i.e., a zero value), the other predicting the number of reports made.[44] In addition, the models controlled for the count of reports an individual made for the other type (i.e., when predicting the number of incivility reports, including the number of reports of natural deterioration as a predictor), thereby accounting for overall reporting activity.[45] As with previous models, full regression results are reported in Appendix C.

The models verified the relationship depicted visually in Figure 3.2. Those who had a greater desire to enforce social norms were more likely to have reported at least one public incivility (i.e., less likely to be a zero; $\beta = -0.24$, O.R. $= 0.79$, $p < .01$), and both territorial motivations predicted more such reports (benefit community: $\beta = 0.83$, O.R. $= 2.29$, $p < .001$; enforce norms: $\beta = 0.40$, O.R. $= 1.49$, $p < .05$). In contrast, wanting to benefit the community was associated with a higher likelihood of having reported any issues of natural deterioration ($\beta = -0.26$, O.R. $= 0.77$, $p < .01$), and neither motivation predicted more reports. In sum, a desire to benefit the community appeared to be associated with custodianship in general, but a desire to enforce norms was exclusively associated with reports of man-made incivilities.

Different Types of Custodianship?

If the reporting of incivilities and natural deterioration are, respectively, expressions of the caretaking and defense components of territoriality, it raises the question of whether they manifest differently in neighborhoods. Here I examine two ways that this might be true: geographic distribution of each type of report and whether individuals specialize in one type or the other.

Geographical Distribution of Caretaking and Defense

One area of particular interest is how caretaking and defense interact with the geography of the city. For instance, because reports of incivilities have the potential to be more personal, people might be expected to react more strongly to them when they are closer to home. One way to test this question is by assessing whether individuals who have reported both types of issues tend to make one closer to home than the other (i.e., a within-subjects design).[46] There was a small but significant difference between the two, with reports of incivilities sitting closer to the reporter's home (*mean* = 214.3 m vs. 482.4 m; $t = 2.29$, $p < .05$ for log-transformed values). Another approach would be to ask what proportion of each type of report occurred in the reporter's home neighborhood. Returning to the clustering technique from earlier, I found that only 21 percent of incivilities were outside the reporter's home neighborhood, compared to 30 percent for natural deterioration ($\chi^2_{df=2}$ = 179.8, $p < .001$). Similarly, 21 percent of individuals reported any incivilities outside their home neighborhood versus 27 percent for natural deterioration. Combined, these multiple analyses indicate that individuals make a greater effort to address incivilities when these problems occur closer to home.

Specialization in Caretaking or Defense

A potentially more interesting question is that of specialization and whether individuals tend to pay preferential attention to one type of issue over the other. This would stand to reason if the two behaviors are driven differentially by the two components of territoriality and if those components vary across individuals. One way to model this question is to examine the proportion of reports of incivilities across individuals with the same total number of reports and see if most people have the expected mix of call types or if those who specialize in one or the other are over-represented. To illustrate, let us limit our attention to individuals who have made five custodial calls ($N = 995$). This might include anywhere from zero to five reports of incivilities (i.e., exclusive reporting of natural deterioration or incivilities, respectively). Because ~20 percent of custodial calls are for incivilities, if the two types of reporting are substitutable, then the most likely proportion of such reports for an individual would be the same (one out of five), and others would vary around this. We would estimate that 41 percent of individuals would have this ratio in their reporting.[47] Instead, only 18 percent of this group made one report of an incivility. There was a corresponding increase in those who exclusively reported natural deterioration (60 percent vs. a predicted 32 percent) or incivilities (4 percent vs. a predicted 0.03 percent).

Extending this analysis, I calculated expected counts for every feasible combination of number of total custodial reports and social control reports ($N = 419$).[48] As in the previous illustration, expected and observed counts were then transformed into proportions of individuals at that level of reporting activity. The left panel of Figure 3.3 charts together the relationships between these expected and observed proportions and the percentage of incivility reports. As described, the expected proportions were highest when incivility reports were nearly 20 percent of reports, and then descend close to zero at the highest level of social control reporting. In contrast,

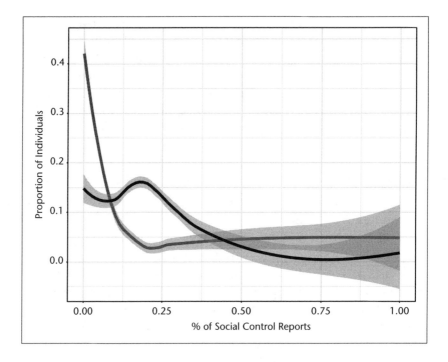

the observed counts were greatest for those who exclusively report natural deterioration and incivilities, and were lowest in the very ratio of "mixed calling" that would be expected to be highest. The right panel of Figure 3.3 illustrates this relationship further, plotting the percentage difference between observed and expected counts of individuals across the range of percentages of social control calls.[49] Note that this difference is most pronounced for those who specialize in reporting man-made incivilities.[50]

Conclusion: Motivations in the Commons

The findings here illuminate a phenomenon that has been largely obscured. Very little is known about the ways in which individuals contribute to the maintenance of the commons, and the territoriality thesis presents a specific explanation for why they do: because they identify with the space in question and, in turn, want to take care of it and defend it from both natural deterioration and denigration by others. The studies presented in this chapter supported this premise. First, we saw that

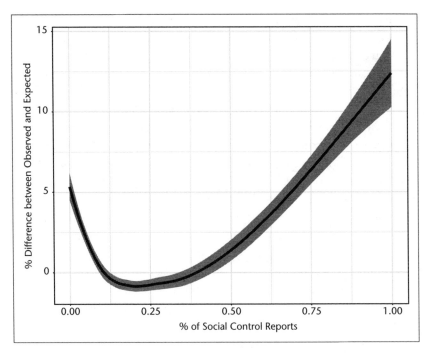

FIGURE 3.3 Evidence for specialization by custodians on issues arising from either natural deterioration or incivilities. The left panel compares the expected and observed proportion of custodians for different combinations of the two classes of issues. The right panel shows the percentage difference between the expected and observed proportions.

custodial reports were anchored by the home, evidence that perceived ownership is driving the decision to take action on a pothole, streetlight outage, graffito, or other instance of deterioration or denigration in the public space. Furthermore, by marrying the 311 data set with a more traditional survey protocol, we found that 311 users who expressed higher levels of territoriality tended to make more reports over a greater geographic range surrounding their homes.

While the evidence here is specifically for the urban commons, it provides a novel tool for understanding other commons as well. Nearly all research on the sustainability of commons to date has treated the contributions of individuals as an expression of "cooperation," but this perspective is simply a metaphor reflecting the public impacts of the behaviors in question. It is not a rigorous description of their underlying motivations. In fact, when theorists and practitioners take the metaphor of cooperation seriously, they reach the erroneous conclusion that material incentives are the only motivation for individuals to care for these communal spaces. On the contrary, we saw here that a desire to increase property values was in no way predictive of custodianship. This single-minded approach misses the other organic motivations that might drive human behavior and the contextual variables that can elicit them. Territoriality may lead to collective benefits via the maintenance of the commons, but it is rooted in a care for the spaces themselves. It is not inherently cooperative, nor is it inherently selfish. It needs to be discussed on its own terms, meaning that theory and practice have to consider how people interact with the local landscape, be it urban or otherwise, when designing programs intended to support the commons.

The results of this chapter offer initial lessons on the distribution of custodianship within and across communities, and how the actions of individual residents result in success or failure in the maintenance of the commons. The first such lesson is a counterpoint to a major assumption in commons research. Although nearly all simulation models and theoretical treatments take the stance that the majority of the population must be "cooperators" for a community to be viable, the results here suggest that this sort of threshold is unrealistically high. Only 10 percent of Bostonians reported a public issue through a registered account during the six years being analyzed. To put a finer point on it, that same percentage was closer to 5 percent for any given year. This is an extreme example of the classical Pareto principle, which states that a small proportion of individuals are responsible for most or all of the contribution to collective outcomes. The second lesson moves beyond existing thought on the commons and introduces a new layer to its analysis. We saw that custodians might specialize in either of two manifestations of territoriality, caretaking or defense, suggesting a *division of labor;* that is to say, individual community members differ in the contributions they make to the commons, and comprehensive maintenance is only possible through the combination of their efforts. The next chapter further examines this division of labor and how it leads to a community's collective efficacy in the maintenance of the urban commons.

CHAPTER 4

Division of Labor in the Commons

WHILE IN COLLEGE, I spent a summer working for the U.S. Forest Service in the Idaho panhandle. I was stationed in a small town that existed almost entirely as a government-subsidized outpost. Once the seasonal employees left each September, the remaining year-round population was approximately 25 people. The town consisted of two clusters of about a dozen buildings straddling a narrow river—affectionately referred to as "the crick"—with Forest Service–owned bunks a hundred meters up the hill. The post office sat at the main entrance to the town, and adjacent to it was a single modest, well-tended lawn, probably the only thing in this vast wilderness of conifers, elk, mountain lions, coyotes, moose, squirrels, and birds of various sorts that resembled what urban New Englanders would call a "park," albeit without enough space for a playground or picnic area.

One morning, I was walking through the center and chanced upon a man with a set of gardening tools and a wheelbarrow working on the park. I asked him, somewhat naively, what he was doing. He informed me that he was tending the grass. When I asked if he owned it, he responded that he did not. What stuck with me, though, was his explanation for why he did it: "I decided to do it once many years ago and I guess people just end up expecting you to keep doing it." Despite his gruff, somewhat resigned attitude toward his semivoluntary position as Keeper of the Commons, it encapsulated the discrete roles that each of us takes in the functioning of the public domain. In a town so small, this was on display in a variety of ways. The postman had worked there for long enough that he was able, upon some prompting, to recite the name and post office box number of everyone in town. There was the restaurant–bar–general store, which would sell you groceries or use the same items to cook meals for those dining in. The town had a one-room schoolhouse, and I worked with the sons of the teacher who had educated everyone in the town from kindergarten to fifth grade. There were other, less formal roles as well, such as that of my fellow seasonal employee whose job was to identify and track rare and notable species. If during the day I saw a bird of prey that I did not recognize, I knew whose door to knock on.

My memory and description of this small town might be a bit reductionist, but it serves to illustrate in simple terms how public society relies on and inherently creates a *division of labor:* individuals contribute to the public good in different ways, and only through the combination of their efforts can they fully address collective needs. In the case here, the society was small enough that each task—postman, schoolteacher, Keeper of the Commons—fell to a single person or family, but in urban areas these roles comprise many subtasks that are undertaken by multiple individuals. This is apparent as we turn to custodianship in the urban commons. We have already seen that many 311 users specialize in which public issues they report, concentrating either on instances of natural deterioration or on incivilities perpetrated by other individuals. Taking this logic further, neighborhoods are not a uniform topography of houses and streets but rather a pastiche of main streets and side streets, of residential, industrial, commercial, and institutional spaces. Individuals might differ in their inclination to act in each of these cases, and the commons will depend on all of their efforts.

Building on the work of Chapter 3, this chapter seeks to articulate how the behavioral dynamics we have already seen determine the overall maintenance of the commons, a question that is critical to any society. Put another way, the focus here is on how the actions of individual community members result in collective efficacy, or the ability to accomplish a shared task. I propose a division-of-labor model for this relationship, which distinguishes types of actors and the tasks they address. This is in contrast to the simpler cooperator–free-rider model that is more popular in commons research. Importantly, my proposed approach acknowledges that commons might vary in the types or quantities of tasks that they generate, which in turn determines the types of actors that each needs. This is something that existing research does not consider. I evaluate this new approach by concentrating on the relative contributions of two groups of custodians that we met in Chapter 2: typical custodians, who only occasionally make reports; and exemplar custodians, who do so with some regularity. The implication, though, is that a similar logic might be fruitfully applied to other types of commons.

The analysis occurs in three parts. First, I reexamine the neighborhood audits from Chapter 2, assessing whether the two types of custodians are each independently necessary for a neighborhood to effectively respond to instances of deterioration—what we might refer to as collective efficacy in the maintenance of the urban commons. Following this, I further explore which types of tasks each group might be more inclined to address based on their respective level of territoriality. This second step not only demonstrates the need for both groups but also specifies how they complement each other. The chapter ends by considering how this approach strengthens our understanding of the operation of the commons, and particularly how different types of actors are responsible for the impacts of contextual factors, such as socioeconomic status. Each of these three questions, most notably the second and third, requires considerable analytic work. As with previous chapters, sections begin with the conceptual framing and conclude with a summary, so that readers can engage with the methodology to whatever depth they desire while still accessing the substantive points herein.

What a Division of Labor Looks Like

In Chapter 3, I discussed how research on the maintenance of the commons typically reduces individuals into two groups: "cooperators" and "free riders." This model relies on a number of simplifying assumptions. We have already seen that the term "cooperation" serves to describe an individual's contributions (or lack thereof) but does not capture the true motivations of a behavior that is in fact rooted in territoriality. The current chapter attends to a second simplifying assumption of the cooperator–free-rider model. By defining individuals as either contributing or not, the model implies that the maintenance of the commons entails a single task or set of closely related tasks. One exception has been the treatment of the enforcement of social norms through punishment as an independent behavior that makes a second-order contribution to the commons.[1] Apart from this, there has been little effort to differentiate between the tasks that contribute to sustainability.

Chapter 3 has suggested that real-world commons are more complicated than a single-task model might imply. The two components of territoriality motivated different contributions to maintenance: a desire to benefit the community was associated with reports of natural deterioration, such as streetlight outages; and a desire to enforce social norms was associated specifically with reporting man-made incivilities, such as graffiti. Furthermore, we saw that individuals tended to specialize in one or the other of these two forms of custodianship. This suggests that individuals not only vary in their contributions but do so in a manner that is sufficiently systematic to indicate a division of labor in the maintenance of the commons.

Collective Efficacy and the Many Tasks of the Commons

Looking closely at any given common, one will observe a variety of activities that contribute to its maintenance. Take the example of certain Japanese villages nestled in the mountains, originally described by Margaret A. McKean[2] and cited at length by Elinor Ostrom,[3] in which villagers have held local forests and meadows in common since at least 1600. Though each village has its own specific set of rules for doing so, they all collectively harvest shared resources, such as feed for animals for the winter, guaranteeing the even distribution of both effort and products. To be included in these harvests, however, each community member must do their part: "There were written rules about the obligation of each household to contribute a share to the collective work to maintain the commons—to conduct the annual burning (which involved cutting nine-foot firebreaks ahead of time, carefully monitoring the blaze, and occasional fire-fighting when the flames jumped the firebreak), to report to harvest on mountain-opening days, or to do a specific cutting of timber or thatch."[4] These obligations are then policed by "detectives," who, depending on the village, might be paid patrolmen, a rotation among eligible males, or even an open-ended system in which any citizen is authorized to report violations.

The example of Japanese mountain villages illustrates how collective efficacy in the maintenance of a single common can entail many distinct tasks. The same situation might be imagined for any other commons. Going further, Ostrom put forward eight design principles that she argued were essential to long-enduring common public resources, some of which described types of tasks that would need to be completed by the community.[5] In addition to explicit stipulations for and limitations on resource access, these also included the need for monitoring compliance, the effective implementation of sanctions for violations, and mechanisms for conflict resolution. These additional institutions might be considered second-order contributions to the maintenance of the commons, as they ensure that people will behave in ways that will sustain the commons. Consequently, between basic maintenance and the institutions that help it to persist, the average common relies on a diverse array of activities. This implies that there might in turn be variation in skills and motivations across the population that lead each individual to engage more actively in some tasks than in others, creating the basis for a division of labor.

The urban commons is seemingly a simpler case because it rarely involves allotting a limited resource. One will note that there are no complex institutions in place regulating the right to walk down a sidewalk. Nonetheless, the urban commons presents its own diversity of tasks, and collective efficacy in the comprehensive maintenance of these spaces and infrastructure requires attention to each of them. We have already seen the distinction between natural deterioration and man-made incivilities. Furthermore, the geography of the city is a heterogeneous patchwork of different zonings and land uses, and any given neighborhood comprises a combination of main streets and side streets, as well as residential, commercial, industrial, and institutional spaces. It is not enough to assume that an individual's inclination toward custodianship is consistent across these varying contexts. Rather, just as the two components of custodianship motivate different types of tasks, there may be individual differences in whether a person takes action on disorder or deterioration in one space versus another. This would suggest that there are multiple ways for an individual to contribute to a common. It may be that the predilection for each of these tasks varies independently, but there is also the possibility that they are linked in some manner. For example, if an individual who reports on main streets is also more likely to report incivilities, it would indicate a more robust typology of actors. Such a situation would be the definition of a division of labor, with multiple groups of actors who contribute in distinct ways and whose efforts combine in the overall maintenance of the commons.

Attention to a division of labor would create a more nuanced view of the maintenance of the commons than the cooperator-free-rider model and would offer a more general template for considering how the actions and interactions of individual community members combine to create collective outcomes. In this light, the maintenance of the commons is just one example of a shared challenge, and the insights here could be extended to the realization of collective efficacy defined more broadly, whether it be the socialization of children, the prevention of crime, advocacy with public agencies, or something else. Importantly, by addressing the question of "how" collective efficacy is realized, a division-of-labor approach also allows us to quantify the patterns of behavior that actualize the well-known relationships between contextual factors and institutions. First, though, it is necessary to determine how to quantify the components of this division of labor.

The Behavioral Composition

Describing collective efficacy, whether in the maintenance of the commons or otherwise, in terms of the discrete actions and interactions of community members presents a conceptual difficulty.[6] Collective efficacy refers to a community's capacity to respond to a given task or challenge created by local events and conditions. This implies a certain consistency, meaning that the response of a community to a future event is predictable based on how the community has handled similar situations in the past. This is at odds with the phrase "discrete actions and interactions," which isolates each of these events and considers them in terms of the proclivities of the individual actors that participate in them. How, then, can we bridge these two levels of analysis? One valuable tool for such an exercise is the concept of *social regularities*. Seymour Sarason originally argued that behavioral regularities—patterns of action and interaction—are critical for understanding the basic operation of a social setting.[7] Building on this, Edward Seidman recast behavioral regularities as social regularities, arguing that they shape and are shaped in large part by social relations and norms, as well as other contextual factors.[8] He defined social regularities as the subset of social processes that feature some level of consistency (i.e., are regular in their frequency), and he underscored the primary importance of those that, like collective efficacy, influence outcomes for both the group and its individual members.

Because social regularities describe the linkage between the actions and interactions of individuals and collective outcomes, they provide a natural framework for us to bridge these two levels of analysis. To do so, we must first consider the dynamic of a single event of interest and how a series of them constitute or do not constitute a regularity. For example, the maintenance of the urban commons comprises events that require the coincidence of two things: a violation of a social norm in a public space, and someone who moves to address the situation. A few questions then follow. First, given the presence of a violation, what is the probability that the average community member will take action on it? This parallels most existing work on collective efficacy, capturing the generalized level of a social regularity across a population. A more nuanced question, though, would be how much this tendency varies across the members of the population. We might refer to this variation as the *behavioral composition* of the neighborhood, or the embodiment of a social regularity in terms of the propensity of each individual to contribute to it.

The behavioral composition might be described in any number of ways. Examples include the mean level of activity, variance in activity levels, the maximum level of activity, or any other statistical feature derived from the levels of activity and their distribution. It is incumbent on the researcher to determine which of these best captures diversity in a particular regularity and its implications for collective outcomes. In the current case, the possibility of a division of labor calls for a typology, or categorizing actors based on the types of actions they are more likely to undertake. This allows for the creation of measures that quantify the representation of these groups in a given community, capturing the overall capacity to address each of the diverse array of tasks and contexts presented by the urban commons. This matching of subsets of community members to specific tasks provides a level of detail that would be absent in a single summary statistic of tendency across the population, such as mean or variation.

Behavioral Composition and the Urban Commons: A Typology of Custodians

Chapter 2 presented an initial attempt to divide custodians into two groups, arguing that they might represent different resources in neighborhood maintenance: "typical" custodians, who only sporadically take such action and over a narrow range near their homes, and "exemplars," who do so with greater regularity and geographic coverage. I defined them formally as those who made two or fewer public reports in a year (90 percent of custodians) and those who made three or more (10 percent of custodians), respectively. This dividing line was chosen for two reasons. First, it is where the distribution flattens and the tail begins, suggesting qualitatively different groups of individuals on each side (i.e., the "elbow test"). Additionally, the proposed behavioral differences between the two groups included not only the frequency of reporting but also the geographic range of custodianship, and this cut point created the greatest distinction in the latter.[9] The following analyses use this typology to examine the presence of a division of labor in the maintenance of the urban commons.

Testing for a Division of Labor in the Urban Commons

Testing for a division of labor in the maintenance of the urban commons entails two main steps. The first is to examine not only whether typical and exemplar custodians each contribute to the urban commons but also whether they are independently necessary—that is, a lack of one cannot be compensated for by an abundance of the other. This is critical to a division of labor interpretation, as it would indicate that each contributes in a way that the other does not. The second step will then examine which tasks and spaces in particular these two groups might differentially attend to, more directly articulating the division of labor they create. As noted, these two analyses, particularly the second, entail considerable methodological work, which is why each begins with the conceptual question and concludes with a nontechnical summary.

Analysis #1: Are Both Types of Actors Needed?

The first test for a division of labor in the urban commons is whether typical and exemplar custodians (i.e., the behavioral composition of a community) are both required for maintenance. To answer this question, let us return to the neighborhood audits presented in Chapter 2. The reader will recall that these audits identified streetlight outages and broken sidewalks, and used them to assess a community's overall custodianship. Put another way, these audits provided an objective measure of collective efficacy in the maintenance of the urban commons across the neighborhoods of Boston. The first step to evaluating the division-of-labor model, then, is to reconceptualize that initial analysis—which was intended to reveal biases in 311 reporting across neighborhoods—to determine the extent to which typical and exemplar custodians combine in this shared task.

The relative value of typical and exemplar custodians in the maintenance of the urban commons might be described by one of four models, which fall into two categories. The first two, the *foundational actors model* and the *communitarian model,* assume that variation in neighborhood-level outcomes is determined primarily by the distribution of one behavioral type or the other. The latter two, the *additive model* and the *collaborative model,* depict situations in which both groups contribute to the collective outcome. Each of these four models has been observed in some manner in previous neighborhood work.

1. The *foundational actors model* posits that the actions of prominent individuals are central to the collective outcome. This is seen most famously in William Julius Wilson's description of "truly disadvantaged" urban ghettos.[10] He pointed out that the problem was not that the average resident was poor but that *all* residents were poor. The resultant lack of strong role models undermined a variety of social processes, including the creation of a local culture of advancement and achievement. In a separate example, Kennedy, Piehl, and Braga have shown that "high-crime neighborhoods" are in fact the result of ~3 percent of local youths perpetrating gun violence.[11] This model would predict that the distribution of exemplars would be most important to maintenance.

2. The *communitarian model* posits that the critical factor for collective outcomes is the overall volume of actors. Clear et al. uncovered such a case in their research on incarceration and the social organization.[12] In high-crime neighborhoods, it is not unheard of for as many as 20 percent of adult males to be incarcerated at any given time, leaving notable holes in the social network. It is not that any one individual is the key bridge between multiple subpopulations within the neighborhood but rather that the sheer volume

of loss will inevitably eliminate connections, leaving the neighborhood socially fragmented.[13] In the current case, this model would predict that the distribution of typical custodians would be most important to maintenance.

3. Of the two models that incorporate both types of actors, the *additive model* is the simpler, positing that members of the two groups make the same type of contribution to the collective outcome, differing only in the magnitude of their impact. Thus, a single exemplar and a set of typical custodians who generate the same quantity of activity would be interchangeable. This model would predict that the distributions of both exemplars and typical custodians have independent effects on maintenance.

4. The *collaborative model* captures the essence of a division of labor. In this case, the two groups make qualitatively different contributions to the collective outcome and therefore are not interchangeable, but are both necessary. The classical example of this is traditional civic institutions and activism, in which leaders must catalyze and organize collective action, while goals can only reach fruition if a handful of "foot soldiers" are also involved.[14] This model would specifically predict an interaction effect, in which neighborhoods with both exemplars and typical custodians would be more effective at maintaining public spaces than would neighborhoods high in only one or the other.

The goal of the foregoing analysis will be to determine which of these four models best captures the relative importance of typical and exemplar custodians.

Quantifying Collective Efficacy and the Behavioral Composition

Testing the relationship between the distribution of typical and exemplar custodians and collective efficacy in the maintenance of the urban commons requires the coordination of two data sets: the neighborhood audits originally presented in Chapter 2 and the database of 311 users. Before this can be done, important decisions need to be made about how to utilize each.

NEIGHBORHOOD AUDITS. Our audit identified 244 streetlight outages in 72 of Boston's 156 census tracts, and the assessment of all sidewalks in the city ($N = 27,388$; on a 0–100 scale, 100 = no panels requiring replacement) found 1,168 (4 percent) sidewalks that generated requests for repair. The results of these audits are described in greater detail in Chapter 2, but one point in particular bears repeating. Those initial analyses revealed significant variation across neighborhoods in the likelihood of (1) reporting streetlight outages within two months of identification and (2) making one or more reports of a broken sidewalk. Importantly, this validates one of the primary assumptions of this chapter, which is that neighborhoods have a characteristic level of collective efficacy in addressing issues in the public domain.

DATABASE OF 311 USERS. As done previously, custodians were categorized into typical custodians, who made one or two reports regarding public issues in a year (90 percent of custodians in 2011, the year of the audits), and exemplar custodians, who made three or more in a year (10 percent of custodians). Using estimated home locations, I tabulated the number of typical custodians and exemplars for each neighborhood.[15] In determining the best way to quantify this distribution, however, we must first account for the spatial dynamics of custodianship, which entails the coincidence between an issue at a specific location and an individual who takes action on it. For this reason, we are concerned specifically with the coverage offered by each group. Typical custodians generally attend to the narrow region surrounding the home and must in turn combine to cover the broader neighborhood. Consequently, their overall value is best described in density per square mile. On the other hand, exemplars act as custodians over a multiblock radius and are therefore likely to report issues throughout the neighborhood. This would indicate that the raw count of exemplars would give the best approximation of their total coverage. A second consideration is choosing the correct time window for measuring actors. Because sidewalk assessments were conducted primarily over the course of 2011, I limit the analysis to custodians in that year. The streetlight outages occurred within a more precise time window, meaning it is most appropriate to focus on reporter activity in the months just preceding the streetlight audits. Based on the analyses of reliability conducted in Chapter 2, I utilize a three-month time window.[16]

As in Chapter 3, it is necessary to address the potential bias present in the 311 data set and how it might hinder the current analysis. In tabulating the typical and exemplar custodians living in each neighborhood, we must assume that registered accounts are an accurate estimation of the distribution of users across neighborhoods. However, registered users only generate about half of the reports of public issues, and there is reason to believe that some populations would be more inclined to register than others. Consequently, those neighborhoods whose residents register at lower rates would be more effective at reporting issues than would be indicated by the representation of registered custodians in the database. To address this weakness, I run the foregoing analyses twice, once only with counts of custodians and then again incorporating measures of median income and proportion who are black, Hispanic, or immigrant (log-transformed when necessary) as a robustness check.

Collaboration between Typical and Exemplar Custodians

A series of regressions adjudicated between the four models for how the behavioral composition leads to collective efficacy: foundational, communitarian, additive, and collaborative (complete results for all models are reported in Appendix D). For sidewalks, neighborhoods with a greater density of typical custodians or more exemplars were more likely to generate reports, explaining 30 percent of the overall variation (typical reporters: $\beta = .38$; exemplars: $\beta = .29$; both p-values $< .001$). This indicates contributions by both typical custodians and exemplars to maintenance, which is consistent with the additive and collaborative models. The latter of these, though, further stipulates that each of the two groups not only contributes but is independently necessary. Analytically, this would be reflected by an interaction effect between the two types of actors,[17] which was significant ($\beta = .13$, $p < .05$; change in variance explained: $F = 3.88$, $p < .05$). As illustrated in Figure 4.1a, this indicates that the combination of both a density of typical reporters and many exemplars best ensured that a community would report a broken sidewalk.[18]

The same analysis produced similar results for streetlight outages. Neighborhoods with a higher density of typical reporters ($\beta = .28$, $p < .05$) and more exemplars ($\beta = .30$, $p < .05$) were more likely to report an outage to the city services department. When placed in the same model, the two were comparably strong predictors (typical custodians: $\beta = .26$; exemplars: $\beta = .23$; both p-values $< .10$), but, in the end, the interaction effect between them was the lone predictor in the final, best-fitting model ($\beta = .36$, $p < .01$).[19] This again supports the notion that a community's overall

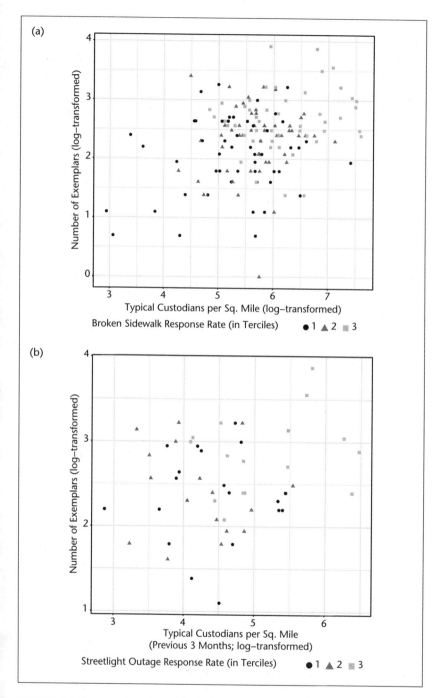

FIGURE 4.1 Scatter plots depicting the increased likelihood of (a) requests for sidewalk paving and (b) reports of streetlight outages in neighborhoods with both a greater density of typical custodians and a greater number of exemplars.

efficacy in maintaining the urban commons is greatest where both the density of typical custodians and the number of exemplar reporters are high.

As noted, this analysis makes the assumption that registered accounts are an accurate estimation of the distribution of users across neighborhoods. To check the robustness of the current findings, the regression analyses were repeated, incorporating measures of median income and proportion who are black, Hispanic, or immigrant (log-transformed when necessary). These additions left the original results unchanged.[20]

Summary: Collaboration in the Urban Commons

Here we see preliminary evidence that collective efficacy in the maintenance of the urban commons fits a collaborative model. That is to say, the effective maintenance of a neighborhood depends on the contributions of two different types of custodians: typical custodians, who take action only occasionally and near their homes, and exemplar custodians, who take action more often and over a greater geographic range. Importantly, these two groups appear to be nonsubstitutable, meaning that the overabundance of one cannot compensate for a lack of the other. The reason for this, however, is not immediately clear, and will be the focus of the next analysis.

Analysis #2: The Distinct Contributions of Typical and Exemplar Custodians

If both typical and exemplar custodians are necessary for neighborhood maintenance, then it follows to ask how each contributes to this task. To do so, let us consider what we know about the ways in which they express custodianship. Typical custodians report one to two issues per year and almost exclusively on their street block of residence. In contrast, exemplars are actively vigilant, reporting issues with discernible regularity over a somewhat larger region. When cast this way, it becomes clearer why a neighborhood might need both, as their distinct patterns of custodianship may lead each group to address issues that the other cannot or will not. Take the hypothetical example of two streetlight outages in a neighborhood, one on a traditional residential street and the other on an undeveloped street with empty lots. In the former, the residents of that street might be motivated to take direct action—it very easily could be someone's only 311 report of the year. The latter case may lack typical custodians who claim the space as their own, meaning it would fall to an exemplar who is attentive to issues over the broader neighborhood. A neighborhood will regularly experience each type of issue, meaning effective upkeep depends on both types of actors.

We might then consider how typical and exemplar custodians contribute to the urban commons on two dimensions: (1) the types of issues that might arise, categorized, as in Chapter 3, as man-made incivilities and natural deterioration, and (2) the heterogeneous land use of the city, including residential, industrial, commercial, and institutional zoning and the distinction between main and side streets. Because this analysis does not rely on the neighborhood audits, we are again able to use the full span of the data set (3/2010–12/2015, available through the Boston Data Portal).[21] This enables us to consider a third type of "custodian" involved in neighborhood maintenance: city employees. Many employees of city agencies identify unaddressed issues and submit them as new work orders as part of their daily activities. Given their official role and their greater presence around government-owned areas, such as schools, they likely contribute to this process in a manner distinct from that of community members. As in previous chapters, the reports are mapped to addresses, but here we look at the street ($N = 24{,}730$ attributed to a census tract in Boston, 14,124 of which generated at least one request for service through 311) on which they occurred as well as the census tract. I use user accounts to differentiate the three groups of custodians, though in this case I define exemplars as those making four or more public reports, owing to the extended time span of the data.[22]

Three Types of Custodians, Three Roles

An initial assessment indicated that the three types of custodians contribute approximately equally to the maintenance of Boston neighborhoods in terms of the overall volume of reports, with typical custodians accounting for 36 percent of reports, exemplars for 31 percent, and city employees for 33 percent. This sets an important baseline for the analysis moving forward, but we should be careful to recognize its true interpretation. One will note that public constituents with registered accounts are responsible for more than twice as many reports as city employees are. Furthermore, about half the reports are anonymous, meaning that public constituents report approximately four times as many issues as city employees do. We might also assume that those who make anonymous reports are probably more similar to typical custodians than to exemplars, meaning that typical custodians are actually responsible for the bulk of reporting activity.

This section opened with a series of thought experiments as to how these three types of actors might contribute in different ways. Here we can more formally test these and other such hypotheses, with a particular eye toward how each group's respective territoriality interacts with the range of tasks and contexts presented by the urban commons. In terms of types of issues, Chapter 3 already presented evidence that reports of man-made incivilities more commonly come from those who are inclined toward the enforcement of social norms. Because of this personal nature and motivation, one might expect constituents to make such reports more often than city employees. Similarly, exemplars, with their greater overall activity and concern for the neighborhood, might be more likely than typical custodians to make such reports. Indeed, constituents reported 82 percent of incivilities, and these were more often reported by exemplars than by typical custodians (48 percent vs. 34 percent).

The varied geography of urban neighborhoods harkens back to the delineation of the primary and secondary territories. Whereas the primary territory refers to the areas immediately abutting one's home, the secondary territory refers to shared spaces, such as parks or commercial districts.[23] From this, one might reason that typical custodians focus their custodianship on the primary territory, and exemplars, with their higher levels of territoriality, would be more likely to extend their custodianship into secondary territories. Consistent with this, exemplars reported relatively more issues than typical custodians on main streets (33 percent vs. 29 percent) as well as on nonresidential streets (34 percent vs. 28 percent). In contrast, the reports of city employees had a geographic profile that reflected their professional roles, featuring a disproportionate number of reports on streets with industrial (44 percent) and exempt zoning (i.e., government buildings; 40 percent).

MULTILEVEL ANALYSIS. To examine differences in the roles of the three types of custodians more comprehensively, I ran two multilevel regression models that nested reports in streets and streets in tracts (i.e., a three-level model). The first of these models predicted the likelihood that a constituent-generated report was made by an exemplar rather than a typical custodian, and the second predicted the likelihood that a report was made by a city employee rather than a constituent. As in other places in this book, multilevel models allow us to test the effects of variables at each level while simultaneously controlling for characteristics of all other levels.[24] They also extend the question of geographic context to variation between census tracts, which vary on population density and their primary land usage (residential, downtown, industrial/institutional, such as a college campus, or park). See Appendix D for all model details.

The two models acted as formal confirmation of the descriptive analysis presented earlier. First, an issue was more likely to be reported by an exemplar rather than a typical custodian if it occurred on a main street ($\beta = 0.26$, O.R. = 1.29, $p < .001$) or any type of nonresidential street ($\beta = 0.22 - 0.50$, O.R. = 1.25 – 1.65, all p-values < .001) and if it referenced a man-made incivility ($\beta = 0.54$, O.R. = 1.72, $p < .001$). In addition, holding all else constant, constituent-reported issues were more likely to be made by exemplars if they were in census tracts classified as being industrial or institutional ($\beta = 0.20$, O.R. = 1.22, $p < .01$) and with greater population density ($\beta = 0.01$, O.R. = 1.01, $p < .001$). Meanwhile, an issue was more likely to be reported by a city employee if it occurred on a main street ($\beta = 0.33$, O.R. = 1.39, $p < .001$) or any type of nonresidential street ($\beta = 0.42 - 0.57$, O.R. = 1.52 – 1.77, all p-values < .001), particularly those with industrial uses. Man-made incivilities were dramatically less likely to be reported by city employees ($\beta = -1.10$, O.R. = 0.33, $p < .001$). Issues in census tracts in industrial/institutional ($\beta = -0.29$, O.R. = 0.75, $p < .01$) or downtown regions ($\beta = -0.42$, O.R. = 0.66, $p < .01$) were also less likely to be reported by city employees, as were issues in areas with greater population density ($\beta = -0.01$, O.R. = 0.99, $p < .01$).

From Territoriality to a Division of Labor

We now can make two clear statements about a division of labor in the maintenance of the urban commons. First, there are two groups of custodians, which I have dubbed typical and exemplar custodians, and the latter express greater levels of territorial motivations than the former. Second, the two groups tend to specialize in the maintenance of different tasks and spaces. Typical custodians focus on natural deterioration on residential streets, presumably in areas near their homes. In contrast, the efforts of exemplars extend into the "shared" spaces of a neighborhood; they also tend to be more attentive to man-made incivilities. Though each of these two facts describes aspects of a division of labor, they do not guarantee that differing levels of territoriality *cause* typical and exemplar custodians to contribute in distinct ways. Alternatively, exemplars may engage in these additional behaviors simply as a by-product of their greater activity. To probe this question, we return to the survey data, limiting our analysis to those respondents who acted as custodians during 2012 and their reporting during that year ($N = 439$). A series of general linear models used the two territorial motivations (benefiting the community and enforcing social norms), status as a typical or exemplar custodian (as a proxy for overall activity), and demographic characteristics to predict whether an individual had reported at least one public issue that was (1) on a main street, (2) on a nonresidential street, and (3) a man-made incivility.

The elevated activity of exemplars was primarily responsible for their distinct contributions. It was the strongest predictor of having made at least one report that was on a main street ($\beta = .93$, O.R. $= 2.53$, $p < .001$), that was on a nonresidential street ($\beta = 1.98$, O.R. $= 7.24$, $p < .001$), and that was a man-made incivility ($\beta = 2.01$, O.R. $= 7.46$, $p < .001$). Territoriality was unimportant apart from one case: a greater desire to enforce social norms predicted a greater likelihood of having reported a man-made incivility ($\beta = .32$, O.R. $= 1.38$, $p < .001$). This illustrates an indirect, two-step pathway in which territoriality leads to greater activity, which in turn increases the likelihood that an individual will report more types of issues in more varied contexts.[25]

Summary: Distinct Contributions to the Commons

The two analyses presented in this section articulate a division of labor in which typical and exemplar custodians make distinct contributions to the maintenance of the urban commons. The former group specializes in reporting issues of natural deterioration on residential side streets, whereas the latter are critical for addressing man-made incivilities in general and all types of issues in "shared" spaces—main streets and those with nonresidential zoning. In sum, each is necessary for comprehensive neighborhood upkeep. Giving further nuance to this story, we saw that city employees act as a third type of custodian that also contributes to the maintenance of the urban commons in their own characteristic ways, emphasizing industrial and institutional (e.g., government-owned) zones.

Looking more closely at typical and exemplar custodians, the differences between them are consistent with their levels of territoriality, but it appears that territoriality itself is only indirectly responsible. Instead, the elevated activity that arises from a higher level of territoriality best explains exemplars' tendency to report over a greater range of spaces. Theoretically, this provides new insight on the distribution of behaviors between the primary and secondary territory. As an individual's territoriality for the neighborhood increases, their custodianship is prone to break through the invisible boundary between the primary and secondary territories. Once he or she has done so, though, they are likely to report anywhere in the broader region, from main streets to industrial back roads, independent of their original level of territoriality. The only exception to this was that the specific desire to enforce social norms still inclined individuals to report man-made incivilities. A practical implication is that if a program could expand the reporting activities of individuals independent of their territoriality, it would feasibly increase levels of reporting in the shared spaces of the city, an idea we return to in Chapter 6.

The results here give credence to a division-of-labor model that might be applied to other commons as well as to other cases of collective efficacy in shared tasks and challenges, whether they explicitly refer to a common or not. Before exploring how one would go about extending the model in this way, however, it is worth asking how valuable the division-of-labor model is. The problem with traditional models of the behavioral dynamics of the commons is not so much the assumptions themselves—assumptions of course make the models more tractable—but the extent to which they obscure reality. The next section evaluates whether the traditional model of the commons, with its assumption of a single type of actor who contributes in a single way, and the division-of-labor model come to the same conclusion about which neighborhoods are most likely to be effective at preventing and counteracting disorder. If the two are not in agreement, then there is evidence that the extra nuance of the division-of-labor model is not only useful in detailing the on the ground process of maintenance but is also necessary for understanding collective outcomes.

From Context to Outcomes: Behavior as the Missing Link

A division of labor in the maintenance of the urban commons is enlightening in its own right, but it also offers a potential missing link for traditional analyses of when and where communities achieve collective tasks. For example, nearly all research on collective efficacy has been exclusively at the neighborhood level, examining how contextual characteristics, such as concentrated disadvantage and ethnic composition, predict generalized outcomes. They in turn skip over the individual-level patterns of behavior that are responsible for these outcomes. A focus on the behavioral composition makes it possible to examine how contextual characteristics affect and in turn operate through these patterns of behavior to impact a community's outcomes. In the terminology of the commons literature, we could look at this as how context and institutions influence behavior to determine long-term sustainability.

Looking specifically at the urban commons, we can ask how neighborhood characteristics predict the effective contributions of typical and exemplar custodians, which are in turn responsible for the maintenance of the urban commons. It is well established that certain contextual factors, such as wealth, home ownership, and ethnic composition, strongly predict neighborhood maintenance in urban neighborhoods, typically measured as physical disorder. In analyzing this question, this section will compare the interpretations of the two models we have seen throughout this chapter: the traditional cooperator–free-rider model and the division-of-labor model. The former considers the proportion of cooperators in a population—essentially, a per capita metric—as the determining factor for commons maintenance. Attention to a potential division of labor, however, demands consideration not only of different types of actors but also of the practical dynamics of the tasks they attend to, including their frequency and distribution within a space. Because neighborhoods might differ in these tasks and contexts, their need for typical custodians and exemplars will similarly vary, and the division-of-labor model would capture this in ways that the traditional model would not.

The key to the foregoing analysis is whether the two models identify the same contextual factors as predictors of effective maintenance of the commons. If they do, then the assumptions of the cooperator–free-rider model are not so great a deviation from reality that they lose track of fundamental relationships between context, behavior, and outcomes. However, if there are differences, they would indicate that the added nuance of the division-of-labor model provides insights we would not otherwise have had. This analysis will utilize measures of median income, population density, and ethnic composition from the U.S. Census Bureau's ACS (2010–2014 estimates).

Using Context to Predict Effective Custodianship

Part I: The Cooperator–Free-Rider Model

Because it is more straightforward both statistically and conceptually, let us begin with the analysis of the cooperator–free-rider model traditionally utilized in the study of the commons. To do so, we estimate the proportion of custodians within a community (i.e., number of custodians divided by adult population), making this essentially an analysis of the characteristics that predict custodianship per capita. An initial regression found that individuals were on average more likely to be custodians in richer neighborhoods ($\beta = .25, p < .05$), those with fewer black, Latino, and Asian residents (black: $\beta = -.17$, $p < .05$; Latino: $\beta = -.32$, $p < .001$; Asian: $\beta = -.28, p < .05$), and those with a lower population density ($\beta = -.19, p < .01$). This model holds two distinctions from the division-of-labor model. First, it treats behavior per capita rather than in terms of the specific types of tasks that might present themselves. Second, it only acknowledges one type of actor who contributes to the maintenance of the commons. To create a hybrid between this model and the division-of-labor model, we can relax the second assumption and allow that there are two types of actors and analyze their respective per capita representations separately. Unsurprisingly, typical custodians per capita were associated with the same factors as custodians on the whole (income: $\beta = .25, p < .001$; black: $\beta = -.17$, $p < .05$; Latino: $\beta = -.32$, $p < .001$; Asian: $\beta = -.28$, $p < .05$; population density: $\beta = -.19, p < .01$), as would be expected, as they account for 90 percent of custodians. Exemplars per capita, however, were associated only with fewer Latino and Asian residents (Latino: $\beta = -.23$, $p < .01$; Asian: $\beta = -.23, p < .01$). Importantly, this second set of models still ignores how variations in urban form can influence the types of tasks that arise in a particular commons.

Part II: The Division-of-Labor Approach

QUANTIFYING THE IMPLICATIONS OF A DIVISION OF LABOR. The division-of-labor model considers two questions: (1) What are the needs of the region, based on the kinds of tasks that can be expected? (2) To what extent does the behavioral composition of its population correspond to these needs? The maps in Figures 4.2a and 4.2b illustrate just how much the answers to these questions can vary depending on the organization and form of a given neighborhood. Taking two specific illustrations, the Back Bay, pictured in Figure 4.2c, is a dense, mixed-use neighborhood that has some areas whose maintenance is more reliant on typical custodians and others that are more reliant on exemplars. In contrast, West Roxbury, pictured in Figure 4.2d, is a residential neighborhood with a suburban design and is more reliant on typical custodians. The question of maintenance from this perspective is how well the behavioral composition of a neighborhood matches its needs.

To quantitatively estimate the "need" each neighborhood has for each type of custodian, as captured in the maps in Figure 4.2, I first calculated the expected number of issues to be reported on each street segment by an exemplar and by a typical custodian (based on its land use and other characteristics, parameters drawn from the models presented in the previous section) and then summed all streets within a tract.[26] For simplicity, this analysis is limited to instances of natural deterioration. The first step then is to correlate each of the two measures of need with the corresponding prevalence of custodians.[27] Generally speaking, neighborhoods with a greater need for typical custodians had more of them, and the same was true for exemplars (typical custodians: $\beta = .61$, $p < .001$; exemplars: $\beta = .53$, $p < .001$), reflecting substantial alignment between the needs of a community and its behavioral composition. Nonetheless, these correlations were far from perfect, indicating that many census tracts were either overachieving or underachieving in each category. We can think of these residuals as indicators of the strength of "coverage" by a particular group.

WHICH NEIGHBORHOODS ARE MOST EFFICACIOUS? We now have two measures that reflect the extent to which the prevalence of each of the two types of custodians is sufficient to satisfy the needs of a neighborhood, taking into account its particular land use and organization. If the distribution of these measures is associated with a set of contextual variables different from those that predict the number of custodians per capita, it will confirm that this more nuanced model is necessary to fully understand sustainability. Indeed, this was the case. As with the per capita models, coverage by exemplar and typical custodians was associated with median income

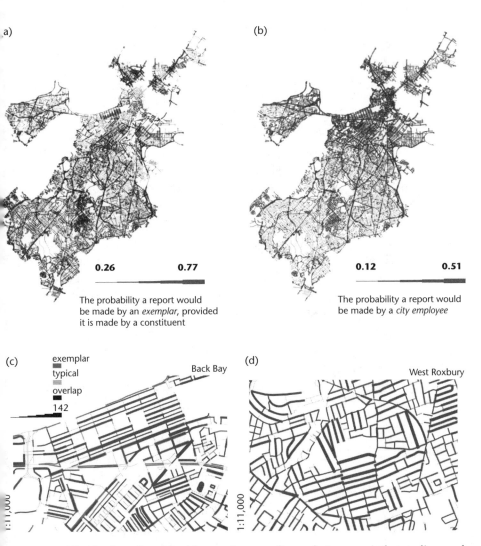

FIGURE 4.2 Distribution of need for (a) exemplar custodians relative to typical custodians and (b) city employees relative to custodians for all streets in the city, highlighting the greater need for exemplars along major thoroughfares and in downtown regions, and for city employees in industrial and institutional pockets. Insets compare the need for exemplar and typical custodians for (c) Back Bay, a relatively densely populated, mixed-use neighborhood with some areas where maintenance is more reliant on typical custodians and others that are more reliant on exemplars, and (d) West Roxbury, a residential neighborhood with a suburban design, leading to a greater reliance on typical custodians.

(typical: $\beta = .41$, $p < .01$; exemplar: $\beta = .29$, $p < .05$), but the similarities ended there—coverage was *positively*, rather than negatively, associated with greater population density (typical: $\beta = .46$, $p < .001$; exemplar: $\beta = .40$, $p < .001$) and was not associated with any aspects of ethnic composition.

Summary: The Extra Nuance of the Division-of-Labor Model

This section has consisted of a lot of data acrobatics and an ample number of findings, but the main point, that the neighborhoods of a city are not facsimiles of the same commons, is succinctly captured in Figure 4.2, which compares Back Bay, which is downtown, to the more suburban West Roxbury. Each neighborhood has a unique organization and structure that requires a particular combination of typical and exemplar custodians. These are just two examples of many, but they illustrate the weakness of the assumptions of the traditional cooperator–free-rider model. The maintenance of the commons is not a single task and, as such, is not realized by a single type of actor. As we saw in the analysis, this assumption led the traditional model to erroneous conclusions about the neighborhood characteristics that determined collective efficacy in the maintenance of the urban commons. The more nuanced division-of-labor model was necessary to properly reveal how demographic and social characteristics influence the interaction of the local population with its geography and the tasks it presents.

The cooperator–free-rider model prescribed a per capita approach that focused specifically on the proportion of custodians in a population. This found that neighborhoods with greater affluence and fewer minorities were more likely to have a greater representation of custodians. This is valuable information, telling us more or less which individual or contextual characteristics increase the likelihood of the average person to act as a custodian. They provide credence for the concern that disadvantaged and disenfranchised populations have lower engagement with 311, a point we will return to in more detail in Part III.[28] Thus, the per capita approach offers a certain type of insight on who participates and when they do so, and could be useful in understanding the broader prevalence of other characteristics whose level is distributed across individuals or households, such as the physical disorder of buildings.

The question at hand, however, was not so much which individuals are more likely to act as custodians but rather which neighborhoods are most effective in the maintenance of public spaces and infrastructure. A per capita approach is insufficient to answer this question, because it does not account for the possibility that the varied structure and organization of a city's neighborhoods leads them to differ markedly in the number and types of custodians they require. For example, a largely residential neighborhood like West Roxbury will be able to rely primarily on typical custodians, whereas a neighborhood like Back Bay that is dominated by the "shared" spaces of commercial or industrial zones needs a strong representation of exemplars. Taking these additional elements into account led to divergent conclusions regarding which neighborhoods are effective in addressing deterioration and denigration to the urban commons and which are not.

The most striking disagreement between the cooperator–free-rider and division-of-labor approaches was around population density. The former found that neighborhoods with greater density had fewer custodians per capita. This would be consistent with the concept of diffusion of responsibility, wherein individuals are less likely to take action on shared problems when they perceive that there are many other individuals who might also do so.[29] However, the second set of analyses found that coverage was *higher* in neighborhoods with greater density, likely owing to the simple fact that with more people present there are more opportunities for someone to take action, even if each individual is less likely to do so. In addition, the traditional analysis found that the greater presence of any minority group predicted fewer custodians per capita. When controlling for the expected volume and nature of reports, however, these aspects of the community did not predict coverage in any way. This suggests that such groups tend to live in neighborhoods that, by their land use and form, might require fewer custodians, and thus their lower rate of custodians per capita is not an issue. Some might argue that this ignores the possibility that more disadvantaged neighborhoods experience more issues, particularly in terms of man-made incivilities. This is a valid point, but two things are worth noting. First, the regressions controlled for median income, potentially accounting for some or all of this imbalance across neighborhoods. Second, the per capita analysis did not permit this either, meaning the coverage analysis certainly eliminates a large portion, if not all, of any perceived lack of effectiveness of minority communities in leveraging 311 to maintain their particular set of public spaces and infrastructure. That all said, the two models did agree on one thing—that median income predicted not only more custodians per capita but also the greater capacity of a neighborhood to address public issues.

Extending the Division-of-Labor Model

This chapter has articulated a division of labor in how the members of a community combine to realize collective efficacy in maintenance of the urban commons. This model is an advance over previous approaches in its acknowledgment of the potential for multiple types of actors and might be extended to elucidate the sustainability of other commons around the world and, even more broadly, the dynamics of various collective challenges and tasks that fall outside the commons. A major hurdle was the very challenge of bridging between individual-level patterns of behavior and the collective outcomes they influence, requiring a solution that was jointly conceptual and methodological. First, attention to *social regularities* required a description of the basic mechanics of custodianship and thereby the patterns of action and interaction that result in public maintenance. This enabled us to then quantify these patterns in terms of the *behavioral composition* of a neighborhood, divided into two types of actors who contribute to maintenance in distinct ways: typical custodians, who report only occasionally, focusing primarily on instances of natural deterioration on residential streets, and exemplars, who report more frequently and over a greater range of contexts and types of issues. Second, it was necessary to think critically about how the tasks themselves are distributed across spaces. The ensuing analysis uncovered the role of land use and urban form in determining how the nature of maintenance varies both within and between neighborhoods. In the end, these analyses not only uncovered a division of labor in the maintenance of the urban commons but also revealed that this approach provided novel insights regarding the contextual factors that predict how effective a given neighborhood would be in maintaining the commons.

To demonstrate how we might apply the steps laid out here to other collective tasks, let us turn our attention to a classical example from the urban context, the problem of managing adolescent groups in public spaces. Such groups might become a nuisance or even dangerous if not properly monitored. For the sake of illustration, we can begin with the assumption that the dichotomy of typical and exemplar custodians is relevant to this case, though we will return to this later. What I have termed exemplars have been of interest to many previous writers, as they are responsible for the most evocative expressions of public discipline. Jane Jacobs refers to "characters" who offer consistent "eyes and ears on the street."[30] Another example is Mary Pattillo-McCoy's Ms. Spears, a respected elder in the Chicago neighborhood of Groveland who was prepared to redirect behavior whenever and wherever she deemed appropriate.[31] These individuals are probably the easiest (and most fun) to observe and describe because of their persistence in enforcing social norms, but they are unlikely to be the only ones with attentive eyes and ears. Similar to typical custodians, there are others who act episodically, responding specifically when adolescents have become unruly in a space near their home or business. As with the earlier example of a streetlight outage, these two groups would presumably take action in overlapping but nonequivalent sets of situations, making both of them necessary for the comprehensive management of the neighborhood.

Intervening with unruly adolescents, however, differs from reporting a streetlight outage in ways that may have implications for both the typology of relevant actors and the contextual factors that moderate their desire to take action. Most apparently, whereas 311 reports are made in isolation, intervening in social disorder requires interpersonal interaction. Adolescents are much more likely to ignore adult admonitions than the Department of Public Works is to ignore a work order. Ms. Spears, for example, probably felt empowered to discipline children in public because she knew their names and their families. Pattillo-McCoy also details how relationships can *deter* action.[32] There are cases in which an individual might choose not to intervene precisely because she knows the kids and would prefer to avoid conflict. In this way, the relationships of a community may play a magnified role in people's responses to social disorder, acting as the scaffolding that can either facilitate or inhibit an individual's ability to redirect people's behaviors in the public space. This might also lead to a more complex typology of actors, with typical and exemplar custodians further divided into additional categories based on their social integration.

We might apply the same approach to any collective task of interest. In urban neighborhoods, examples might include the construction and management of a community garden, motivating against the closing of a local fire station or the opening of an unwanted store, or the leadership of a parent-teacher association. Likewise, as noted, many of the commons across the world clearly contain multiple tasks. Even for those in which there would seem to be a single action of interest—for example, how many cattle one chooses to graze on the commons—Ostrom's design principles make it clear that the efforts of organization and management themselves entail distinct contributions.[33] These should not be ignored; as many studies have shown, the regulatory institutions that promote group-beneficial behaviors are often as important as the group-beneficial behaviors themselves. Once a researcher has identified a collective task of interest, he or she must then answer the following questions: What are the dynamics of the primary contributions to the task? Who are the relevant actors, and what are their patterns of contribution (or lack thereof)? How do these actors reinforce each other, and where do they play complementary roles? How do they mediate the role of contextual factors? These steps will determine whether a division of labor is in operation and, if so, how it works.

Conclusion: The Behavioral Dynamics of the Commons

The long arc of research on the commons has entailed the proposal and debate of institutions and contexts that predispose, coerce, or otherwise encourage members of a community to act in the collective best interest. The behavioral dynamics of the commons—the patterns of action people undertake, their motivations for doing so, and how they combine to realize (or fall short of) maintenance and sustainability—have remained something of a mystery, and models of the commons have consequently relied on a number of simplifying assumptions. This has similarly been true for the operation of collective efficacy in urban neighborhoods, where we know a lot about *whether* and *where* communities will achieve shared goals but little about *how* they do so and *who* is responsible. The past two chapters have begun to fill this gap by examining the particular case captured by 311, with the anticipation that it could act as a model for other contexts and challenges.

As we consider the discoveries summarized in these past two chapters, we see the lessons from Part I on how best to work with novel digital data. Some of the requests received by 311 clearly contribute to the maintenance of the urban commons, but it was not immediately apparent how to interpret these actions. Through a series of analyses and the use of a survey, we were able to demonstrate that the maintenance of the commons relied on territoriality, not, as assumed by most behavioral models, cooperation or even material investments. Furthermore, we found that the two components of territoriality, caretaking and defense, contribute to the maintenance of the commons in distinct ways. This deductive, theoretically driven analysis of custodianship at the individual level then gave way to an inductive question for which there was little reason to nominate a "preferred" or most likely hypothesis: How do the members of a community combine to determine collective outcomes? The result was the articulation of a division of labor in which typical and exemplar custodians and city employees each contribute to maintenance in distinct ways. Importantly, the findings rejected the simplifying assumptions embedded in the cooperator–free-rider model of the commons, indicating that the more nuanced division of labor model is a conceptual and methodological advance that might be applied more generally to collective efficacy and to commons across the world.

The detailed findings of Part II have been largely academic but can be put to good use, helping us to reconceptualize how institutions can effectively manage the behavioral dynamics of the commons. The 311 system itself is a modern, technologically enabled member of this class of institutions, and it is well suited to the more nuanced interpretation of the commons presented here, as it clearly violates the assumptions that constrain existing models of the commons. It does not appear to elicit group-oriented behavior but rather facilitates a natural tendency to care for spaces and objects with which one identifies. Nor is its use by community members unidimensional. Rather, it empowers both typical and exemplar custodians, who contribute to the urban commons in their own ways. Herein lies the practical value of the theoretical exercise of the last two chapters. Part III will capitalize on this opportunity, exploring how we might translate these insights into additional refinements and innovations in the maintenance of the urban commons. In doing so, it realizes a major promise made at the outset of this book: that scientific advances and improvements to policy and practice can be mutually reinforcing pursuits.

Government in the Age of Civic Tech

CHAPTER 5

Partnering with the Public

ESTUARIES AND WETLANDS are an often overlooked instance of a common. Though they do not produce much in the way of immediately useful resources for humans, they are critical to the overall stability and health of the watershed. They buffer the impacts of storms and flooding, recharge the groundwater, store excess carbon, and act as a refuge and breeding ground for many species of wildlife, thereby helping to sustain biodiversity. For this reason, many environmental groups hold the preservation of these unique and valuable areas as a critical part of their mission. Tom Langen, a biologist at Clarkson University who specializes in the study of wetlands, worked with one such group that sought to convince private landowners to donate any wetlands in their holdings for conservation. The environmentalists brought to the landowners what they believed to be an enticing opportunity to contribute to the protection of lands vital to the watershed they called home. This logic appealed to their sense of a common good and their desire to promote it. Unfortunately, it swayed few people.

What did convince people to donate their land to the program, as Langen recounts, was concern for their legacy. Whereas most landowners were not especially motivated by the opportunity to preserve the watershed, they were enticed by the idea that the land would be donated in their name, in which case their contribution to the watershed would be attributed to them in perpetuity. The environmental group quickly reoriented its outreach strategy, concentrating on the opportunity for individuals to leave the land in their name to the conservation project rather than having it pass into other hands through sale or inheritance, at which point their legacy would end.

Just like a 311 system, the wetland preservation story entails a collaboration between an institution and the public in the maintenance of a common. Particularly instructive about this case are the distinct motivations the two parties had. The environmental group was concerned with protecting the wetlands for the broader public good, but the private landowners were attracted by the creation of a legacy. Until the environmental groups understood this, their outreach was ineffective, because they were selling their own motivation rather than speaking to the interests of their audience. A similar thought process is visible surrounding 311, which is one of the newest manifestations of *coproduction*, or government programs that directly involve constituents in the design and delivery of services. Proponents of "civic tech" often treat 311 and related innovations as expanding the channels for civic engagement or political participation and in turn classify custodianship with behaviors like voting, volunteering, and donating to civic groups. But is this just an assumption based on the fact that it is a government program intended to involve the public in the delivery of services? As the story of wetland preservation demonstrated, targeting the correct motivations is critical to the success of a program; otherwise it will likely fail to garner much participation.

Here we see an opportunity to convert the insights from Part II into practical value—in short, to transition from what we can learn from urban informatics to what communities can directly gain from such work. Building on our newfound understanding of territoriality as a major motivation for custodianship, Part III of this book will address more fully the motivations that drive use of 311 and the ways in which these insights can support additional refinements to such programs. In doing so, it also evaluates the promise held by civic tech for communities and how such innovations are best designed. This chapter further probes the question of why people use 311. There is no reason to believe that territoriality is the *only* motivation relevant to custodianship, and thus we consider whether it also arises from a desire to be engaged civically or politically, or what I call a *civic disposition*.

Testing the relative importance of territoriality and a civic disposition for the usage of 311 is more than just a question about a single program.

It is also an opportunity to examine coproduction's more general assumption that a civic disposition is the primary motivator for participation in any government program. We will see here that there is a need to move beyond this narrow perspective to one that acknowledges that a given coproduction program might engage any of the numerous facets of human psychology, depending on the nature of participation it requires. This lesson is especially valuable as civic tech expands the variety and nature of such programs. This work builds on a project I undertook with Dietmar Offenhuber of Northeastern University, Jesse Baldwin-Philippi of Fordham University, Melissa Sands of the University of California Merced, and Eric Gordon of Emerson College.[1] Chapter 6 then builds on these insights to assess a series of public interventions and experiments that seek to increase participation in 311. Importantly, they are designed and evaluated in light of the motivations that they seek to engage. Overall, these two chapters illustrate how civic tech can enable effective coproduction if paired with a thoughtful examination of when and why individuals would be interested in participating in a given program.

Collaborations between the Government and the Public

As I have noted before, the proliferation of 311 systems and allied programs has been part of the broader trend of civic tech. Just as computational social science has promised to leverage data to transform our understanding of human behavior, this movement has seen digital technology as a catalyst for diversifying and strengthening the ways that people can contribute to their local communities and to society in general. One subset of this work has focused specifically on the lines of interaction between municipal governments and their constituencies. Previously, such interaction centered primarily on town hall meetings and other public forums, which tend to be dominated by a small, relatively vocal subset of the community. The limitations of this system have often left both government officials and the constituents they serve wondering what exactly was accomplished.[2] The hope has been that "Gov 2.0" will be able to leverage the two-way communication capacities of modern web tools to solve these sorts of challenges.[3] Stephen Goldsmith and Susan Crawford have also lauded such efforts as establishing a new form of public administration that is responsive to the needs of the public in near real time.[4] And others have argued it will transform public deliberation and the crafting of public policy.[5]

The promise of civic tech lies in more than just expanding communication between government and the public. The hope is that it can be the basis for what Benjamin Barber calls "strong" democracy, in which constituents are consistently involved in various aspects of designing, managing, and delivering government services.[6] This idea may not be as novel as it appears at first blush, however. Rather, it puts a technological spin on a long-standing concept in political science and public administration referred to as *coproduction,* or programs that directly engage constituents in the planning and implementation of government services.[7] Whereas classical examples of coproduction have included parent-teacher associations and community policing, civic tech has facilitated other forms of participation in government, including, of course, public deliberation, but also participatory budgeting[8] and planning new community developments.[9]

As coproduction programs increase in number and popularity, they raise a question that has long faced such efforts: What motivates individuals to participate in a government program? This knowledge is critical because the success of coproduction programs stands and falls with constituent participation. Relative to the extensive literature on coproduction writ large, this question has received only a small amount of study.[10] More importantly, it has not been updated to account for the variety of coproduction programs that have emerged in recent years, including the proliferation of civic tech. Traditional theory has treated participation in a coproduction program as an intrinsically civic (or political) act and thus driven by a broader tendency to take part in activities that contribute to society (e.g., volunteering, voting). I refer to this unidimensional characterization of participation as the *public-as-citizen* model. Civicness is only one of many human motivations, though, and I argue that a given coproduction program might capitalize on any of them. I refer to this more expansive view as the *public-as-partner* model, in that it treats each member of the public as a multifaceted partner whose various capacities enable him or her to contribute in multiple ways.

Coproduction: A Brief History

In the 1970s, the Workshop in Political Theory and Policy Analysis at Indiana University introduced the concept of coproduction, offering it as an alternative to the prevailing practice at the time of administering government programs in a wholesale fashion through large, centralized bureaucracies.[11] They argued that this should be tempered by a more localized approach that incorporated the public into service delivery.[12] Philosophically, coproduction embodied the democratic ideals of citizen access to and participation in government. In a practical sense, such programs would improve services by allowing members of the public to tailor implementation to community needs. If this latter concept sounds similar to Elinor Ostrom and her colleagues' emphasis on localized institutions as the most efficient solution to the problem of the commons, it should. Ostrom herself was one of the primary actors in the workshop and wrote a handful of prominent pieces on the subject.

One of the most eloquent descriptions of coproduction comes from Ostrom's 1996 essay on the subject, defining it as "one way that synergy between what a government does and what citizens do can occur."[13] From this, she reasoned that coproduction could make services more efficient and effective, but only if the efforts of these two entities were complementary and nonsubstitutable. Taking 311 as an example, the maintenance of the urban commons consists of two different activities that might be divided between government and the public. Urbanites observe and can report instances of deterioration or denigration in public spaces during their daily movements, and city agencies provide the professional expertise and equipment for fixing them. While this illustrates the potential advantages of coproduction, it also highlights the dependence of coproduction on the participation of the public and, in turn, the importance of understanding when and why members of the public would choose to do so.

Coproduction saw a decline in popularity during the 1990s, owing to the emergence of "the new public management," an effort to make bureaucracy operate more like private industry.[14] This perspective cast members of the public as "customers," rather than potential collaborators in the delivery of government services. Interest in coproduction has seen a resurgence, however, in the last 10–15 years, as the new public management has been replaced with the more consonant paradigm of "new public governance," which views service delivery as the collaborative co-ordination of various partners.[15] Such collaboration might involve multiple government agencies working in concert to address a particular need but has also lent itself well to Ostrom's stance that coproduction improves delivery systems by leveraging the complementary capacities of both government and citizens.[16] Enthusiasm for coproduction has been further fueled by the advent of modern web technologies. Proponents of civic tech have capitalized on these novel resources to create new mechanisms for communication and collaboration between the government and the public, enhancing the potential for true partnership.

In the years since Ostrom and her colleagues introduced coproduction, thinkers have expanded it to encompass a variety of different arrangements. The level of activity and responsibility attributed to the public can vary considerably across examples. In the most basic case, Stephen Osborne and his colleagues have argued that all service delivery entails coproduction because the recipient of the service must necessarily participate in its consumption.[17] At the other extreme, there are cases in which the public is the primary or sole deliverer of the services, such as when expert patients assist in the provisioning of health care.[18] Additionally, Tony Bovaird has illustrated ways in which coproduction can go beyond service delivery to include the planning and design of policies and programs.[19] Others have also extended the model to account for collaborative arrangements between government and community organizations or nonprofits.[20] For our purposes here, 311 is specifically a case in which individual members of the public participate in service delivery, but it might also offer insights on individual contributions to the planning and design of services as well.

Public as Citizen or Public as Partner?

By definition, coproduction programs depend on the participation of the public and are unlikely to be effective without it. For this reason, a critical question is why members of the public do or do not choose to participate in a given program. Most work to date, however, has focused on govern-ments and how they can better construct channels or distribute resources in ways that will make programs more accessible.[21] This emphasis on whether the public is able to coproduce has left little understanding, how-ever, of why someone would want to do so.[22] Central to this latter ques-tion is how one conceptualizes constituents and their role. As recounted by John Clayton Thomas, as public administration has evolved in the last 40 years, so has its perspective on the public.[23] From the 1970s into the 1980s, a period that also saw the original rise of interest in coproduction, members of the public were "citizens" with a major stake and interest in shaping policy and its implementation. In the 1990s, the philosophy of new public management[24] treated the public as "customers" whose needs must be fulfilled. More recently, new public governance has emphasized collaboration across agencies and sectors, treating members of the public as an additional "partner." The first and last of the three perspectives on the public are the most important for our purposes here because each presents a particular way of thinking about the active role that constituents might take in governance.

Existing research on participation in coproduction programs has largely focused on the public-as-citizen model. This is embodied by a popular metaphor that refers to coproduction programs as a "bridge to citizenship" by which participation will entrain and encourage involvement in civic life.[25] This perspective treats participation in coproduction as an overtly civic or political action, reflecting a generalized *civic disposition* that manifests in a broader pattern of political participation, including behaviors such as voting and volunteering. There are clear weaknesses to this approach, the most apparent being that this proposed by-product of coproduction programs has been little tested,[26] and the few studies that have tested it have found little evidence that other civic and political behaviors actually predict participation in coproduction.[27]

The lack of support for the *public-as-citizen* model calls for an alternative conception of the motivations that might drive participation in coproduction programs. As the new public governance and civic tech diversify the ways in which government seeks to collaborate with the public in service design and delivery, it raises the question of what it means to think of members of the public as partners. To inform this, let us think about how agencies and organizations become involved in the process of governance. In such cases, the potential of each organization to contribute to a program is not exclusively dependent on its will to provide a public good (i.e., the equivalent of civic disposition at the organizational level); in fact, there are cases where this does not appear to be the case at all. For example, in Ghana, the Public Road Transportation Union is a private association that collects taxes from buses and taxis on behalf of the government in exchange for extensive control over the transportation sector,[28] an activity that speaks little to a desire to provide a public good. Rather, the manner and extent of a contribution by an agency or organization is determined by their specific capacities in that domain.

We might then define a partner as an entity with characteristic facets and capacities that can contribute to the collaborative process of governance. When one applies this definition to members of the public, it is apparent that the public-as-citizen model takes a narrow view of why constituents would be motivated to participate in a coproduction program. Indeed, humans are endowed with a diverse array of motivations that extend far beyond a capacity for civicness, and in theory a coproduction program might appeal to any one of these. To make effective use of this knowledge, we might turn to the psychological concept of modularity, which states that a given motivation is oriented toward certain goals or tasks. As such, it is responsive to relevant cues and contexts and will manifest itself in behaviors surrounding those goals.[29] In this view, a motivation will be relevant to coproduction if a program's activities evoke the cues or call on the behaviors associated with that motivation. This perspective enables us not only to expand our attention to motivations beyond a civic disposition but also reason what types of motivations would be relevant for any given program.

The one systematic attempt to identify multiple motivations for coproduction was made by John Alford.[30] He proposed three types of nonmaterial rewards that might contribute to one's willingness to coproduce: intrinsic rewards, such as increased self-esteem from efficacious action; solidary incentives, arising from a desire to contribute to the group; and expressive values, or normative beliefs about societal issues. Alford's nonmaterial rewards offered an important advance, but they did not go far enough in that they were still generalized incentives, applicable to any coproduction program. Instead, an important value of the public-as-partner model as I have described it is that it permits the motivations of interest to vary across coproduction programs, depending on the nature of participation. In a practical sense, this broader view becomes increasingly necessary as new public governance in general and civic tech in particular further diversify the ways that constituents might participate in the design and implementation of policy. Indeed, part of the strength and appeal of coproduction programs is that they can leverage actions that have not previously been part of the governance process.

To summarize, the public-as-partner model provides a distinct perspective on participation in coproduction by considering any of the diverse array of human motivations as being potentially relevant to a given coproduction program. It expands on the public-as-citizen model by opening up the possibility that participation in coproduction could entail more than just a civic disposition, and it poses the previously unexplored corollary that different coproduction programs rely on distinct sets of motivations. If this were found to be true, it would call for a program-by-program approach when implementing, evaluating, and promoting coproduction. It also raises a second, complementary question: In actuality, how important is a civic disposition to coproduction?

Applying the Public-as-Citizen and Public-as-Partner Models to 311

The 311 system's collaborative model for the maintenance of the urban commons makes for an effective comparison of the public-as-citizen and public-as-partner models because the two make divergent predictions about the motivations that would lead a constituent to identify and report an issue in the public domain. The majority of research on 311 has taken the former approach, classifying 311 reports with other forms of political participation or civic engagement, such as voting.[31] This would stand to reason, as issues in the commons are everyone's problem but no one's formal responsibility, meaning efforts to address them might be consciously civic or "for the greater good." This logic, however, would appear to be a reiteration of the traditional model of the commons, which characterized contributions as a manifestation of "cooperation." Part II of this book has already noted that a major weakness of this approach is that it uses the consequences of a behavior to infer the motivations, rather than considering the action itself on its own terms. As importantly, each of these studies has assumed this interpretation of 311 reporting to be true without directly validating it.

In contrast, when thinking of the public as a multifaceted partner, we might ask what other motivations are engaged during acts of custodianship. I have already argued at length that such behaviors are a manifestation of a fundamental human capacity for territoriality, and I have presented multiple lines of evidence to this effect. Nonetheless, it certainly does not preclude the possibility that a civic disposition plays its own independent role in motivating participation in 311 or even that it might account for the previously observed association between territoriality and custodial reports; for instance, it is possible that those with a higher civic disposition also express greater concern for their neighborhoods and that a higher civic disposition in turn is responsible for both that concern and custodianship.

The goal here is to test the distinct hypotheses arising from the two models. The public-as-citizen model predicts that usage of 311 to report public issues would be a function solely of a civic disposition and thereby greater in those who are also more active in other civic and political activities (e.g., voting). The public-as-partner model would predict that 311 reporting would be greater in those with higher territorial motives. Though we have already seen evidence of this relationship in Chapter 3, here we retest it while simultaneously considering any effect of a civic disposition, which I did not do before. It is worth noting, however, that the hypothesis is not that territoriality would be active across coproduction programs or uniquely responsible for usage of 311, but simply that this motivation is particularly relevant to the form of participation required by 311 systems.

Testing the Public-as-Citizen and Public-as-Partner Models

To test the public-as-partner and public-as-citizen models, we return to the user survey presented in Chapter 3. The current analyses supplement the two survey scales measuring territoriality—benefiting the local community and enforcing social norms—with two additional pieces of information about individual users. First, the survey also included a series of items about participation in civic activities. Second, my colleagues and I linked survey responses and 311 behavior to public voting records. These two additions provide the necessary measures for civic disposition. Additionally, rather than a simplistic analysis of "participation," these analyses use the methodologies from previous chapters to describe the custodial habits of 311 users in multiple ways, including whether someone was a custodian or not, the volume and geographical range of such activity, and whether they acted as a custodian in various spaces across the urban landscape. This permits a more nuanced assessment of how civic disposition and territoriality might explain different aspects of 311 reporting. Importantly, the focus on measuring and analyzing individual-level behaviors here is unique among studies that have compared 311 usage to political participation, offering a number of advantages:[32] (1) it avoids the ecological fallacy, permitting a "true" individual-level interpretation; (2) it links objective behavioral measures from multiple databases with self-reported behaviors and motivations; (3) the multilevel models permit us to control for differences between neighborhoods in the number of public issues that might need attention, thereby factoring out similarities inherent in living in the same environment; and (4) this is one of the only studies of this sort that has isolated reports of a particular type of interest rather than just counting 311 calls of all types in an indiscriminate fashion.

Before proceeding with this analysis, it is important to recall a few details from the original presentation of the survey sample. The sample was notably more white, educated, and middle-aged than the overall population of Boston (see Table 3.1 in Chapter 3), though it is unclear how much it differed from the demographic composition of 311 users. The sample was also above average in its use of 311. It had an overrepresentation of custodians, and those custodians made more reports than would be expected by chance. These biases should be taken into account when considering the results reported here, though, as before, we have to consider whether the underrepresented groups would in fact have different relationships between territoriality, civic disposition, and custodianship. It is not clear whether or why this would be the case. The higher level of custodianship in the sample does, however, give us greater power to compare between groups and to understand the motivations of highly active custodians. Additionally, because the survey included 311 users of all types, we are able to compare custodians to noncustodians while accounting for confounding factors that may lead them to know of and use the system in the first place.

Measuring Civic Disposition

The survey asked respondents to indicate whether they had participated in each of nine civic or political activities in the previous six months (e.g., attended a meeting for a local community group or government agency; see Table 5.1 for a complete list of items and their prevalences). Contacting a government official or agency was the most widespread behavior (70 percent), though this might be inflated if some respondents included

TABLE 5.1 Comparison of participation in civic activities, voting, and territorial motives between custodians and noncustodians

	Custodians	Noncustodians	Total
Civic activities and political participation			
Signed a petition about a social or political issue	208 (48%)	119 (49%)	327 (49
Volunteered with a local or national civic group	194 (45%)	105 (43%)	299 (44
Donated to a local or national civic group	244 (57%)	126 (52%)	375 (55
Used social media to engage with a local or national civic group	150 (35%)	90 (37%)	240 (36
Contacted a government official or agency	316 (73%)	163 (67%)	479 (71
Participated in an online discussion or blogged about a political issue	125 (29%)	72 (30%)	197 (29
Participated in a march, protest, or demonstration for a political cause	28 (6%)	20 (8%)	48 (7%
Sent a letter to the editor of a local or national newspaper	36 (8%)	31 (13%)	67 (10%
Attended a meeting for a local community group or government agency	218 (51%)	112 (46%)	330 (49
Voted in 2011 municipal election	181 (42%)	89 (37%)	270 (40
Territoriality			
Benefit community	4.39 (0.78)	4.20 (0.90)	4.32 (0.8
Enforce norms	3.42 (1.21)	3.36 (1.28)	3.40 (1.2
Material interests			
Maintain property values	2.56 (1.57)	2.47 (1.49)	2.53 (1.5
Total	431 (64%)	243 (36%)	$N = 674$

311 as being a government official. For most other civic activities, including volunteering, signing a petition, donating to a civic group, and attending a community meeting, about half of the sample reported participating. The average individual participated in three activities (*mean* = 2.98, *median* = 3), and 109 respondents (15 percent) had not participated in any. Henceforth we analyze the activities as a sum rather than as individual activities.[33]

We identified 562 survey respondents in public voter records by linking on names and addresses. We assumed that those who could not be matched in this way were not registered and therefore did not vote.[34]

Voting provides a valuable measure of civic disposition, as it is the most common and basic manifestation of citizenship, and here we focus particularly on whether each individual had voted in the most recent municipal election, which was in 2011. This is for two reasons. First, conceptually, voting in a municipal election is the most appropriate parallel for studying participation in a municipal program.[35] Second, from a measurement perspective, voter turnout in local elections tends to be exceedingly low, especially during odd-numbered years, as there are no concurrent federal elections. This makes it a more salient indicator of civicness.[36] As with reports of civic activities, voting in the 2011 municipal election was elevated in our sample. We had a record of voting for 40 percent of the survey respondents compared to a 24 percent turnout rate for all registered voters that year.

Civic Disposition, Territoriality, and Custodianship

An initial descriptive analysis found little relationship between a civic disposition and custodianship. Custodians were no more likely than noncustodians to participate in any of the nine civic activities or to vote (see Table 5.1; $\chi^2_{df=1} = 0.00 - 2.86$, all p-values = ns), nor did custodians and noncustodians differ in total number of civic activities (*means:* custodians = 2.99, noncustodians = 2.95; t-value = 0.28, $p = ns$). In contrast, custodians reported a greater motivation to benefit the community (*means:* custodians = 4.40, noncustodians = 4.21; t-value = 2.78, $p < .01$), though the same was not true for the desire to enforce norms (*means:* custodians = 3.44, noncustodians = 3.39; t-value = 0.55, $p = ns$).

Multilevel Analysis

To formalize the analysis of custodianship, civic disposition, and territoriality, I again utilize multilevel models. As in Chapter 3, these models allow us to control for demographic characteristics and for confounds arising from the opportunities for reporting issues created by one's neighborhood context. Though a major reason for using multilevel models was the potential for similarities between neighbors owed to a shared residential environment, I place all details testing for the presence of such clustering at the neighborhood level (i.e., τ and its significance) in footnotes as it is a bit tangential to the main theme. One difference between the sample analyzed here and that in Chapter 3 arises from the decision

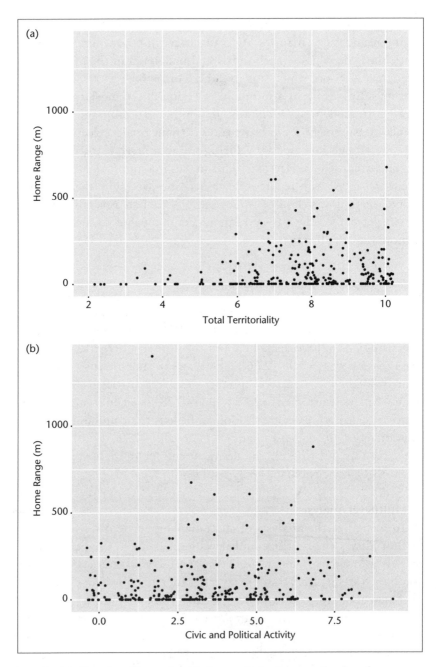

FIGURE 5.1 Dot plots illustrating (a) the correlation between the size of an individual's home range and a combined territoriality score and (b) the lack of the same correlation with total civic and political activities.

to leave the measure of material incentives out of the analysis given its general impertinence in previous analyses. This allows us to include 12 additional respondents who had omitted that item but had completed all of the other measures of interest and who were not part of the analysis in Chapter 3.[37] Major results from the analysis are represented visually in Figures 5.1 and 5.2; complete results are reported in Appendix C.

The findings from these models were consistent with the descriptive comparison of custodians and noncustodians above. Users of 311 who participated in more civic activities or had voted in the 2011 municipal election were no more likely to act as custodians (civic activities: O.R. = 0.96, $p = ns$; voting: O.R. = 1.21, $p = ns$). Those who expressed a greater desire to benefit their community were more likely to act as custodians (O.R. = 1.33, $p < .05$), confirming earlier analyses.[38]

Custodianship across the Urban Landscape

As in Chapter 3, we can go further than a simple comparison of custodians to noncustodians to take account of the varied ways that individuals interact with the geography of a city. People have a home neighborhood but also visit other neighborhoods for work, travel, and recreation. We can attend to this in two ways. First, we can flexibly define a person's "home neighborhood" through the geographic clustering of an individual's reports. From this, we derive two measures: the number of reports made within one's home neighborhood and the geographic range of custodianship in the home neighborhood.[39] Second, we utilize items from the survey that asked individuals whether they used 311 in various locales, including their neighborhood of employment, where they visit friends and family, or on their commute. These analyses are necessarily limited to custodians.[40]

Individuals who expressed a greater desire to benefit their community or to enforce social norms had home clusters that were both larger (benefit community: O.R. = 2.36, $p < .01$; enforce norms: O.R. = 1.32, $p < .05$) and had more reports (benefit community: O.R. = 1.26, $p < .01$; enforce norms: O.R. = 1.22, $p < .001$). Notably, those participating in more civic activities had home clusters with *fewer* such reports (O.R. = 0.86, $p < .001$), but the range of reporting around the home was neither larger nor smaller (O.R. = 1.08, $p = ns$). Having voted was unrelated to either measure (reports: O.R. = 0.96, $p = ns$; size: O.R. = 0.92, $p = ns$). Figure 5.1 visualizes these

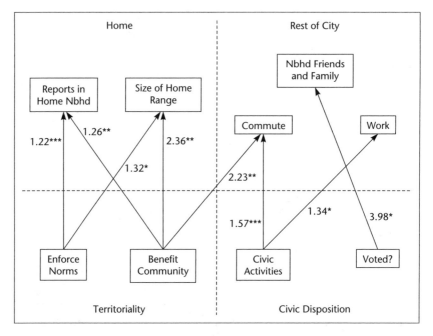

FIGURE 5.2 Schematic depicting the dichotomous relationship between territoriality, civic disposition, and the geography of custodianship.

relationships, illustrating how the size of one's home range correlates with territoriality but does not correlate with civic and political activities.[41]

In order to better understand reporting *outside* the home neighborhood, we turn to the survey items about where people report issues. In the survey, 28 percent of custodians reported that they used 311 to report issues while on their commute, 24 percent in the neighborhood where they work, and 13 percent in the neighborhoods of friends and family. Those who expressed a greater desire to benefit the community and participated in more civic activities were more likely to state that they reported while on their commute (benefit community: O.R. = 2.23, $p < .01$; civic activities: O.R. = 1.57, $p < .001$), but only civic activities were associated with a greater tendency to report in the neighborhood where one works (O.R. = 1.34, $p < .05$). Those who voted were more likely to report from the neighborhood of one's family or friends (O.R. = 1.38, $p < .05$).[42]

Summary: Observing the Public's Role as Partner

The findings here strongly support the public-as-partner model of co-production. Consistent with the analyses in Chapter 3, the two components of territoriality—seeking to benefit the community and enforcing social norms—were associated with custodianship. Those with a greater desire to benefit the community were more likely to act as custodians, and both components of territoriality predicted more reports and a broader geographical range of reporting in the home neighborhood. Additionally, those with a greater desire to benefit the community were more likely to report while on their commute. These relationships are crucial to explaining global usage of 311 because, as we have seen, most reporting occurs in the reporter's home neighborhood. In contrast, indicators of a civic disposition were predictive of reporting exclusively in contexts outside the home neighborhood, including at work, while on one's commute, and in the neighborhoods of friends and family. These are much less frequent contexts for the use of 311, diminishing the relative importance of a civic disposition to the functioning of a system as a whole.

Beyond the relative importance of territoriality and civic disposition to 311, the geographic patterns of the results revealed something of a dichotomy in how these motivations interact with the urban landscape, as illustrated in Figure 5.2. Territoriality explained 311 reporting in the home neighborhood, exactly where such motives should, by definition, be stronger. Meanwhile, 311 reporting outside the neighborhood was more strongly explained by a civic disposition, though, notably, these relationships were only moderately consistent, as three of six possible relationships between indicators of civic disposition and locales beyond the home neighborhood were significant. This seems fitting, as the decision to report throughout the city is similar in spirit to a desire to participate in activities that contribute to society more broadly. In fact, this distinction mirrors the assumptions of the public-as-citizen model and the public-as-partner critique. The former ignores the basic motivation to maintain public spaces over which one has a sense of ownership, which is foundational to the collaborative arrangement of 311. It is only when individuals break through this invisible boundary of personal interest that a civic disposition becomes a relevant factor.

The results confirm that 311 data should not be used to assay political participation, which many authors to date have done.[43] This is especially true when the data are aggregated to assess an individual or neighborhood's volume of activity. We do find, however, that reports outside a reporter's home neighborhood (i.e., those not included in the home cluster) could arguably be used as an indicator of a civic disposition. Leveraging this methodology to interpret 311 participation in this manner would require the analysis of reports nested within individual accounts, as done here. This is not to say that the data cannot be used to test hypotheses about how relationships between constituents and government can influence participation, which is the focus of some existing studies, but rather that it would be inaccurate to treat 311 reporting as a proxy for activities such as voting or volunteering or as the primary motivation for such behaviors.

A New Perspective on Coproduction and Civic Tech

Traditional perspectives on coproduction treat a tendency toward civic and political behavior, or what I have referred to here as a civic disposition, as the fundamental basis for participating in and contributing to government programs. A similar set of assumptions is embedded in the stated mission (and very name) of civic tech, which seeks to enable a civic disposition. As an alternative to this public-as-citizen model, I argue that those studying and implementing coproduction programs should think of members of the public as partners—individuals who have an array of facets and capacities, any of which might be incorporated into the collaborative process of governance. The public-as-partner model encompasses and extends the public-as-citizen model, acknowledging a civic disposition as one of many motivations that might be active in coproduction. Consequently, it permits a more nuanced assessment of participation. Whereas the public-as-citizen model assumes that a single generalized motivation is uniquely applicable across programs, the public-as-partner model's more expansive approach anticipates that programs might differ in the specific motivations that they engage, depending on the particular nature of participation each requires. This latter consideration becomes even more valuable as civic tech rapidly diversifies the number of ways that constituents might contribute to the design and delivery of services.

Importantly, the public-as-partner model does not dismiss a civic disposition or other generalized motivations for participation in government programs as irrelevant but simply distinguishes between them and motivations that are more specific to the participation required by a given program. The analysis of 311 presented here clearly illustrates the complementary roles that these two types of motivations might play, suggesting a series of considerations that we might explore for each.

Program-Specific Motivations

The division that emerged between territoriality and civic disposition was geographic in nature, situating the former in the home neighborhood and the latter in other spaces around the city. This would raise the question, though, of how specific a motivation is to any given program. Attending to concerns in one's home neighborhood certainly is not unique to 311 systems, in which case "program-specific" refers more to the particular form of a program and others that cue similar motivations. For example, community policing, one of the original inspirations for attention to coproduction, depends on the enforcement of social norms and expectations by local residents and, in turn, their territoriality.[44] It would stand to reason that the same motivation might be central to participation in any coproduction program that would require individuals to take action surrounding the upkeep, beautification, or defense of their neighborhood.

Coproduction programs are diverse, however, and many are not centered on neighborhood spaces. In rural France, families participating in the Villa Family program act as hosts to elderly tenants as a localized substitute for nursing homes.[45] In the United Kingdom, the Sure Start program provides new mothers with in-home consultations with existing mothers.[46] In many developing countries, community members are trained to deliver health services in rural areas in order to supplement an otherwise limited formal health sector.[47] Meanwhile, civic tech has only expanded the ways that constituents might engage in governance, as illustrated by efforts to involve residents in community development decisions through virtual environments[48] and to crowdsource solutions to Boston's snow-removal problem during the record-breaking winter of 2014–2015.[49] Each of these programs relies on its own characteristic set of motivations.

I have listed a disparate set of programs to illustrate how broadly participation in, and thus motivation for, coproduction might vary. That said, it is likely that there are other themes that link the goals and activities across multiple programs, leading them to call on one or more of the same motivations. For example, Ostrom describes how two Nigerian communities had differing success rates with a public school system owing to the value that local parents placed on formal education.[50] In parallel, Melissa Marschall found that parents in Detroit, Michigan, with higher education were more engaged in discussions regarding school issues.[51] We see then how two programs in different cultures can tap similar motivations thanks to a shared focus on childhood education. Short of proposing a full taxonomy of coproduction programs and the motivations that they engage, this simply demonstrates how the public-as-partner model might inform further theory and practice. Program-specific analysis will reveal both distinctions and overlaps in motivations across programs in a manner that will resemble the organization of human behavior, with programs clustering around particular motivations that are most closely related to the major societal challenges that coproduction programs seek to address. In turn, policymakers and practitioners can leverage these consistencies to give greater context to participation in any given program.

Generalized Motivations

Even if there are motivations that are generalized across coproduction programs, it is clear that it is no longer sufficient to assume that they are universally responsible for all forms and levels of participation. Consequently, a new question of interest is how a generalized motivation is relevant to a given program. Here we saw a civic disposition responsible for custodianship that fell geographically beyond the natural bounds of territoriality. This insight might have implications for other place-based programs but would be less helpful for understanding participation in, say, parent-teacher associations or community health care delivery. While a civic disposition may play a role in these latter two as well, it will manifest in a way specific to the program. Similarly, we might think of Alford's nonmaterial rewards, including solidarity incentives and normative beliefs, as classes of motivations that might take multiple forms, depending on the program in question.[52] For example, territoriality is strongly associated with social relationships within the neighborhood.[53] In contrast, Marschall found no evidence that neighborhood social relationships influenced greater involvement around school issues, likely because that particular social context has little bearing on the behavior in question.[54] Individuals and communities also differ in their normative beliefs and therefore might vary in how they respond to the values promoted or embodied by a particular program.

Another way to think about generalized motivations, particularly civic disposition, is along the spectrum of constituent participation, from the receipt of services to the planning and design of programs. The 311 system sits midway along this spectrum in that constituents direct the allocation of services but are not involved in the design of the system. To its one side are programs in which the public's only role is to receive services. It has been argued that these too are a form of coproduction because individuals are not merely passive vessels but must accept and utilize the services if the program is to have any impact.[55] Program-specific motivations would seem largely if not uniquely responsible for participation in such cases, as an individual's desire for services would be rooted less in a civic disposition than in the anticipated benefits, which will clearly vary depending on the nature of the service. Take the example of flu shots, which are important not only for individuals but also for preventing the spread of disease throughout a population. Though this might support an argument that one has a "civic duty" to receive a flu shot, we have already seen multiple cases, from estuaries to streetlight outages, in which such rhetoric is ineffective. Instead, people are more likely to decide whether to receive a flu shot based on whether they believe that it will keep them or their family members healthy while not exposing them to unwanted side effects.[56]

For programs on the other end of the spectrum, which involve the public in some mixture of planning, design, and implementation,[57] a civic disposition is increasingly relevant. Especially when participation requires one to join an organization that meets regularly, sometimes with government officials, this would seem to appeal to the same motivations that were measured as civic activities in the survey presented here—donating, volunteering, advocating, and voting. Nonetheless, these programs necessarily target particular topics, creating situations, such as the one observed in this study, in which a civic disposition will combine with other motivations to drive participation. In the case of 311, territoriality was an initial requirement for being a custodian in the first place, but custodians with a greater civic disposition were more likely to report across the city. This reflects one particular way that motivations synergize in influencing participation—that the program-specific motivation is a prerequisite, enabling a civic disposition to have an impact. As similar research is conducted on participation in other programs, it will become clear whether this is typical or whether there are other ways in which these motivations interact.

Next Steps: Theoretically Informed Innovation

The public-as-partner model transforms our understanding of how coproduction programs operate. This is timely given the rapid proliferation of civic tech, which is currently experimenting with the number of ways in which the public can be incorporated into governance. Practically, the model offers a framework that can inform the organization, implementation, and evaluation of these programs. We might understand this by revising the metaphor that describes coproduction. I noted earlier that traditional rhetoric casts coproduction programs as a "bridge to citizenship" that calls on and bolsters a civic disposition,[58] a perspective that is similarly foundational to the philosophical inspiration of civic tech. The public-as-partner model suggests an alternative metaphor, that coproduction acts as a lever translating motivations into civic impacts. Many of these motivations, such as territoriality in the current case, are not inherently civic, yet the program channels them into positive outcomes for the community. As public administrators continue to use coproduction programs, including those considered civic tech, to engage constituents in new and creative ways, they will likely call on more and more behaviors that were not previously part of the governance process. In many cases, modern data collection will also provide a detailed window into the patterns of participation, as they did here. This in turn will both call for and facilitate a case-by-case investigation of these various levers in order to identify the motivations that each is harnessing for the collective good.

Metaphors, of course, have their limits, but thinking about coproduction programs as levers can assist those managing or implementing them to better understand their work. In this way, the current chapter has set the theoretical basis for a practical reorientation of the management of coproduction programs. If we know which motivations a program is leveraging, one might ask whether it is appropriately designed to do so. For example, returning to the lesson of wetlands preservation at the beginning of this chapter, do outreach efforts speak to the constituent's interests and concerns, or are they falling on deaf ears? Similarly, program evaluation should consider the motivations whose presence or absence is responsible for the observable level of participation. Especially when a program is seeing disparities across demographic or socioeconomic groups, this information might help administrators avoid the perpetuation of existing inequities.[59] Chapter 6 builds on these opportunities, assessing the effectiveness of three innovations that sought to expand the reach of Boston's 311 system. Distinctively, these projects—from conception, to design, to evaluation—were informed by a theoretical understanding of territoriality, civic disposition, and any other motivations that might drive custodianship.

Experiments in Coproduction

KURT LEWIN, one of the founding fathers of social psychology, attempting to dispense with any argument that theory and practice are distinct and incompatible goals, quipped that there is "nothing as practical as a good theory." In reality, there is often a gap between efforts to advance theory and the everyday activities of practitioners, but, to echo Lewin, this certainly need not be the case. Theory is simply a framework for organizing and explaining facts, and thereby it offers a basis for extrapolating existing knowledge to new contexts. Its translation into innovations and refinements in policy and practice is its promise to society and, as I have argued throughout this book, the foundation for collaborations between academics and public officials within the context of urban informatics.

Let us illustrate the practical value of a good theory with a tale of two theories—each of which has appeared repeatedly in previous chapters—and the evolution of crime prevention in the United States. In the early 1980s, Wilson and Kelling proposed broken windows theory (BWT).[1] One of the multiple appeals of BWT was its explicit identification of a causal mechanism in the generation of crime: physical and social disorder encourages the escalation and expansion of delinquent behavior. This made for a straightforward translation into new law enforcement policies that targeted low-level misdemeanors in order to preempt violent crime, most famously in the form of New York City's zero-tolerance policing program. In these regards, BWT seems a highly useful theory. Unfortunately, as summarized in Chapter 2, further scientific testing has repeatedly cast doubt on its foundational principle, as elegant as it might be, and there is limited if any evidence that disorder actually causes crime.[2] In their seminal evaluation of BWT, Sampson and Raudenbush found that a community's collective efficacy in the enforcement of social norms has greater influence on local crime rates.[3]

The apparent importance of collective efficacy set the stage for another shift in policing strategies, this time to community policing. Though community policing programs have come to vary widely in their implementation,[4] they all seek to implement formal law enforcement in a manner that reinforces the local community's ability to manage the behavior of residents and visitors. Evaluations of this trend have found that community policing is effective in lowering crime and creates more positive relationships between police and the communities they serve.[5] This latter benefit appears particularly important in light of the tensions we have seen in recent years in places like Ferguson, Missouri, and Baltimore, Maryland. It would be revisionist history to say the proponents of collective efficacy invented community policing, as the concept existed for at least a decade before Sampson and Raudenbush's work. Nonetheless, it had taken a back seat to broken windows policing in the late 1980s and early 1990s, and the research on collective efficacy provided renewed evidence for its value. I have in fact been in numerous meetings with police departments and other agencies and community groups that serve neighborhoods in which practitioners speak explicitly about "supporting collective efficacy" in the community. A practical theory indeed.

Is the public-as-partner model articulated in Chapter 5 a practical piece of theory? To take a devil's advocate approach, it uses accessible terms such as "citizen" and "partner" but only as labels for abstracted definitions of the bases of human behavior. Similarly, what does it mean for a behavior to be rooted in territoriality? This would seem to fall outside the realm of the practical. Yet, if we can translate these concepts into applications for a given program, the public-as-partner approach becomes a useful tool for policymakers and practitioners. From this perspective, the lesson might be articulated more simply. Directors of 311 programs and other public officials should think of participation less as a proxy for civic engagement and more as an expression of care and concern for the places that matter to an individual. It is rather intuitive, then, to realize that those places are most often going to be near the home. This framing provides a road map for evaluating the program and developing future refinements in its implementation and outreach, and a similar distillation is possible for any coproduction program.

The goal of this chapter is to make good on the public-as-partner model's application to 311 and to use this as a case study in the evaluation of civic tech. In doing so, it embodies the virtuous cycle of learning and application offered by urban informatics. The data generated by the 311 system supported novel insights on human behavior, which in turn inspired evidence-based innovations in policy and practice. Specifically, the chapter addresses two main questions. First, does attention to territorial motives improve the effectiveness of the system? Second, to what extent can new interventions engage a civic disposition and construct the hypothesized bridge to citizenship promised by coproduction and civic tech alike? For both of these questions, we will also consider the pressing concern of the "digital divide," and the extent to which such innovations can be used to increase access to technologically driven city services by disadvantaged groups.

We examine the questions at hand through three experiments surrounding Boston's 311 system. The first looks at program outreach and whether a message that targets localized sensibilities ("Clean up Dudley Square!") is more effective than one that appeals to people's care for the broader city ("Clean up Boston!"). The second is the introduction of BOS:311, a smartphone app that makes it convenient to report issues from anywhere. This increased accessibility raises the possibility that users might more easily break through the invisible boundaries of their "territory" and even form a greater connection with their community and city. The third experiment is an effort to build greater communication with BOS:311 users by sending them thank you notes that include pictures of the work that they instigated, including repaved potholes, fixed streetlights, and the like. This program also carried the hope that it would not only drive continued usage of the system but also elicit greater custodianship for the broader city, both in sentiment and in action.

The Flyer Study: An Experiment in Outreach

The primary goal of outreach for any government program is not only to inform people about it but also do so in a way that encourages participation. Many efforts around outreach focus on whether members of the population are able to participate. For example, Morten Jakobsen recently tested whether a language-learning program for the children of immigrants in Denmark could increase participation by providing parents with resources for practicing at home.[6] In contrast, the public-as-partner model provides a basis for developing interventions that attend to the public's desire to participate. As noted in Chapter 5, every human motivation is oriented toward particular tasks and is activated by a characteristic set of cues that are relevant to those tasks. In turn, messaging around a coproduction program would gain the greatest traction if it spoke to those psychological cues.

The lessons of the previous chapters suggest that outreach for the 311 system would be most effective if it spoke to territoriality. Drawing from the modern definition of human territoriality presented in Chapter 3, this could be treated in practice as appealing to people's psychological ownership of the space. We have seen repeatedly that custodianship is anchored by the home and the abutting spaces, though for a substantial number of Bostonians their efforts to maintain the neighborhood extend into shared spaces, such as commercial streets and parks. A program of outreach that can speak to one's identification with this geographical level, at once localized but also collective, would in theory be the most effective in encouraging participation. Boston lends itself well to this challenge thanks to its long history as a "city of neighborhoods" and the well-established names attributed to many regions of the city. Thus, we might ask whether messaging that encourages people to help "Fix Potholes in Eagle Hill!" or "Fix Potholes in Dudley Square!" outperforms more generalized exhortations to "Fix Potholes in Boston!"

In 2013, I conducted this very study in collaboration with the directors of the city of Boston's 311 system and the Mayor's Office of New Urban Mechanics. The study was executed as part of a course I was teaching on social psychology methods. The students helped to develop the flyers advertising the 311 system, which reflected the two types of messaging (i.e., the "treatments"), and we distributed those same flyers door-to-door in 10 neighborhoods dispersed throughout the city. In order to maximize the value of the experiment, we concentrated on disadvantaged neighborhoods that appeared to be underutilizing 311. Though the experiment itself was definitively low-tech, its evaluation was made possible by the 311 system's data. The "before" assessment of custodianship already existed, and the "after" measures, which would inform us as to the effectiveness of the different types of messaging, were forthcoming. Importantly, the value of the experiment sat at the intersection of science and policy: in determining which type of messaging would be more effective for outreach surrounding 311 systems, it also evaluated the practical relevance of the territoriality thesis.[7]

Designing a Field Experiment

The field experiment required two main components. First, we needed to design flyers that could accommodate minor adjustments in geographical reference, permitting our two proposed treatments, dubbed *Neighborhood* and *Boston*. Second, we had to create an experimental design that could evaluate the relative impacts of these treatments. Because we had no way of knowing whether the specific individuals who received the flyers subsequently used 311, we treated neighborhoods as the unit of analysis. As such, the question was whether neighborhoods receiving one treatment or the other exhibited a greater increase in custodianship.

The Flyers

We constructed the flyers, which are pictured in Figure 6.1, around three main components, two of which were manipulated for the purposes of the experimental treatment. At the top was a headline stating, "Potholes in [Location]? Get Them Fixed!" Depending on the treatment, this referenced either Boston or the name of a local neighborhood (e.g., Eagle Hill). Second, each flyer included an image of a pothole (drawn from the database of images generated by reports submitted via the smartphone app that is the focus of the next experiment) and a description of where that pothole had been found. The *Neighborhood* treatment used an image of a pothole from the local neighborhood and gave the nearest intersection in the caption, thereby priming care for neighborhood spaces. The *Boston* treatment used an image of a pothole from a major street that crosses the city and gave no specific intersection (i.e., "Tremont St."), emphasizing the generality of the message. Finally, both versions of the flyer contained instructions on how to contact the Mayor's Hotline.

The Experiment

The goal of the study was to assess the extent to which the two different messaging approaches—one highlighting the local neighborhood, the

FIGURE 6.1 Example flyers from the *Neighborhood* treatment (left) and the *Boston* treatment (right).

other highlighting Boston—were effective in eliciting custodianship in a neighborhood. We also compared the *Neighborhood* and *Boston* treatments to *Control* neighborhoods that received no flyers. With finite manpower, we conducted the experiment in only a small subset of the city, utilizing a matching design that created triplets of census tracts with similar characteristics in the same region of the city (based on planning districts, such as Fenway and South Boston). This effectively controlled for not only demographic and socioeconomic characteristics but also regional patterns, as well as previous levels of custodianship. We selected five matched triplets, each in a different planning district. In order to maximize the potential effect of the intervention, we made certain that three of these were located in the city's three most disadvantaged districts and that they also ranked lowest in custodianship 311.[8] Two-person teams distributed flyers throughout the neighborhoods on a single weekend in April 2012. We chose April because it is a period with a rapid increase in reporting, owing particularly to potholes resulting from the spring thaw. Our goal was to deliver a flyer to every housing unit in the neighborhood.[9] In order to make the task more manageable, we selected a single representative census block group (CBG) for each tract. This had the additional benefit of helping us avoid contagion effects, as we selected CBGs that did not border each other from within tracts that did.

The Effect of the Flyers

The main outcome of interest was the volume of reports of public issues in each CBG following the distribution of flyers. To control against the same quantity in the previous year, we analyzed the percentage increase (decrease) in reporting between the six-week period following the distribution of flyers in 2012 and the same period in 2011. Because of the non-normal distribution of this measure, as well as the very few degrees of freedom, here we use the multinomial test, which evaluates the likelihood of a specific ordering of each of the triplets.

As shown in Figure 6.2a, CBGs receiving the *Neighborhood* treatment had the greatest percentage increase in reporting in four of the five triplets. In the fifth triplet, the CBG in the control treatment had the greatest percentage increase. This outcome supports the hypothesis that the *Neighborhood* flyers were more effective in encouraging reporting ($p < .05$).[10] In contrast, one will note not only that no CBG in the *Boston* treatment had the greatest percentage increase in its triplet but also that it had a greater percentage increase than the control treatment in only two of five cases.

Importantly, the same pattern was not visible for nonpublic reports (e.g., request for recycling bin; see Figure 6.2b). The CBG in the *Neighborhood* treatment had the greatest percentage increase in this class of calls in only two of five triplets and had the second-greatest percentage increase (or the second-lowest percentage decrease) in reports in the three other triplets. In fact, one of the two CBGs with the *Neighborhood* treatment that led its triplet with the greatest increase in nonpublic reports was the only CBG in the *Neighborhood* treatment not to lead its triplet with the greatest increase in public reports. This suggests that the increase in custodianship in CBGs with the *Neighborhood* treatment was not merely an expression of increased knowledge about the system.

Summary: Priming Territoriality to Elicit Custodianship

The "flyer study" found that outreach for the 311 system was most effective when it spoke to people's attachment to the spaces around their homes rather than a broader opportunity to contribute to the maintenance of Boston. Neighborhoods that received a flyer whose message primed territoriality had a greater increase in reports of public issues

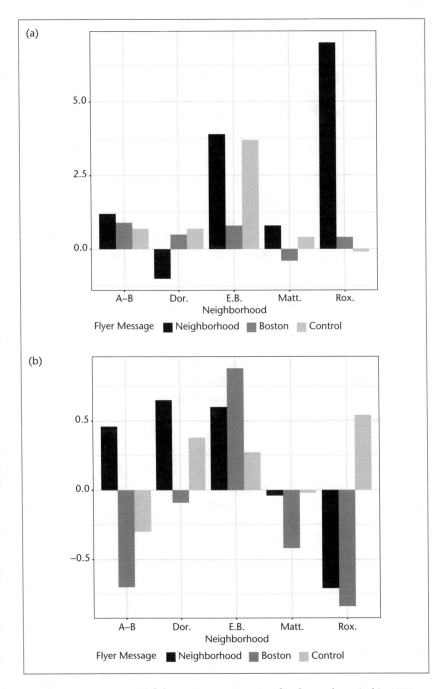

FIGURE 6.2 Proportion of change in 311 reporting for the study period in 2012 relative to the same period in 2011 for matched triplets for (a) public issues and (b) personal needs.

Note: Labels indicate planning district. A-B = Allston-Brighton, Dor. = Dorchester, E.B. = East Boston, Matt. = Mattapan, Rox. = Roxbury.

than those receiving either a flyer with a Boston-centric message or no flyers at all. This effect was independent of an overall increase in use of the system, suggesting that the flyers were effective specifically in encouraging custodianship rather than merely informing individuals about the Mayor's Hotline. In stark contrast, the results found that a flyer encouraging people to help clean up Boston was no more effective than distributing no flyer at all. Though the results of the experiment are consistent with the territoriality thesis, one might wonder whether, alternatively, the messaging primed an in-group psychology, thereby stimulating protective behavior. Even if this were the case, however, it would be more of a complement to the territoriality thesis than a true alternative. In situations where there is perceived collective ownership, territorial and in-group motivations are not independent. Rather, the psychological mechanisms underlying territoriality are employed for a space defined by the in group. In other words, if an in-group psychology were active, it would be relying on territoriality to accomplish the goals of maintaining the local space.

The results provide additional evidence for the territoriality thesis of the urban commons while also demonstrating its practical ability to shape outreach for 311 systems and allied programs. That said, it suffers from some of the limitations of traditional field research. Because of our procedure of distributing flyers door-to-door, we were forced to construct a relatively small sample that also had to conform to the stringent requirements of the matching procedure. Consequently, the analysis consisted only of multinomial tests rather than a stronger, more detailed analysis of the differences between the treatments. The study did benefit from modern technology, but not to the fullest extent possible. The 311 data permitted a straightforward evaluation of the experiment because they were already being collected both before and after the experiment. We did not, however, embed the messages themselves in any web-based communications and applications. The next two experiments explore the potential to expand use of these technologies for the 311 system.

BOS:311: Evaluating an Icon of Civic Tech

To this point, all of the analyses in this book have analyzed 311 reports without differentiating between the various channels by which the city of Boston accepts service requests, including the hotline and online tools. In doing so, we have ignored the original 311 innovation and one of the icons of civic tech: Citizens Connect, now renamed BOS:311, is a smartphone application that allows people to describe and take a picture of an issue and submit it directly to the 311 system without the need to dial the hotline and interact with an operator. When Boston introduced Citizens Connect in 2009, it became the first municipality to successfully integrate a smartphone application into its 311 system. The tool was lauded both in local outlets, such as the *Boston Globe*,[11] and nationally, as an illustration of how digital technology can make government services more accessible and responsive. Chris Osgood and Nigel Jacob, the co-chairs of the Mayor's Office of New Urban Mechanics and the initiators of the project, were recognized by *Governing* magazine as Public Officials of the Year in 2011 for this and related projects.[12] The app has since given rise to a number of daughter apps, including the City Worker app, which enables employees to directly add cases to the agency's cue; Citizens Connect Text, which permits reporting by text message; Commonwealth Connect, which extends the tool to other municipalities throughout Massachusetts (which will be the focus of Chapter 7); and an updated version of the app, rebranded BOS:311, released in 2015.

By comparing the use of Citizens Connect and BOS:311 (hereafter BOS:311) to more traditional channels (e.g., hotline and self-service internet portal), we have a unique opportunity to evaluate the potential of civic tech. Civic tech promises to increase interactions between the government and the public on multiple dimensions—not only diversifying the number of channels for interaction but also expanding the activities these interactions support, thereby inviting in a broader and more representative set of the public. These goals are rather ambitious, and they do not always acknowledge the possibility that the digital divide may result in certain populations having less access to the tools that civic tech offers. Cesar McDowell and Melissa Chinchilla, for example, have argued that civic technologists spend too much time focusing on civic engagement and not enough on creating civic inclusion.[13]

Nonetheless, proponents of civic tech argue that it will do more than just expand engagement and will transform the way individual members of the public view their relationship with the government and, more generally, their ability to contribute to society.[14] This, however, is essentially saying that civic tech will succeed in constructing the elusive "bridge to citizenship" originally proposed for coproduction. Some have already questioned whether this is possible. Internet theorist Evgeny Morozov has decried what he calls "slacktivism," or online activities that convince participants that they are "making a difference" when in reality they have contributed very little.[15] Expressing a similar concern in a more tempered manner, Ethan Zuckerman distinguished between "thin" engagement, which requires relatively simple action on the part of the participant, and "thick" engagement, which requires reflection, problem solving, and full consideration of the societal implications of an action.[16] He does not necessarily describe the latter as universally preferable, but he says that we should understand in any given case which one a particular program needs and which one it is actually eliciting.

The analysis of BOS:311 here will evaluate the two proposed values of civic tech: increasing the effectiveness of public services and further incorporating participants into civic life. In doing so, it will get at an important tension. Suppose that BOS:311 expands usage in critical and valuable ways but there is no evidence that it energizes a civic disposition. Would that undermine the premise of civic tech? Or does it simply mean its proponents must be more precise in that the word "civic" does not necessarily refer to the motivations of the user but more to the public value he or she might contribute?

The following analysis tests how BOS:311 achieves three goals related to civic tech. First, does BOS:311 engage users from new populations or with different motivations? It will include an analysis of demographic differences between traditional users and BOS:311 users, attending especially to the concern that the value of technology-driven innovations might be limited to young, affluent individuals who have the resources and expertise to capitalize on smartphone applications. We will also consider whether the app attracts people with lower or greater levels of territoriality than traditional channels. Second, does BOS:311 increase the frequency and geographic range of custodians? Even though cell phones enable people to call 311 from anywhere in the city, there may be something additional to the level of convenience the app affords. This question also provides an opportunity to further test the robustness of the territoriality thesis, as it is possible that the narrow geographic range found in previous analyses is driven largely by the predominance of hotline calls. Third, does the app elicit thin or thick engagement? Using items from the survey, we can assess how much BOS:311 connects users to both their local community and the city writ large. If we find no support for the hypothesis that BOS:311 engenders greater civic disposition, we may need to reconsider how we discuss civic tech and its operation more generally.

Data for Evaluating BOS:311

Between March 1, 2010, and December 31, 2015, 7,313 users made 96,304 requests for service via BOS:311 that included geographic reference, and 42,887 were for case types that reflected custodianship. Of these, 15,975 were attributed to 4,345 registered accounts. It is worth noting that the app interface prompts users with a small number of popular case types, including graffiti removal, streetlight outages, and potholes, and an option for Other, which generates a custom dialog box. Cases reported this last way are classified as General Requests within the system. As a result, the proportion of General Requests from the app is about six times that of other channels (55 percent vs. 9 percent). Although comments indicate that many of these issues would qualify as being in the public domain, not all are, so the analysis opts for the conservative approach of omitting them.[17] We can also evaluate the effects of BOS:311 through the survey of 311 users, as 188 (28 percent) of the survey respondents were BOS:311 users.

There are two challenges to assessing differences in reporting patterns between BOS:311 users and those who use other 311 channels. First, there is good reason to believe that there are differences between the two populations that lead them to select one medium or the other for reporting issues. Consequently, the implementation of BOS:311 is best described as a quasiexperiment.[18] Two traditional solutions to such a situation are either to match individuals on key factors that might influence the outcome variables of interest or to control for those factors in a regression.[19] In this first step of the analysis, which will analyze the entire 311 database, we pursue the former approach. Unfortunately, 311 accounts do not include demographic information on users, so the only datum available for matching is residential location. This leads again to the use of multilevel models to compare individuals to those residing in the same neighborhood (in this case, CBGs), assuming that this will control for a substantial amount of the preexisting differences between the BOS:311 and traditional user groups.[20] When analyzing the survey sample, we are able to avoid this problem, as we can include demographics.

A second weakness, which bears on the need for multilevel models to compare individuals living in the same neighborhood, is that the vast majority of BOS:311 users provide their e-mail address as their point of contact; only 9 percent of the 4,345 people who made custodial reports through the app had home addresses on file, compared to nearly half of all custodians. To overcome this challenge, we can approximate an individual's home as lying within the census geography from which he or she most often made reports (see Chapter 2 for more details on the process and validation).[21] It is additionally necessary to estimate the geographical range of custodians lacking a home address. I do so by estimating each individual's "home" as the centroid of the census block in which he or she is believed to live and then measuring the distance of every report they made from that point.[22] A linear model was used to transform raw results from these estimations so that they might be comparable to the exact distance measures used to this point. As will become apparent, however, these numbers are not completely transferable, as they overestimate the size of ranges at the lower end of the distribution.[23]

Question #1: Does BOS:311 Engage New Types of Users?

Demographics

An initial way of thinking about BOS:311's impact is whether it attracted new and different types of users. Most simply, we observe that 70 percent of BOS:311 users made zero reports through the internet portal and hotline, meaning they have interacted with the system exclusively through this channel. We can further probe who these individuals are in two ways. First, we can test whether certain demographic characteristics of census tracts predict the density of BOS:311 users to be greater (or less) than that of the local density of traditional 311 users. As we have seen before, this approach can be informative in terms of per capita participation but is vulnerable to the ecological fallacy. We can also examine demographic differences between the BOS:311 and traditional users who participated in the survey.

Over the six-year span of the 311 data, BOS:311 users lived in every census tract, though the total number varied broadly, from 2 residents to

236 (*median* = 34 residents). In terms of proportion of the population, about 1 percent of the average tract's population were BOS:311 users, and no tract's population included more than 4.5 percent BOS:311 users. A regression found that this distribution was most strongly associated with the proportion of residents who held a professional degree or greater (i.e., bachelor's, master's, or doctorate; β = .61, p < .001).[24] The regression controlled for the number of traditional users in a census tract, meaning that higher levels of education predicted greater usage of BOS:311 *over and above* that which would be implied by the baseline usage of the hotline and internet self-service portal. Additionally, neighborhoods with greater Asian (β = .20, p < .001) and Hispanic populations (β = .32, p < .001) had more BOS:311 users than expected.

Turning to the survey, we can see clearly in Table 6.1 that BOS:311 users and traditional users had distinct demographic profiles. The former appear to be more likely to be male, white, between ages 25 and 44, and to hold a master's degree. A regression confirmed these impressions (white: O.R. = 2.86, p < .001; age: O.R. = 0.64, p < .001; education: O.R. = 1.28, p < .001; male: O.R. = 2.23, p < .001). This tells a story similar to that of the earlier tract-level analysis, demonstrating clearly that BOS:311 appeals predominantly to those with higher levels of education. One striking difference between these two analyses is the different conclusion surrounding ethnicity. Two effects may be in play. First, the survey interpretations potentially suffer from the underrepresentation of minorities relative to Boston's population, causing them to appear particularly uncommon among BOS:311 users as a result of sampling bias. Contrastingly, it could be that some heavily Hispanic and Asian neighborhoods are also popular with young, white renters. Examples include Chinatown and Allston, each of which are majority minority but near downtown centers and major universities. Thus, there is a need for further exploration of this particular question.

Territoriality

In addition to whether BOS:311 invites a new demographic profile, one might also ask whether it engages a different set of motivations. To do this, we can use the survey and multilevel models to examine whether BOS:311 users expressed levels of territoriality different from those of traditional 311 users while also controlling for demographic characteristics and neighborhood effects. The average BOS:311 user reported a greater

TABLE 6.1 Demographic comparisons between survey respondents who used BOS:311 and those who exclusively used traditional channels

	Trad. users (%)	BOS:311 users (%)		Trad. users (%)	BOS:311 use (%)
Gender			*Ethnicity*		
Male	215 (44)	121 (64)	White	371 (76)	166 (88)
Female	271 (56)	67 (36)	Black	53 (11)	7 (4)
			Hispanic	15 (3)	2 (1)
			Asian	9 (2)	2 (1)
			Other	38 (8)	11 (6)
Education level			*Age*		
High school or less	34 (7)	2 (1)	18–24	9 (2)	1 (1)
Some college	75 (15)	15 (8)	25–34	67 (14)	49 (26)
Professional degree	11 (2)	6 (3)	35–44	98 (20)	62 (33)
Associate's degree	33 (7)	4 (2)	45–54	126 (26)	49 (26)
Bachelor's degree	161 (33)	65 (35)	55–64	108 (22)	17 (9)
Master's degree	139 (28)	80 (43)	65–74	67 (14)	9 (5)
Doctoral degree	33 (7)	16 (9)	>75	11 (2)	1 (1)

desire to benefit the community ($\beta = .18$, $p < .001$) but a lower desire to enforce social norms ($\beta = -.13$, $p < .01$). On the one hand, it might seem counterintuitive that the app would appeal to one territorial motivation and not the other, but this is consistent with the general marketing of BOS:311 and the system more generally. It is typically pitched around "[making] Boston more beautiful" and less about defending one's neighborhood. Importantly, we cannot confirm whether these differences existed before downloading BOS:311 or whether they emerged after, or even in response to, the use of BOS:311. Nonetheless, they would seem to indicate that BOS:311 users express even more caretaking for their neighborhood than traditional users do but are less defensive of it, indicating a moderately different type of user.

Question #2: Are BOS:311 Users More Active Custodians?

At first blush, app users were approximately as active as users of traditional channels, with 68 percent making a single report and 85 percent making three or fewer reports (versus 65 percent and 89 percent for users of traditional channels). This is based on an analysis limited to reports through the app. If, however, we take into account that 30 percent of BOS:311 users used the other channels, they do in fact exhibit greater overall activity, with only 51 percent making a single report and 74 percent making three or fewer. BOS:311 users had an estimated median geographical range of 120.4 m, compared to 74 m for traditional users (Wilcox test: $p < .001$). This was accompanied by a higher chance of having a range greater than 800 m (24 percent vs. 11 percent). Though these differences are certainly measureable, it is worth noting that the average app user is still acting as a custodian exclusively within a range of fewer than two blocks of home.

To do a more formal analysis of these differences, we can again compare BOS:311 users and traditional users living in the same CBG to each other using multilevel models.[25] Consistent with the initial descriptive statistics, both models found that BOS:311 users were more active reporters than were traditional users living in the same neighborhood (frequency of reporting: $\beta = 1.06$, $p < .001$; geographic range of reporting: $\beta = 2.43$, $p < .001$). Unpacking these parameters, we find that the average custodian using traditional channels living in the average neighborhood was expected to report approximately two public issues (2.05) and have an estimated geographic range of 110 m.[26] In contrast, the average custodian using BOS:311 living in the average neighborhood was expected to report approximately six public issues (5.93) and have an estimated geographic range of 226 m.[27]

What Matters: The App or App Users?

Thus far, we have learned three things about BOS:311 users: (1) they are largely individuals who were not already using the 311 hotline; (2) they tend to be more highly educated and express greater caretaking for their neighborhoods than traditional users; and (3) they report public issues more often and over a greater geographic range than traditional users. This raises the question of whether differences in reporting can be attributed to the smartphone application itself or result from the distinctive predispositions of those who have chosen to download and use it in the first place. We can use the survey to pursue this more nuanced analysis. In previous chapters, use of the survey has been limited to those with confirmed addresses, but here for the first time we use estimated census tracts of residence in order to incorporate more BOS:311 users, as very few had addresses on record.[28] The models that follow predict frequency and geographic range of reporting in exactly the same way as those presented in Chapter 3, except that they include BOS:311 as an additional predictor of custodial activity.

Indeed, we find that BOS:311 users reported more public issues than those using traditional channels ($\beta = 0.25$, $p < .01$), even when controlling for demographics and attitudes (though these effects remained as observed in previous chapters). The overall impact, though, is less dramatic, indicating only about one more report than for a traditional user with the same demographics and level of territoriality.[29] BOS:311 predicted a greater geographic expansion in custodianship than previously seen, amounting to approximately 200 m ($\beta = 0.45$, $p < .001$). Within their different levels of activity, however, BOS:311 users and traditional users reported the same mix of issues. BOS:311 users were no more or less likely to report natural deterioration ($\beta = 0.10$, $p = ns$) or man-made incivilities ($\beta = -0.15$, $p = ns$).

Question #3: Does BOS:311 Create a Greater Connection with the Community?

One of the hopes behind BOS:311 and other civic tech is that it will elicit thick engagement from users, thereby constructing the bridge to citizenship anticipated by coproduction. This requires actually helping Bostonians connect with their communities. Our survey also included a series of questions regarding how well 311 facilitated such interactions and sentiments. Two referenced the neighborhood level ("[It's helpful for] seeing who cares about your community" and "[It's helpful for] connecting you with others in your community"), and one referenced the level of the city ("[It's helpful for] connecting you with the city of Boston"). Using models similar to those that were limited to custodians, we see a mixed result. BOS:311 users did report a greater sense of connection with the broader city through the app ($\beta = 0.36$, $p < .05$) but a *lesser* connection with others in their community ($\beta = -.56$, $p < .01$). This latter result was emphasized by the fact that BOS:311 users averaged 2.10 on connecting with the community, indicating that it was generally seen as not being a component of the system (falling under the Likert-scale neutral point of 3).

Summary: The Nuanced Success of BOS:311

The impact of BOS:311 is characterized by both successes and short-comings. On the positive side, it attracted new users, as 70 percent had never used the other 311 channels. The overall population of BOS:311 users also reported more public issues and exhibited this custodianship over a greater geographical range. Each of these positive discoveries, however, comes with qualifications. First, the expansion of BOS:311 was limited largely to those with a higher level of education, doing little to narrow any digital divide in access to government services. There is some suggestion that Asian and Hispanic neighborhoods have more BOS:311 users than would be expected based on their use of traditional channels, but this will require further examination. Second, greater reporting by BOS:311 users is largely driven by those using the app in conjunction with traditional channels. This is not problematic on its own, as the city of Boston never intended the app to replace or stand apart from the rest of the system. It does mean, however, that this global tendency toward more frequent reporting is driven only by the 30 percent of app users who utilize multiple channels and not by the app itself. Third, though BOS:311 users have expanded geographical ranges, they are still reporting largely from their home neighborhood. The consensus of the analyses is that app users have approximately a 100–200 m greater range than traditional users, still seating them squarely within a quarter mile of their homes.

Caveats aside, BOS:311 has tangibly increased custodianship in the city. Nonetheless, it appears to fall short of the thick engagement to which civic tech aspires. One of the goals of BOS:311's founders and managers is to increase custodianship not only in action but in sentiment, and thus stimulate further participation in civic life. We cannot determine from the current study design whether BOS:311 actually leads to other forms of civic and political participation, but we were able to describe the connection it does or does not create between users and their community. The app appears to impart to users a connection to Boston as a whole, which is an important breakthrough. In Chapter 5, we demonstrated that it is this broader geographical perspective that links a civic disposition to custodianship. However, the behavior itself does not bear this out, as people are still reporting largely in their own neighborhoods. In contrast, the app has engendered less of a connection with users' local communities, the very locus of their custodianship. Thus, one might quip that BOS:311

users have acknowledged the bridge to citizenship but have not necessarily crossed it, either by extending their custodianship geographically or intensifying it locally.

311 Talks Back: Bringing Public Works Out of the Shadows

Each of the first two interventions successfully increased custodianship by engaging or amplifying territoriality. The flyer experiment made the home neighborhood more salient. BOS:311 made reporting issues more convenient but within the limitations of people's natural range of custodianship. We have yet to see an innovation, however, that constructs the promised "bridge to citizenship" by engaging a civic disposition and eliciting reporting beyond the bounds of the home neighborhood. The city of Boston conducted a third policy experiment that pursued this in a nearly literal sense, taking advantage of BOS:311's capacity for two-way communication to increase direct interaction between providers of basic city services and the users of 311. In 2014, the city began sending messages to individual BOS:311 users when their requests were closed. These messages typically included some picture as evidence of the completed job, such as a worker filling the previously cracked sidewalk, or a team standing next to the streetlight they had replaced. The hope was that these messages would emphasize the commitment of the government to public mainte-nance and thereby validate and reinforce participation by the public, pos-sibly even leading to the persistent engagement anticipated by proponents of civic tech.

The city of Boston conducted this experiment in messaging in col-laboration with three professors interested in how such interactions can influence trust in and engagement with government: Ryan Buell and Michael Norton, professors at Harvard Business School, and Ethan Porter at the University of Chicago. Their inspiration stemmed from a marked decline in Americans' faith in government over the past few decades.[30] Part of the problem appears to be that there are many programs and ser-vices provided by government that most people do not understand or even know of. This has been referred to by Suzanne Mettler as the "submerged state."[31] Take the example throughout this book of the maintenance of public spaces and infrastructure, which traditionally is a task that occurs quietly and without fanfare. When the work is being done most efficiently, it is hard to notice because problems have been fixed so rapidly. When there are issues with the public infrastructure, it is quite easy to blame it on public works employees, whether it is their fault or not. In this way, it falls into that set of thankless tasks that fit the adage: "If you're being noticed, you're not doing your job correctly."

Buell, Porter, and Norton hypothesized that trust in government might be bolstered by bringing the submerged state to the surface through greater transparency. This was rooted in a similar discovery they had gained through studies of the private sector: when people can see evidence of the effort being invested in a product, they rate it as being of higher quality, are more satisfied with it, and are more grateful toward the company that made it.[32] Transparency might hold a similar value for the relationship between government and the public. Importantly, Buell, Porter, and Norton were not advocating for transparency in the sense of the Sunlight Foundation's push for Open Data or the Freedom of Information Act but rather for an operational transparency that reveals how work is accomplished. This would give government a chance to draw attention to its successes, thereby making the case for its own legitimacy and crucial role in society. The BOS:311 messages were a clear instance of such communication, and they provided a unique opportunity to observe whether operational transparency might not only engender trust but also encourage sustained participation in a government program. Like the other studies in this book, Buell, Porter, and Norton's study exploited the continuous nature of 311 data for evaluation. They examined specifically whether BOS:311 users who received the messages actually made more reports or reported a greater variety of case types in the following months.[33] I have since worked with them to analyze also whether the messages encouraged a greater geographic range of reporting, as this would be the best evidence that the messages evoked a civic disposition.

The Experiment

In September 2014, the city of Boston released a new version of BOS:311[34] that permitted city departments to send messages to the user who made the request when it was closed. The city leveraged this capacity to send closure messages that included images of the work performed or the city workers who performed it. These acted as a visual confirmation of the work done to fulfill their service request. The new version of BOS:311 was "pushed" to all individuals who already had BOS:311 installed on their phones. It diffused rapidly, achieving more than a 95 percent penetration rate within three months. Reporters received the new closure messages with accompanying images only if the work team responsible for a particular case uploaded one.

As in the analysis of BOS:311 usage itself, this is more appropriately described as a quasiexperiment, because the messages were not randomized across users. Whether and when a 311 user experienced the "treatment" of operational transparency depended on two things: (1) having downloaded the new version of BOS:311 and (2) having made a report that was later responded to with an image of the completed work. For this reason, exposure was staggered across multiple months, with some individuals experiencing it earlier than others. Methodologically, we can best specify the effects of the treatment by analyzing whether and how an individual's reporting behavior changed after receiving the visual confirmation that their request had been closed. Over the 14 months following the initial implementation of the new version of BOS:311, 21,786 users were exposed to the treatment.[35] The study analyzed each individual's behavior in each month following their initial installation of the app through panel models that included fixed effects for each user, thereby controlling for an individual's more general tendencies. The models tested the frequency and geographical range of reporting in a given month while controlling for how many total requests an individual had made before that month, the proportion of those requests that were closed (i.e., to control for objective satisfaction), and the amount of time since downloading BOS:311. This amounted to a final sample of 371,992 person-months.[36] See Appendix E for all model details.

Impacts of Closure Messages

The most apparent and consistent finding was that the messages from the city were successful in eliciting greater use of BOS:311, with those who had received one making more reports ($\beta = 0.81$, $p < .001$). As might be expected, this effect was strongest in the first month after receiving the message ($\beta = 1.63$, $p < .001$) but persisted for as long as a year (all β for 11 months or fewer after exposure $> .39$, p-values $< .001$). An intriguing wrinkle to this finding was the way the messaging interacted with satisfaction with the system. Unsurprisingly, if the city had successfully closed more of an individual's requests, he or she was more likely to use the app more often ($\beta = 1.60$, $p < .001$), but this also modulated the effect of transparency ($\beta = 18.07$, $p < .001$). The effect of messaging was only present if an individual's requests had been regularly fulfilled by the city. In contrast, if the city had not consistently fulfilled the user's requests, the message actually *depressed* reporting. This effect was nonlinear, though, with messaging having the greatest impact on people who had ~80 percent of their requests fulfilled (more details are available in Appendix E).

The effect on reporting range was more equivocal. It seemed as though those who had experienced the transparency messages made reports over a *narrower* range rather than a broader one ($\beta = -0.33$, $p < .001$), though this effect was tempered by whether the message had been received that month ($\beta = 0.18$, $p < .001$). Likewise, those who had received at least one closure message were no more likely to report outside their home cluster ($\beta = -0.17$, $p = ns$). Before we interpret the transparency messages as causing people to report closer to home, however, we should note that the results translate to reports being about 20 m closer to home than otherwise expected. It is very possible that the statistical significance of the result is an artifact of the large sample size. Even if this is not the case, the actual difference in reporting distance is pretty negligible in practical terms.[37]

Summary: Operational Transparency Increases Reporting, but not Range

The success of the BOS:311 closure messages has a certain irony to it. In some ways, the goal of operational transparency is most resonant with the 1990s philosophy of new public management, in which government sought to satisfy its "clients" with techniques developed by the private sector. Indeed, the primary spirit is to effectively communicate the work being done *for* the public. Nonetheless, within the collaborative context of a coproduction program, encouraging the use of services is actually equivalent to eliciting more participation. This raises the question of how BOS:311 users are interpreting the messages. Do they see them as evidence of a service provider doing its job effectively or as a signal that a collaborator is living up to its end of the bargain? It is not clear which users interpreted it in each way, or whether this would influence their behavior.

One will note that the messages failed to lead to a broader geographical range of reporting. Building on this discovery, I would posit that any hope for the bridge to citizenship would rely on communications that cast the relationship between government and the public as one of collaborative partners rather than service provider and client. If the public sees themselves as clients, using services will be driven by their basic inclinations. We would then expect exactly what we saw here—greater participation but still within the invisible boundaries of one's own "territory." But if the public perceives themselves as active collaborators in a joint effort to maintain the urban commons, they might be inclined to expand their custodianship to more spaces. This is speculative at this time but is worth considering in future experiments in operational transparency.

Conclusion

This chapter has described three policy experiments that evaluated innovations to Boston's 311 system. As a whole, they reiterated the role of territoriality in motivating custodianship while also highlighting the limitations its importance creates for eliciting greater participation in the program. They also made clear just how challenging it is to construct an effective bridge to citizenship in the manner anticipated by proponents of coproduction or, analogously, to instigate the thick engagement so sought after by civic tech. The flyer experiment found that neighborhood-oriented messages, which in theory targeted territorial sentiments, were more effective than messages that reference Boston as a whole. BOS:311 was successful in eliciting more frequent reporting over a greater geographical range, but the magnitude of this latter effect was relatively modest (~100–200 m), seemingly constrained by territoriality. Furthermore, BOS:311 users reported little connection with the local community, epitomizing thin engagement. Similarly, the messages that provided BOS:311 users with visual confirmation that their requests had been completed led to increased reporting of cases. Again, this elevated activity did not lead to a meaningfully broader geographic range of custodianship.

I take from these results three main lessons for 311 systems and the collaborative model of the maintenance of the urban commons. The first is that territoriality not only matters but should also be a prominent consideration when designing outreach, messaging, and implementation for such programs. The administrators of 311 systems and their colleagues should probably anticipate that even when they succeed in eliciting more participation, the increases will occur near the home of each individual user. This knowledge on its own is powerful because it calls for a more targeted geographical approach. Rather than assuming that generalized increases in participation will be useful, a city's leaders might focus on encouraging custodianship in neighborhoods or even on streets that have lower levels of engagement with the program. This leads to the second lesson. Although I have spent a lot of time highlighting how BOS:311 and the closure messages did not succeed in their grander vision of constructing a bridge to citizenship, they did increase custodianship in the city. This is no small feat, and it also highlights an important caveat that we have not yet addressed in much detail, that just because an individual engages in custodianship either predominantly or exclusively in spaces adjacent to her home, that does not mean she attends to *all* of the issues within that radius. For the vast majority of Boston's 311 users, there are clearly opportunities for them to be more engaged, even in the few blocks surrounding their homes. Programs that make this a reality are offering tangible value. Third, I do not want the reader to conclude that there is no such thing as a "bridge to citizenship." These are just three initial experiments, and there are certainly other innovations that might successfully connect territoriality with a civic disposition and break the invisible geographic boundary of the "home neighborhood."

Are these results problematic for coproduction and civic tech? I would argue "No," but it depends on how you define success in each context. For coproduction, these experiments further indicate the need for the public-as-partner model. Coproduction programs are effectively leveraging a variety of different motivations, but to assume that a civic disposition is either largely or solely responsible for participation creates a substantial blind spot. Similarly, the difficulty for civic tech is semantic, resting on the distinction between civic motivations and civic impacts (i.e., positive impacts on the public good). Personally, I believe that civic tech has done its job if it has tangible impacts, be they via thin or thick engagement, but for those who see the goal as bolstering civic motivations, the results here are underwhelming. Of course, as discussed in Chapter 5, a civic disposition might play a greater role for other programs, especially when they require a greater time investment or hands-on interaction with public officials and other community members. This adds to the assessment by some that civic tech's effect on civic life will be more incremental than it is transformative.[38] In the end, it appears that proponents of both coproduction and civic tech need to take a pluralistic approach when considering why people might participate in a given program or activity.

Returning to the broader themes of this book, the progression of Parts II and III has illustrated the virtuous cycle of science and policy made possible by urban informatics. The 311 system generated a data set that was able to advance our understanding of how community members contribute to the maintenance of the commons. These very insights supported a new perspective on how programs such as 311 most effectively encourage public participation, suggesting a series of innovations. These innovations then took the form of experiments that could be evaluated through the 311 system's data, further assessing and adding nuance to theories about why people report issues to city services departments. Thus the cycle begins anew. Whether this process concluded with more or less support for civic tech was irrelevant to this story, as it would illustrate the opportunity to learn and iterate on policy in a dynamic fashion either way. One particular concern that has arisen, however, is that of the digital divide and whether civic tech is expanding engagement only for those with ready access to smartphones and related tools. This, however, is not the only digital divide that threatens to beset urban informatics. As we will see in Part IV, the rapid emergence of technological tools has created haves and have-nots in other dimensions as well—between cities of different sizes and between the public, private, and nonprofit sectors.

Digital Divides
in Urban Informatics

CHAPTER 7

Extending 311 across
Massachusetts

IN SPRING 2015, the White House Office of Science and Technology Policy (OSTP) convened representatives from a handful of cities and their university partners in the Eisenhower Executive Building in Washington, D.C. The question for the day was: How do we build a national consortium that supports city-university partnerships in their efforts to create public good through the utilization of modern digital data and technology? The meeting was inspired by an emerging tension. On the one hand, there was a great opportunity for urban informatics to transform cities, but on the other hand, the full realization of this opportunity was hindered by the tendency for each city to become its own isolated laboratory. The hope was that the proposed consortium would facilitate learning and collaboration across cities, whereby advances in one locale could be implemented in another, or large-scale projects could be pursued simultaneously in multiple cities.

Shortly thereafter, OSTP and Carnegie Mellon University formally announced the MetroLab Network (or MetroLab), signed onto by 25 mayors and university presidents and deans. Founding members included some of the usual suspects mentioned repeatedly in this book, such as New York and NYU's Center for Urban Science and Progress, Chicago and the University of Chicago's Urban Center for Computation and Data, and Boston and the Boston Area Research Initiative, but also less obvious hubs for civic innovation, such as South Bend, Indiana, and Notre Dame, Houston and Rice University, and Memphis, Tennessee, and the University of Memphis. The network has since grown to more than 40 members and has hosted conferences on water, big data and human services, and sensor implementation. In its effort to expand the reach of technology-driven innovations in urban policy and practice, MetroLab has come up against a newly emerging digital divide between cities for which such advances are within reach and those for which they are not. As major metropolises forge the way, translating novel digital data and technology into new tools and policies, it is unclear whether and how smaller municipalities will be able to do the same. MetroLab sees these distinctions even among its membership, which is to say nothing of the disparities between those 40-plus member municipalities and the hundreds of cities nationwide that have not yet joined.

In common parlance, the term "digital divide" typically refers to how the poor are less able to afford computers, high-speed internet plans, and other digital tools necessary to keep up with their more affluent counterparts. This is the theme we observed in Part III as we examined penetration of the 311 system and the BOS:311 app across populations. It can also be used as an umbrella term for any case in which one group is seeing marked gains in its ability to utilize digital technology while others are being left behind. Part IV focuses on two such divides that have opened up in the world of urban informatics. In this chapter, I attend to the divide facing the MetroLab between technologically advanced cities and those that are trying to catch up, despite fewer resources and opportunities for collaboration. Chapter 8 then turns to the second divide, which is present among the institutions of a single city. Even where urban informatics is thriving through the efforts of city governments, universities, and private corporations, there has been little incorporation of the community. This is implicit in MetroLab's emphasis on city-university partnerships, and the general lack of discussion on what a city-university-community partnership would look like. Community organizations, the institutions that sit closest to the public, are largely unable to tap the deep intelligence contained in modern digital data, meaning they are missing an opportunity to better understand and advocate for the communities they serve. We will explore the difficulties created by both of these digital divides and possible mechanisms for solving them through empirical case studies, effectively using the tools of urban informatics to identify and address the challenges the field faces.

I will examine the first digital divide of urban informatics through a case study of a single program that tests the ability to transfer data- and technology-driven programs across municipalities. Commonwealth Connect, an effort of the Massachusetts government, sought to extend the city of Boston's BOS:311 app to any municipality in the state, regardless of its size or existing technological infrastructure. The study occurs in two parts. First, the data from the Commonwealth Connect app are largely analogous to Boston's 311 data, and the methodologies developed in previous chapters will help us to evaluate levels of adoption across municipalities and in turn assess the exogenous factors that might determine the local effectiveness of such efforts. As we will see, an initial lesson from these analyses is that effectiveness lies far more with government implementation and utilization of the tool than with the characteristics of the local population. For this reason, the second part of the study is a survey of public officials who helped to implement or manage the system. From this, we are able to derive a deeper understanding of how and when such programs are likely to succeed and the hurdles they might encounter.

The Digital Divide

Anxiety about a digital divide first arose in the late 1980s and early 1990s, though in a different form than it typically takes today. Policymakers and practitioners were concerned that the accelerating advancement and proliferation of computer technology in industrial countries would dramatically increase their economic and social advantages over developing nations.[1] The concept was quickly reoriented to describe the same disparity in technological access emerging within industrial countries, where the well-off were buying computers and subscribing to internet plans but the poor could not afford the same amenities. For example, data from the United States National Telecommunications and Information Administration demonstrated that between 1984 and 2000 possession of computers rose from ~20 percent to ~75 percent of households with incomes over $50,000, compared to a rise from effectively 0 percent to ~20 percent for those with incomes of $25,000 or less.[2] As recently as 2015, these same two income brackets had, respectively, 80 percent and

41 percent in-home broadband access.[3] Consequently, the disadvantaged are not able to access many forms of information that have become central to our modern society. The internet is an important tool for finding health services, browsing job postings, or finding directions (or bus schedules) for going to the grocery store. Although one may argue that people operated effectively without these channels of communication until just a few years ago, they have in many ways supplanted previous technologies for gathering the same information. For example, whereas pay phones made it easy for anyone with a quarter to make a call while away from home, the same action now requires ownership of a cell phone. Even when explicitly not necessary, the internet promises benefits that the user would not come by otherwise.

Income has not been the sole factor responsible for imbalances in the use of digital technology. Those who are older and less educated have also been less likely to utilize digital technology.[4] This has inspired a critique of the relatively simplistic model of the digital divide that dominated the rhetoric of the 1990s, which almost exclusively emphasized material access. It was believed that once people could afford computers and broadband, they would then avail themselves of all that the internet had to offer. This assumption was rooted in an earlier theory surrounding mass media known as the knowledge gap hypothesis. Proponents of the knowledge gap hypothesis posited that when advances in mass media occur, only those with higher socioeconomic status are able to afford it, and therefore they have sole access to the information therein.[5] Alexander van Deursen and Jan van Dijk have argued, however, that this fails to acknowledge the complexity of the internet, which, unlike print media or television, requires more active engagement from the user.[6] Therefore, material access is only one part of the digital divide. This has led multiple authors to propose more detailed models of the elements that lead to disparities in the utilization of modern technology. These generally converge on four main components: attitudes of the users, including the intrinsic desire or motivation to engage; material access; skills to effectively utilize digital technology; and the types of usage they undertake, thereby determining what advantages they reap.[7] This is generally cast as a progressive model, with attitudes preceding the decision to gain material access (or not), provided one has the necessary resources; access in turn makes relevant the need for skills, which then enable the choice of types of usage.

Early advances of the more sophisticated model of the digital divide focused on how disparities in skills could create inequality in the benefits gained from the internet. For example, Eszter Hargittai asked participants to complete 17 tasks involving information retrieval through the internet—including finding sports scores, places to do volunteer work, and prices for a 1995 Ford Escort—evaluating how many of these each person could accomplish. More recently, the emphasis has transitioned to gaps in usage.[8] A somewhat striking study of internet usage in the Netherlands found that people with low levels of education and disabled people were using the internet *more* than those who had higher education levels and were employed.[9] This apparent increase in material access was facilitated in part by what is now nearly universal internet access at public libraries. These different demographic groups were not using the internet in the same way, however. Whereas higher socioeconomic status was associated with greater use of the internet for information gathering, news, and personal development (e.g., seeking out job postings), those with lower education and the disabled were more likely to use the internet for games and social interaction.

The differences observed in the forms of internet usage across socioeconomic groups in the Netherlands have been reinforced by other studies. For example, those with lower education are less likely to utilize "eHealth" tools that leverage internet technologies to provide information about health care, facilitate patient-doctor communication, and permit tracking of health data.[10] Additionally, the Pew Research Center found that many less affluent individuals are replacing computers and broadband with smartphones, which are less expensive.[11] However, this decision in turn makes it more difficult to access web sites that provide information about and opportunities for career development. This is a notable case because a decision centered on material access is creating distinctions in the types of usage that can be effectively pursued. In sum, even if we achieved universal access to broadband, skills and personal decisions about usage continue to perpetuate a divide in the benefits that different groups derive from modern technology.

A Digital Divide across Cities

As urban informatics promises to transform urban policy and practice, we see analogs to the four components of the digital divide: attitudes or motivations, material access, skills, and types of usage. The middle two would appear to feature most prominently. Some cities, such as New York, Chicago, and Boston, have had access to the material resources necessary to implement modern data and technology infrastructures. They also have access to extensive skill sets through local academic and private sector partners, making it easier to translate these material resources into insights and tools that allow them to better understand and serve the city. A few city-university partnerships in smaller cities, such as South Bend, Indiana, and Notre Dame, have also undertaken well-constructed collaborations. Although these municipalities presumably have less capital on hand for such projects, the initial expenditures are justified by the cost savings that come from solutions to local problems. Furthermore, the projects were still made possible by the presence of a world-class institution of higher learning. Similar advances have been slower to arrive in other places, and even many of those that have joined MetroLab are still just "trying to figure out" what they can learn and pilot. In this sense, one of the challenges facing the network is to lower the prerequisite levels of material access and skills necessary to implement such projects.

The most common approach for expanding technology-driven policy innovation is to pursue scaling and diffusion; that is, if the technology is developed in a city with high levels of material access and skills, the final product can be implemented for less cost and effort in other municipalities. This approach makes certain assumptions, however. The first is that it is straightforward to take a policy or program from one city and replicate it in another with its own characteristic demographics and physical and social context. This is inevitably going to fall apart for certain cases, but I will set this assumption aside for our purposes here, in part because initial efforts to overcome disparities between municipalities will have to focus on programs that transfer naturally. The second assumption, which is more relevant to the current discussion, is that these innovations are even relevant or useful for other cities. At an objective level, I would argue that the simple answer to this question is, "Yes, they are." While not every innovation in one city might be applicable to another—for example, South Bend's sensor-driven sewer system might not be relevant to cities that do not sit on a river and therefore do not experience backflow during rainstorms—every city could benefit from one or more technologically savvy solutions that can help them better manage and track the systems and services of their community. This is validated by the implementation of 311 systems in over 400 municipalities of varying sizes. In fact, a nonacademic policy analysis of Buffalo, New York's 311 system concluded that the extra cost of the system paid for itself in efficiencies and community benefits.[12] That said, there may be a limit to this logic as we consider towns of only a few thousand people. Furthermore, what if some cities simply do not see these sorts of programs and policies as interesting? Analogous to motivations and attitudes in digital divide parlance, this would be a significant if not irreconcilable barrier to their effective adoption, even given the necessary access and skills.

Here I present a study of a program called Commonwealth Connect, which sought to scale 311 to all interested municipalities in the Commonwealth of Massachusetts. The program leveled material access by subsidizing contracts with a private vendor to implement a single standardized 311 app and database infrastructure for all participating municipalities. By removing this particular hurdle, we can gain greater insight into the influence the other components of the digital divide can have on the effective implementation of a technologically driven program. In doing so, we can pursue three particular questions: (1) To what extent are implementation and adoption determined by the objective benefits that a program promises? (2) Will attraction to such a program be driven by these objective benefits, or can other motivations and attitudes intervene? (3) If municipalities differ in the skills necessary to thoroughly leverage the 311 system and its data, will that influence the perceived benefits of the program over time?

Commonwealth Connect: Scaling BOS:311

There have been many efforts in recent years to bring the advantages of 311 systems to smaller municipalities that do not have the resources to make the initial investment in a new call center and associated data system. One of the more common approaches is to construct a county-level call center that collects service requests for all municipalities and then communicates them to the appropriate authorities. Examples include Baldwin County in Alabama, Los Alamos County in New Mexico, and Henrico County in Virginia. This has mirrored a similar consolidation in 911 call centers, especially in rural areas.[13] The company SeeClickFix offers an alternative, private sector solution to this challenge. They have built a free smartphone app that allows users to report the sorts of issues typically handled by a 311 system. SeeClickFix then contracts with municipalities to organize and transmit all reports within the city or town as a work queue for an annual fee. Whether the mechanism of choice is the consolidation of public sector resources or a private sector product, the results is the same: the implementation of a basic technology in a manner that equalizes material access across municipalities.

Commonwealth Connect merges the public-consolidation and privatization approaches, creating a public-private partnership in the expansion of 311 to municipalities throughout the Commonwealth of Massachusetts. It is a collaboration of the state government, the Metropolitan Area Planning Council (MAPC), the city of Boston's Mayor's Office of New Urban Mechanics, and SeeClickFix. The state invited applications for municipalities to receive subsidized SeeClickFix contracts for an initial year, in the hopes of demonstrating the value of a 311 system and thereby leading the same cities and towns to incorporate the contracts into their annual budgets. SeeClickFix agreed to implement locally customized apps modeled after the city of Boston's Citizens Connect (the precursor of BOS:311), maintaining the public sense of a statewide program. It would also accommodate local rebranding of the app (e.g., Salem Connect in Salem, Massachusetts). Effectively, this setup generalizes the ability to implement the same technology in use in Boston.

Seventy-six municipalities signed up for the first round, and BARI partnered with the MAPC to evaluate the program's effectiveness, a project that occurred in large part thanks to the extensive efforts of Matt Blackburn, who was then a student in the master's program in urban and regional policy at Northeastern University. Here I report the results of this evaluation, with particular attention to what it teaches us about the digital divide between major metropolises such as Boston and the smaller municipalities that might also benefit from the adoption of modern technologies in their policies and practices. Importantly, because Commonwealth Connect seeks to equalize material access across municipalities, we need to consider how skills and preferences for particular uses of digital technology influence adoption by both governments and their communities. As we embark, it is important to note that it is unclear whether our interest should be in the municipality or the individuals living therein. As we have seen in Boston, there are clear differences across individuals in their motivations to utilize 311, and this creates disparities in the utilization of the system across neighborhoods. This would suggest that individual attitudes (often proxied by demographics) drive the impact of technology adoption. That said, it is also possible that each municipality has characteristics that independently influence whether adoption there will be effective. We start here with the first question, examining how patterns of public use across municipalities are predicted by demographic characteristics. This will allow us to assess the extent to which individual-level skills and usage are an effective frame for considering transfers in technology across municipalities and in turn guide our examination of whether and how municipality-specific policies or practices play an additional role.

Data Sources

SeeClickFix provided three complementary data sets for the program evaluation: (1) the report database, analogous to the 311 database generated by the city of Boston; (2) a list of reporter IDs pertaining to municipal officials; and (3) information on how each municipality implemented and promoted Commonwealth Connect. For those who are interested, these are also available as both a downloadable, documented database[14] and interactive map[15] through the Boston Data Portal, the latter including some of the metrics used here to capture levels of adoption across municipalities. To give context to these data, we also accessed population and demographic data for all participating municipalities from the U.S. Census Bureau's American Community Survey, utilizing 2008–2012 five-year estimates.

The Commonwealth Connect platform received 69,994 reports between January 2013 and October 2015. The structure and content of this database were sufficiently similar to that of Boston's 311 system to support the same methodologies we have seen throughout this book. Because SeeClickFix, and Commonwealth Connect by extension, is largely focused on issues with public infrastructure, nearly all case types (and therefore reports) qualified as expressions of custodianship (67,533 reports, or 96 percent). As with Boston's 311 system, SeeClickFix users are able to make requests either anonymously or through a registered user ID, enabling individual-level measures of reporting. SeeClickFix accounts do not include home address as a form of contact, however, so we approximated each registered user's home municipality as the municipality in which they reported most often.

As part of its contract with municipalities, SeeClickFix maintains a list of user IDs associated with municipal officials, enabling those officials to directly add new cases to the department's queue. When we merged this list with the database of requests, we were able to distinguish between those cases submitted that were made by constituents and those created by public officials. This list contained 258 municipal officials from 64 municipalities, who made 24,749 reports.

Finally, Commonwealth Connect tracked the status of each municipality's implementation of Commonwealth Connect, providing an indication of the extent to which each local government had embraced the program. Status was described at two levels. First, some municipalities were in the *implementation* phase, meaning they were in the process of configuring Commonwealth Connect and had yet to hold an official launch or promote it publicly. The seven municipalities still in the implementation phase as of October 2015 were excluded from the following analyses because they had not formally launched the program. Municipalities that had moved past the implementation phase were described as having some combination of *public launch,* defined as one or more events to introduce Commonwealth Connect to constituents; *promotion* to the public through one or more media following its introduction; and *city buy-in,* or internal adoption of the platform. Of the 69 municipalities that moved past the implementation phase, 38 (50 percent) had all three of these elements, 4 (5 percent) had buy-in but limited promotion, 16 (21 percent) had limited buy-in and promotion, and 11 (14 percent) never publicly launched (or had a limited launch).

Public Use across Municipalities

Between the initiation of Commonwealth Connect at the beginning of 2013 and October 2015, there was a notable and consistent rise in usage of the system by constituents. In fact, the rate of increase of typical and exemplar custodians seemed to still be accelerating in 2015, as the absolute increase in users from the 10 months of available data in that year was greater than the total number of users from the previous two years combined.[16] This trend was quite varied in its manifestation across municipalities, however. Malden, Massachusetts, a city of ~60,000 people about five miles north of Boston, led the way with its extensive use of Commonwealth Connect, generating over 16,000 public requests in this time.

The municipality with the next highest level of activity, in contrast, produced just over 5,000 reports, and 80 percent produced fewer than 500 reports.

Custodians per capita in a given year, which captures the total penetration of the program in a municipality, also revealed stark differences in usage. In 2015, Salem had the highest one-year density of custodians, with 15 per 1,000 residents; Malden, its neighbor Randolph, and Nantucket (an affluent island community where the Obamas vacation) came next with five to six custodians per 1,000 residents. Only one-third of municipalities had as many as two custodians per 1,000 residents. This is particularly striking when one considers that the same value for Boston in 2015 was 42 custodians per 1,000 residents. For a fairer comparison, after about two years with a 311 system, Boston had 18 custodians per 1,000 residents.[17] Though this number is more comparable to the Commonwealth Connect municipalities, it is still greater than even the most active of those. It also indicates that many of these municipalities had sufficient time to reach a similar point of maturation in their use of the system. The low penetration of Commonwealth Connect might also be explained by the reliance on smartphones. Even in 2015, six years after its implementation, the BOS:311 app had the more modest penetration of 1.5 users per 1,000 residents. Nonetheless, the limited level of participation has practical implications because it is often the municipality's only formalized 311 channel.

Explaining Differences across Municipalities

As we look to better understand why municipalities saw different levels of adoption of Commonwealth Connect by the public, we examine the relationship between demographic composition and custodians per capita across municipalities. This measure is our focus because it is the best proxy for a community's efficacy in identifying and reporting issues (see Chapters 2 and 4). An important question for this analysis is whether comparisons across municipalities are the same as comparisons across tracts within a single municipality. Whereas the latter exist within a single administrative context, the former are subject to the manner in which the government promotes and embraces the system. If the activity of the government plays a major role in adoption, then we might expect demographics to be less important. The regressions that follow test both demographic and administrative variables. In addition, to control for implementation date, we use participation in 2015 as a point of comparison and control for the total time since implementation. The full results for these models are reported in Appendix F.

Surprisingly, demographic characteristics were thoroughly unrelated to the number of custodians per capita. This was true for median income and proportion of minorities in the population, which best predicted adoption by the public across the census tracts of Boston; education level, which was associated with greater adoption of BOS:311; and home ownership, which is theoretically associated with custodianship. In contrast, two measures of the government's embrace of Commonwealth Connect played a major role. Municipalities had more custodians per capita if the government had promoted Commonwealth Connect publicly ($\beta = .27$, $p < .05$) and if they had more reports by public officials (per 1,000 residents; $\beta = .29$, $p < .05$).

These results offer three lessons. First, and somewhat obviously, for the public to utilize a coproduction program, they need to know about it, and this knowledge comes from government promotion. Somewhat less obvious, however, is that the government needs to model the utilization of the program for its constituents. Members of the public might be more likely to use the app if they observe officials doing the same. Such observation could· occur through the app interface's real-time list of local cases, through conversation with friends and family who work for the government, or some other method. In municipalities that have strongly embraced the app, government employees might also inform members of the public about the convenience of the app when they are in need. All of these relatively minor interactions would increase not only knowledge of but also confidence in the system and further spread its use. The third lesson is methodological in nature. As noted at the opening of the book, the Boston 311 data are limited to a single municipality, and any comprehensive study of custodianship in the commons should consider behavior across a wide range of contexts, from rural to urban. The Commonwealth Connect data might have offered that opportunity, but it would seem that any such cross-city analysis would be hampered by differences between governments in their implementation of the program. This highlights a broader need to establish equivalence between administrative data from different municipalities rather than assuming that it exists a priori.

Why Would a Municipality Implement a 311 System?

The analysis thus far has told a single clear story: adoption by the public depends heavily on the extent to which the government embraces and models its usage. This stands out in the current case because of the broad variation in how much local governments embraced Commonwealth Connect. Some utilized it as the main mechanism for collecting and tracking all work orders, including those identified by city employees, and others failed to even announce that they had signed up for the program. The next logical question, then, is why this variation in utilization and promotion exists. By combining the digital divide literature with perspectives on public administration, I put forward three different hypotheses. First, municipalities might differ in their attitudes toward such programs, based on the objective likelihood of reaping benefits from them. Elinor Ostrom's writings offer a model of when and where there will be greater complementarity between the activities of the government and the public, thereby making a coproduction program more beneficial.[18] If municipal governments operate rationally, then this model should explain which ones would be more likely to embrace Commonwealth Connect. We might call this the *coproduction model.* Two alternative models come from a growing body of literature on "e-governance" that has examined how municipal governments vary in their inclination toward or against the use of technological innovations, with a theoretical foundation in earlier work on policy diffusion. The first of these models emphasizes *administrative culture* and the internal dynamics that make a municipality more or less likely to adopt technological innovations. The second is an *imitation model,* by which new policies diffuse thanks to learning or competition across governments, as each seeks to be at the forefront of current standards in governance. Here we focus particularly on the potential for this to operate via geographic contiguity. The following subsections will expand on each of these in turn and then determine how we might compare them in the case of Commonwealth Connect.

Rational Assessment of Coproduction

As the reader will likely recall from Chapter 5, Ostrom defined coproduction as "one way that synergy between what a government does and what citizens do can occur."[19] Critical to this synergy is that these two forms of "doing" complement each other. As I have already described for 311, the collaborative maintenance of the urban commons requires that urbanites observe and report instances of deterioration or denigration in public spaces and that city agencies provide the professional expertise and equipment for fixing them. Each fulfills their own role with an efficiency that the other cannot. The strength of this complementarity might vary across municipalities, however. To see when this might be the case, we turn to insights from Chapter 4 and the division of labor that arises between government officials and private residents. The results there suggest that we should attend to population density, which increases the effective level of custodianship and lowers the dependence on public employees, and the proportion of residential streets, which are more effectively monitored by the local population.

A second consideration is the ratio between the overhead cost of the program and the benefits it provides. If the optimal point of collaboration does not create sufficient savings to offset the overhead cost, we would not expect the program to be of interest to the municipality. Though Commonwealth Connect has largely removed the initial cost, it has not addressed the multiplier effect, where larger municipalities may see greater total benefits and therefore a lower cost-benefit ratio. This would suggest that larger municipalities are likely to gain more from the program.

Administrative Culture

Recent years have seen considerable research on "e-governance" and when and why governments do (or do not) incorporate digital communication technologies into their work. An influential theory in this domain has argued that e-governance must emerge in stages, progressing from the use of online media to keep constituents informed to more participatory, two-way forms of interaction between government agencies and the public.[20] From this perspective, leveling material access may not be sufficient for fostering effective adoption by municipalities that are technological newcomers. Although such newcomers are in a literal sense capable of implementing Commonwealth Connect, they may be taking an untenable shortcut. Because the administrative culture has not traversed the earlier stages of e-governance, it is unprepared for the responsiveness demanded by the tool.

Evidence suggests that the initial decision to adopt e-governance depends largely on the amount of available resources. Some have found that access to flexible, or "slack," resources makes it possible to innovate.[21] Others have made the broader point that total revenue is a key determinant because it indicates a more complex apparatus that can incorporate new efforts effectively.[22] Caroline J. Tolbert and her colleagues have also found some evidence that wealth of the community, reflected in overall revenue, can play a critical role in the success of the later stages of e-governance, at least at the state level.[23] They also found that the presence of a dedicated IT department was a major predictor of the adoption of e-governance tools.

Imitation

The literature on e-governance also emphasizes the potential role of policy diffusion, or the extent to which governments learn from, copy, and compete with each other, particularly those with similar political, cultural, or geographic features.[24] As Frances Stokes Berry and William D. Berry argue, these external forces might occur through professional networks or geographical contiguity.[25] There is some evidence for each, though primarily at the level of U.S. states. Hyun Jung Yun and Cynthia Opheim, for example, have found that states whose leaders are part of professional networks geared toward technology were more likely to adopt new innovations.[26] For geographic contiguity, there is some historical evidence that states are more likely to adopt policy innovations if surrounding states have already done so, though the effect may differ by the context or nature of the innovation.[27] That said, one study at the municipal level found no such effect for cities in Turkey.[28] Taken together, these various studies suggest that, at least in some cases, municipalities may seek out innovations based on the decisions of their neighbors and colleagues, independent of objective benefits and administrative culture.

Data and Operationalization

To examine the factors associated with the overall implementation of Commonwealth Connect, we will again utilize the data provided by SeeClickFix. The analysis will also include municipal-level census information for population size and density. Additionally, MassGIS records on roads and tax units provided measures of road lengths and their zoning, and the Massachusetts Department of Revenue's Municipal Databank provided details on each municipality's budget.[29] From these contents, we are able to operationalize each of the three sets of hypotheses. First, Ostrom's model of complementarity is assessed using population size (in

1,000s), density, total road length, and the proportion of streets that are residential. Second, the incorporation of technology within administrative culture was difficult to assess directly, as municipalities are not required by the commonwealth to report expenditures or employees working in IT in their annual budget. Because others have found that such features are generally best predicted by overall budget size and annual surplus, I use those measures as a proxy.[30] In order to avoid collinearity between the first measure and total population, I instead use expenditures per capita. Third, I did not have direct access to the professional networks of municipal leaders, so the analysis focuses specifically on geographical contiguity, assuming this will capture many of the cultural and political connections between municipalities as well. For this purpose, the models include spatial lag parameters[31] to examine whether the number of bordering towns with Commonwealth Connect influenced adoption and implementation.[32]

The analysis examined three different outcomes. The first was whether a municipality had joined Commonwealth Connect at all ($N = 351$ municipalities in Massachusetts). The latter two were specific to municipalities who implemented the program ($N = 64$), whether they formally promoted the program (per SeeClickFix records), and the extent to which city employees used it (i.e., city employee reports per 1,000 residents). All results from the regressions are reported in Appendix F.

Testing the Three Models

I analyzed the three models for interpreting adoption in order. First, there was limited support for Ostrom's complementarity model. The only relationship of note was that municipalities with a greater population were more likely to join Commonwealth Connect (O.R. = 1.03, $p < .01$). Otherwise, total population, population density, and road length and zoning did not predict joining, promoting, or employee utilization of Commonwealth Connect. Second, there was no evidence for the administrative culture model, as neither expenditures per capita nor surplus predicted joining, promoting, or utilization of Commonwealth Connect. Finally, we do see some support for the imitation model. Municipalities with more neighbors enrolled in the program were also more likely to have participated in Commonwealth Connect (O.R. = 1.39, $p < .05$). Notably, this measure, like those before it, had no relationship with promotion or utilization of the tool after joining the program.

Summary: The Crucial Role of Government in Driving Public Uptake of 311

This section has presented a two-part analysis of differences across municipalities in the adoption of Commonwealth Connect. The first focused on levels of use among the public, and the lesson was pretty simple: at least at this early stage of implementation, public adoption depended on the municipal government's commitment to the program in word and practice. Municipalities that promoted the system and used it regularly as part of the course of daily service provision also saw active publics. These administrative impacts completely overrode any effect of material access or skills present in the public, at least as proxied by demographic characteristics.

The natural next question was when and why municipalities adopted, promoted, and thoroughly utilized Commonwealth Connect. There were three candidate models for this: the coproduction model, based on Ostrom's[33] work, argued that municipalities would be more likely to join based on the likelihood that it would facilitate a collaborative effort between the public and the government to maintain public spaces and infrastructure; the administrative culture model emphasized the role of internal capacity for and attraction to technological innovations; and the imitation model highlighted the desire of local governments to keep up with the programs offered by neighboring municipalities. The findings were limited but telling. Only total population (a component of the coproduction model) and the number of surrounding municipalities also joining Commonwealth Connect (a component of the imitation model) were predictive of participation in the program. Furthermore, *no measured variable* was predictive of promotion and use of the system once it had been adopted.

We might derive three conclusions from the limited results of the second analysis. First, municipal governments are rational, but only to a certain degree of sophistication. Larger municipalities probably could envision the greater multiplier effect of investing in a program like this. Beyond that, it is likely that few if any took into consideration the particular physical form of their town and its zoning and how that might determine the magnitude of benefits the program could provide. (To be fair, Chapter 4 of this book is the first formal demonstration of those variations in potential benefits, so it would be hard to blame municipalities for not considering this.) Second, it does seem that learning and competition between neighboring municipalities is an effective mechanism for accelerating the adoption of such programs. The third conclusion arises from the inability to predict promotion and utilization of Commonwealth Connect. This suggests that the actual dynamics surrounding these higher levels of adoption are more complex than what can be accessed through quantitative analysis. It may be that more specific, localized processes are determining how the program is implemented in the end. To further explore this, the next section describes a series of interviews conducted with public officials who were responsible for Commonwealth Connect in their municipality.

Implementing Commonwealth Connect:
The View from the Inside

The implementation of a program like Commonwealth Connect can be a complex process. It necessarily consists of the decisions and actions of many government employees from multiple departments and agencies, making it difficult to understand through regression models and related tools. For this reason, BARI, the MAPC, MONUM, and SeeClickFix undertook a second phase of evaluation of the program, in which we interviewed public officials who were designated as the primary contact for the Commonwealth Connect program for 17 municipalities that participated in the Commonwealth Connect program. Through a structured questionnaire, we asked each one to tell us the story of Commonwealth Connect in their municipality, in the hope that the corpus of these interviews would shed greater light on why such programs either flourish or falter.

The Interview Methodology

We conducted the interviews in summer 2015. For each of the 17 participating municipalities, we interviewed either the individual indicated as the primary contact for Commonwealth Connect or a colleague designated by that contact as the best person to interview. We initially generated a random sample that was stratified by three variables: city usage, a dichotomous variable regarding whether the municipality had any reports from identified public officials; high or low constituent adoption,

TABLE 7.1 Classification of municipalities participating in the Commonwealth Connect survey by population density, constituent adoption level, and city employee usage

		City employee usage	
		Yes	No
	Rural		
	High	1	0
	Low	4	3
Constituent	*Suburban*		
adoption	High	3	0
	Low	1	1
	Urban		
	High	2	0
	Low	1	1

based on the median number of custodians per capita over the course of the program (two per 1,000 residents for 2013–2014); and urban/suburban/rural.[34] This made for 12 possible categories (2 × 2 × 3). We created an ideal random sample with two municipalities from each category, but owing to low response rates, we eventually invited additional participants until we had at least one respondent from each category, except those with high constituent adoption and no city launch, as these were very uncommon (owing to the correlation we have already seen between the two forms of adoption).[35] Participation was reasonably well distributed across urban ($n = 4$), suburban ($n = 5$), and rural municipalities ($n = 8$). Not surprisingly, there was greater participation from municipalities that had used Commonwealth Connect internally (12 of 17 participants). Representation for each of the nine categories is reported in Table 7.1.

The survey contained a series of multiple-choice items regarding the adoption, implementation, and future goals for Commonwealth Connect within the municipality, including anticipated benefits from Commonwealth Connect before implementation; whether the program was supported by others within the government; whether it had been adopted as a work-order system or integrated with existing work-order systems; additional uses of the data generated by the program; the mechanisms used for launching the program both internally and within the community; perceived adoption of the app by community members; and overall satisfaction. Most items had a Yes/No structure followed by open-ended responses for elaboration, permitting a qualitative analysis.

Interview Results

Overview of Responses

An initial look at the responses indicates that implementation generally started strongly, with nearly all municipalities describing an internal launch (16 of 17) followed by training for employees in how to use the system (15 of 17).[36] All respondents indicated that they had anticipated some benefit from Commonwealth Connect from the outset, though the nature of those anticipated benefits varied. We asked specifically about the potential to increase constituent engagement, efficiency and responsiveness in service delivery, and the government's technological sophistication. Each of the three benefits was endorsed by more than half of the sample, but increasing engagement was the most prominent (12 of 17 respondents vs. 10 of 17 for the two others). Six municipalities had anticipated all three as potential benefits, whereas eight had only anticipated a single benefit. These two groups seemed equally likely to have utilized the program internally (five of six vs. six of eight). Notably, regardless of initial perceptions, all respondents believed that all three benefits were apparent at the time of the interview, reflecting the effectiveness of the program's stated goals, at least to those overseeing implementation.

Despite these strong beginnings, the program hit some speed bumps as it started to depend on collaboration across departments. Just over half of respondents indicated either "full" or "general" support from others in the government (10 of 17). Similarly, just over half of the municipalities surveyed utilized Commonwealth Connect as part of a work-order system (11 of 17), though unevenly across departments. All of those using it as a work-order system had done so for public works (11 of 17 municipalities), making it the unsurprising linchpin to demonstrating the utility of the system. Some who had success with this initial step extended this function to the mayor's office (five), parks and recreation (three), and public safety (four). The vast majority of those using Commonwealth Connect as a work-order system had city usage (9 of 11), whereas the same was true for only half of the other municipalities (three of six). This would stand to reason, as city usage was defined as having at least one confirmed public official making reports, which would almost automatically follow if the municipality was using Commonwealth Connect as a work-order system. Finally, we can go a step further and see how many municipalities made additional use of the information generated by a 311 system. Eleven of 17 municipalities used Commonwealth Connect data in meetings to assess performance. Seven municipalities indicated that they use it at an even higher level, examining trends and geographic patterns to allocate resources more strategically. More, however (11 of 17), thought they would do so in the future.

Though these findings are suggestive, they are limited in two ways. First, it is difficult to come to robust statistical conclusions based on such a small sample size. Second, the findings make it difficult to distinguish cause and effect; for example, did limited support from others in government reflect limited buy-in, did it inhibit efforts throughout the government to use the system, or both? The open-ended responses from the interviews create the opportunity to further probe the factors that influenced implementation across municipalities. To do this most effectively, I will divide the sample into three groups: (a) those with city usage and high constituent engagement; (b) those with city usage but low constituent engagement; and (c) those without city usage.

Group A: City Usage, High Public Adoption

The six municipalities with city usage and high constituent engagement offer a window into how such programs work at their best. Of these, four had incorporated Commonwealth Connect as part or all of a work-order system, and a fifth was in the process of connecting it to their existing 311 system. In addition, four explicitly indicated further uses of the data. These included spending projections for infrastructure; assessment of performance, such as how long it takes a department to close a particular type of case; "[telling] the story" of the city and the services it provides; and statistical analyses of community needs. Among these, one municipality had a partnership with University of Massachusetts Boston's Collins Center for Public Management to utilize the data more effectively. Another municipality specifically noted that it helped the highway department target impassable roads during snowstorms, generating a big "win" for the program locally.

The successes of Commonwealth Connect in these municipalities do not explain why such successes were attained in the first place. What we see through the surveys is that in each case there was a strong and consistent internal push for implementation. All six municipalities utilized all three media for an internal launch that our survey asked about—announcements, training, and additional informational meetings. Community launches were similarly robust, with all municipalities utilizing at least three different media, including an event, web site, social media, local publications, announcements in public spaces, and mailings. One suburban municipality suggested how this shared enthusiasm might arise. "The town manager [was] very clear" that Commonwealth Connect was a priority, and "leadership made sure all departments participated." This aligns well with Goldsmith and Crawford's argument that technology-focused transformation of municipal governance depends on strong leadership at the top.[37] As we will see, though, this top-down approach is not universally effective.

Group B: City Usage, Low Public Adoption

The six municipalities with city usage but low public adoption gave insight into how initial city uptake might fail to translate into a fully successful implementation. Effectively speaking, however, the category only rightly contains five municipalities, as I exclude one that had recently joined the program at the time of the interview and in the following year had one of the highest levels of public adoption. As we move forward, it is important to note that our definition of city usage—that *any* reports were generated by an account associated with an identified public official—is quite liberal, meaning we can have a city with "usage" but very little overall uptake within the government. This distinction plays a prominent role here, as half of the municipalities in this group indicated little or no internal support from others within government.

Two of the municipalities in this group shared stories that were telling about the critical role that municipal departments play in sustaining the program. First, a rural municipality indicated that the department of public works already had a work-order system and was not interested in utilizing Commonwealth Connect, either independently or as an adjunct to the current system. The representative went on to point out that the "citizens did not pick it up." Though this was true, it speaks to a general assumption on the part of this municipality that uptake was going to happen shortly after the launch or not at all, and that usage did not require further modeling by the government. An official from a second rural municipality told a story that starkly contrasted with the narrative in

Group A that a mayor's leadership drove adoption. In her municipality, she reported, use of the system "was mandated by the town manager, and when something is mandated there can be resistance." This municipality reported robust internal and community launches, and the official with whom we spoke described the system's value in glowing terms. She indicated she was "completely satisfied" with the program, but added that she "would like to see the [municipal] staff take it more seriously. [It is] getting acknowledged, but follow-through is tough."

Other municipalities described similar conflicts around the full utilization and adoption of the system. None indicated that they were currently using the data generated by Commonwealth Connect for additional purposes, and only two had any interest in exploring such options in the future. One rural community stated that there was little need for a true work-order system, limiting the overall value of the program. An aging industrial "city" (classified here as suburban) felt that the population simply was not sufficiently technological for the program to have much impact.

Group C: No City Usage

The five municipalities without city usage illustrated in even blunter terms the sorts of mechanisms that can undermine a program like Commonwealth Connect. In this category, I again set aside one of the municipalities because it had a marked increase in constituent adoption in the following year. Notably, it continued to have no city usage, for which reason I return to it later as its own distinct case. Of the four others, one indicated no internal support, and another described a situation in which support was strong "at the top, but not at [the] implementation level." In both cases, "[Public Works] did not come to the table." A third said the program was only "somewhat supported," though with no elaboration. The fourth did not formally launch the system internally.

The fifth municipality in this category provides an interesting example, as it was the only one we interviewed that had no city usage and, at least eventually, a high level of constituent engagement. The interviewee indicated that the "City Manager was a big champion [of the program]" but that "one department head was not supportive." Interestingly, Commonwealth Connect was used as a work-order system for the Mayor's Office and Department of Public Works but had not been integrated with any internal technology. Work orders were printed out and handed to the worker who would complete them, and no issues were being followed on smartphones or tablets within the department. At the same time, the city had a reasonably strong community launch, had been trying to maintain "word of mouth" campaigns, and even the interviewee solicited the interviewer for additional advice while completing the survey on how to publicly promote the system.

Summary: The Many Ways to Undermine Full Adoption

The main lesson of the survey was that there was no single reason why some municipalities were successful in the implementation of Commonwealth Connect and others were not but that there were many points at which the process might be interrupted. Some rural communities indicated that the basic need for such a system was limited given the low volume of maintenance needs, echoing results from the quantitative analysis. Less extreme, almost all of the municipalities with no city usage or limited internal support had little interest in or understanding of how the data might support other uses, such as performance management or learning about community needs. In some cases, low levels of technological savvy made the system operationally irrelevant. In others, we see intriguing internal power dynamics, as in the three municipalities where a strong directive from the top was either ineffective or counterproductive in galvanizing broad-based adoption across departments. At times, the overall utility of Commonwealth Connect was undercut by an unwillingness to use it as a work-order system, and in some municipalities, it seemed as though the internal launch was only half-hearted. In sum, internal adoption could break down at any point between joining the program, internal launch, or continued reinforcement of its use. This is not all that surprising, but it illustrates the many challenges that might arise in the implementation of such a program, making any given failure largely contingent on the particulars of the local context. This also explains why the initial quantitative analysis failed to discover very much.

A second lesson from the survey offered some explanation for the correlations between the usage of Commonwealth Connect by city employees and adoption of the tool by the public. A few municipalities with city usage but low constituent engagement appeared to disregard the need to model use of the system for their constituents. This appeared to distinguish them from their colleagues in other municipalities who had been successful in translating internal adoption into effective use by the public. The converse was visible in the last example presented earlier, a municipality that had not made much internal use of the system but had succeeded in building sufficient outreach around it to elicit strong community participation. This mismatch between internal usage and marketing is uncommon for political and logistical reasons, but it serves to illustrate the point: even though custodianship is primarily motivated by care for the local space, 311, as a coproduction program, is still a collaboration between the public and the government. Members of the public have to be convinced that the municipality actually believes in the system itself. Without that reassurance, they may wonder whether the city is keeping up its end of the bargain. If not, they may view their efforts as largely ineffectual, whether they believe in the cause or not.

Conclusion

The rapid growth of urban informatics has created disparities across cities in their capacity to leverage technology-driven policies and programs. In simple terms, this emerging digital divide is between large metropolises that have access to both the financial and human resources to develop, implement, and effectively leverage such tools and their counterparts that do not. Placed within the framework put forward by scholars of the digital divide, this would largely point to differences in material access and skills and less to attitudes and choices. The Commonwealth Connect program gave us an opportunity to examine this assumption by making access to a smartphone-based 311 system attainable for all municipalities, effectively eliminating material access as a variable. As a result, we were able to see the extent to which the other components of the digital divide are implicated between technology "haves" and "have-nots" at the municipal level. Doing so also permitted us to evaluate the effectiveness of the scaling approach embraced by consortia like MetroLab and the types of challenges it might encounter.

Attitudes and skills each played prominent roles in determining the effectiveness of Commonwealth Connect across municipalities. Some attitudes were based on objective observations, such as the fact that many rural municipalities made the possibly prudent calculation that they would derive limited benefits from a 311 system. Other attitudes were a bit more subjective, such as a general resistance to technological solutions or, in contrast, the tendency to adopt the program because neighboring municipalities have already done so. In terms of skills, we saw that many municipalities failed to utilize the data in ways that would be beneficial. Just over half took the natural next step of translating the requests into a work-order system, and about the same number used them for performance management. Fewer still used the data in other creative, proactive ways, such as examining resource allocation, communicating with the public about government services, or quantifying public engagement. One might argue that these uses of the data should be classified as choices in the digital divide model, but the interviews suggested that they were rooted in an internal capacity for, or even awareness of, such opportunities.

The story of Commonwealth Connect, however, does not fit neatly into the existing models of the digital divide, suggesting a need for a model that more effectively addresses policy implementation. Put somewhat glibly, it is easier to generalize why the program worked than why it did not. When it was successful, all the necessary actors and institutions were engaged and supportive. When it was not, *something* did not go as planned, but that something could have been at any decision point, resting with any key official or department. Technological solutions are as subject to the complexities of bureaucracy as any government program. This is especially true for something like a 311 system, which requires the buy-in and participation of multiple agencies. In terms of the digital divide framework, the bureaucracy is an additional force that must be considered, strengthening or weakening any of the four other components of the model. For example, the attitudes of some leaders might be critical in that their endorsement is required for success, whereas the skills and vision of those closer to daily operations are essential for the full realization of the program's potential. As such, the bureaucracy is not so much a fifth, stand-alone component to the digital divide model but rather the very context within which the four others must operate during municipal technology adoption.

The practical implications of this chapter are promising. There is evidence that scaling and transferring technological innovations in policy and practice can successfully bridge this particular digital divide, provided the necessary actors are supportive and the bureaucracy is properly navigated. These sorts of challenges are true for any change in governance and should not be taken as unique to the current case. Unfortunately, as discussed at the beginning of this chapter, this addresses only one of two different digital divides arising from urban informatics. Throughout this book, I have discussed modern digital data as being a public resource, and yet the true public—community members and the grassroots organizations and nonprofits that seek to support and serve them—rarely have the analytic skills necessary to utilize them effectively. Chapter 8 takes up this second digital divide facing the field.

Whither the Community?

IN 2010, the Obama administration and the Department of Education announced the Promise Neighborhoods grant initiative. The goal was to support the establishment of "great schools and strong systems of family and community support" within disadvantaged communities, enabling youths there "to attain an excellent education and successfully transition to college and a career."[1] The program's vision was modeled on Geoffrey Canada's Harlem Children's Zone, a hybrid school and community center that had successfully integrated the various institutions responsible for youth services with each other and with the surrounding community. The Harlem Children's Zone has been lauded as an archetype for transforming disadvantaged communities and creating the "promise" that youths growing up there might not otherwise experience, and applicants to the grant program were encouraged to find ways to similarly break down silos between services and to make their relationships with the community more seamless.[2] Since the program's inception, the Department of Education has issued over $100 million in awards to projects spanning the demographic and geographic range of the country. These have included such diverse examples as Knox County, Kentucky, an impoverished, almost exclusively white rural community; the predominantly Latino community in the Los Angeles Promise Zone; the largely black West Philadelphia neighborhood; and the Paskenta-Nomlaki Indians in Corning, California.

Promise Neighborhoods was not a research grant program. It was explicitly intended to fund the planning, organization, and implementation of integrated, community-facing youth services. Nevertheless, recipients have ended up doing plenty of empirical research. In fact, it was required of them. One of the main thrusts in the program description was "learning about the overall impact of the Promise Neighborhoods program and about the relationship between particular strategies in Promise Neighborhoods and student outcomes, including through a rigorous evaluation."[3] The application materials stipulated that a "rigorous evaluation" would have to assess 10 key results, including "children enter kindergarten ready to learn," "youth graduate from high school," and "students live in stable communities." A successful applicant would have to present a clear plan for collecting and analyzing relevant data and would then have to demonstrate success via these metrics to be considered eligible for further funding.

The logic of making funding for social services contingent on an evidence-based approach is sound in theory, but it creates a practical conundrum. Few organizations are equipped with the expertise both to innovate in youth services and to conduct a rigorous, end-to-end evaluation of those services. The most obvious solution to this problem was for a community to partner with a local academic institution that would execute the methodological side of the project; for example, the Knox County and West Philadelphia examples were led in part by Berea College and Drexel University, respectively. This was not a feasible solution for all communities. As we saw in Chapter 7, not every city government has a university partner at the ready, and the challenge is probably even greater for individual neighborhoods, which may not have the institutional connections to construct such a partnership. The result was a vacuum that a handful of nonprofits and academic consortia sought to fill, including the Promise Neighborhood Institute, an effort of PolicyLink, and the Center for the Study of Social Policy in Washington, D.C. I had the privilege to be part of one such group, the Promise Neighborhood Research Consortium, an interdisciplinary team of researchers from across the country. Central to our mission was the construction of methodological tools and guidelines to support Promise Neighborhood grant recipients in their program evaluations.

The challenge presented by the evaluation requirements of the Promise Neighborhoods program reflects the second digital divide facing the field of urban informatics. There is an increasing expectation on the part of funders that community organizations keep up with societal trends by conducting rigorous, data-driven program evaluations, and yet they are severely limited in their ability to do so. That said, the problem goes beyond the challenge of reporting program outcomes. Much has been made of the value that modern digital data, especially open data, offer the public, but who is prepared to execute on that potential? Community organizations are uniquely positioned to identify local needs, and if they were skilled with modern digital data, they could utilize them toward these ends in a way that others cannot. While groups like the MetroLab Network wrestle with the digital divide between cities, far less formal attention is being paid to the digital divide emerging within cities, between those professional institutions that are equipped to work with data and the community members and organizations that are not. Put another way, there is no city-university-community model for urban informatics.

This chapter takes up the role of *infomediaries*, or institutions that can translate data into products that hold public value, in closing the digital divide between data-savvy institutions and the rest of society. Though most work to date has cast infomediaries as consumers of raw data who provide it in more interpretable forms, here I concentrate on the role that community organizations can play in using the data to inform and support programs and services. For this to be possible, however, they need support from other institutions that are skilled in data science. This chapter describes a handful of projects that pursue this ideal, including the Boston Area Research Initiative's program that trains community organizations in the use of its Boston Data Portal. I summarize a survey of training attendees, offering a more direct window into their current utilization of data and attitudes toward "big data." From these results, I seek deeper insights on what an effective city-university-community model might look like, reaching some conclusions but also uncovering a set of unanswered questions.

Big Data and the Public

Returning to a major theme from Part I of this book, the novel data resources that have catalyzed the field of urban informatics, including administrative records, social media posts, and sensor readings, can be a mixed blessing. On the one hand, they create many opportunities for a deeper understanding of the city. On the other hand, the conceptual and methodological challenges they present can be overwhelming. The result is a "data deluge" that has left us awash in information that we do not yet fully understand how to navigate. Writers on the subject, myself included, often characterize the problem as one facing the public agencies, private corporations, and academics who work with data professionally. Less time is spent considering the public—community members, leaders of local organizations and nonprofits, and their associates. The data describe the streets that community members walk, the neighborhoods where they live, work, and play, and even their actions and interactions, and yet such resources are not typically accessible to them. Even when the data are made available, most members of the general public do not have the skills to properly analyze them. They would indeed be lost at sea in the data deluge.

As with other digital divides, we might begin to examine this disparity between data-savvy professional institutions and the public with the question of material access: Could a member of the public access these data and, if so, at what cost of effort and resources? Let us take the most available of the newer forms of digital data, municipal administrative records. Traditionally, access to such data has required a formal request under the Freedom of Information Act (FOIA) and sometimes a charge for the expense of organizing and delivering the data. Under FOIA, the government only has to release data in response to requests, placing the burden of access on the public's time, energy, and ability to identify and request the desired data.

In recent years, the reactive approach of FOIA has given way to the proactivity of open data. This has been instigated in part by groups like the Sunlight Foundation, which have successfully advocated for transparency in government records. It has grown even more as governments and corporations have recognized the potential value of sharing their data with others; researchers and "hackers" are likely to leverage the opportunity to conduct new analyses and build applications that benefit the original data holder, creating something analogous to a low-cost, adjunct R&D team. Consequently, dozens of municipal governments have constructed data portals through which they publish nonsensitive government data, including 311 requests, tax assessments, city-curated mapping files, crime reports, and the like. This has been most prominent in big cities like New York, Chicago, Boston, and San Francisco but has also gained traction in smaller cities. In the greater Boston area alone, the cities of Cambridge and Somerville, both with populations of ~100,000 people, have also constructed open data portals. In parallel, national governments, including those of the United States and Canada, have formed their own open data initiatives and portals, further accelerating the trend.

Proponents of open data have hailed the trend as providing the public with "greater control over their lives and improv[ing] both their material and social conditions."[4] Though this perspective is inspiring in principle, we arrive at a recurring theme in the story of the digital divide. Open data attends to the literal problem of material access but reveals a disparity in skills. Data portals publish large spreadsheets, often with limited documentation, meaning that only those familiar with the tools of data science are equipped to work with them. This is a vanishingly small proportion of the population, an issue that has been noted even by those advocating for open data. A 2014 survey found that 70 percent of the United Kingdom's Open Government Data community (i.e., people involved in the production or use of open data) believed that members of the public lacked the necessary skills to effectively use open data.[5] Similar concerns arose in a survey of Canadians regarding that country's Open Data Initiative.[6] These impressions highlight the fact that solving the problem of material access will not on its own enable the public to make use of municipal data.

The concern of whether members of the public have the skills to work with and leverage data has not been isolated to the open data movement. As data have permeated all aspects of our daily lives, some have argued that "data literacy" is a critical capacity for people in modern society. The term refers to an individual's ability to understand and interpret data and the tools used to organize, analyze, and visually represent information. Even with uniform access, differences in data literacy will result in disparities in the benefits that one might gain from modern digital data. Unfortunately, the problem of data literacy is not a simple one, in part because it encompasses a wide-ranging set of competencies, including "the ability to: formulate and answer questions using data as part of evidence-based thinking; use appropriate data, tools, and representations to support this thinking; interpret information from data; develop and evaluate data-based inferences and explanations; and use data to solve real problems and communicate their solutions."[7] This definition is so broad that it borders on the nebulous, but that in itself is instructive. Data literacy does not comprise a small set of discrete skills but is instead an overarching capacity to reason about and with data. This has led educators to assert that the most effective approach for achieving universal data literacy begins with its incorporation into primary and secondary school mathematics curricula. Some have even experimented with interdisciplinary collaborations that place these forms of reasoning within applied contexts, such as social studies.[8] This is all to say that the problem of data literacy is not a simple one, creating a persistent limitation to the narrowing of this particular digital divide.

Data Infomediaries: Lowering the Needs of Data Literacy

When concerns about the digital divide in internet usage transitioned from disparities in material access to disparities in skills a decade ago, the worry was whether older, less affluent, and less educated individuals with broadband access would be able to effectively utilize their newfound online resources. Similarly, low levels of data literacy across society mean that open data alone is not sufficient to guarantee that the broader public will gain value from these resources. A major difference between these two stories, however, is the level of effort necessary to even out disparities in skills. Whereas a few hours of classes can meaningfully advance an individual's ability to access internet resources, the utilization of modern digital data requires extensive training. Many of the data sets made available through open data portals are foreign even to most academics, meaning the goal of educating large swaths of the population to make effective use of a data portal's contents is simply not feasible. Instead, there is a need to lower that threshold for engagement so that a greater proportion of the population is able to utilize modern data.

A potential solution to the high level of skills required for the use of modern digital data is the *infomediary,* or an entity that translates raw data into value for a particular audience. This value might arise from a new product or service, or even just a more interpretable form of the underlying information. Infomediaries have become increasingly common in recent years. For example, projects such as PolicyMap,[9] Data USA,[10] and the Racial Dot Map[11] have downloaded and reorganized census data into maps, infographics, reports, and other products that are more immediately useful. Many city data portals have also incorporated interactive maps, including Detroit's tax parcel map,[12] CrimeMapping.com's multicity map of crime events,[13] Boston's map of open 311 requests,[14] or, possibly the most impressive in its comprehensiveness, Chicago's Open Grid, which allows visitors to map any public city data set with geographical references.[15] These projects have been a good first step, making information more accessible to those with limited data skills, but they have their weaknesses. First, they tend to isolate a single topic or data source, making them unidimensional. More importantly, second, they rarely transform the data in ways that facilitate interpretations that go beyond a summary of records. As noted repeatedly in this book and elsewhere, a list of records or events without context can be misleading. The third weakness is that they are often one-way; what the infomediary offers may be based largely or entirely on its own internal priorities. As a result, it is not always clear how often or to how many people such portals are useful.

Some have taken a more interactive, community-based approach to the role of infomediary. One such technique builds on Kevin Lynch's seminal efforts to have urbanites draw the map of the city as they perceive it.[16] This has grown into the broader subfield of participatory GIS, with an expansive set of methods for capturing community perceptions of local geography and dynamics graphically.[17] Some have also worked directly with the community to identify the implications of data for them and to represent them in their terms. For example, Rahul Bhargava and his team at the MIT Media Lab have led workshops and built tools for "data therapy," techniques that enable those who are not data scientists to engage meaningfully with data.[18] One particularly interesting product of this work has been a series of "data murals," artistic representations of data and their meaning to a community. In contrast to the portal-based infomediaries, these sorts of projects are better aligned with localized needs and interests. The downside of their specificity, however, is the inability to create a generalizable product.

Each of the two approaches to infomediaries described here—one general and institution driven, the other localized in its motivation and impact—holds value, but there is a middle ground that is largely empty. How does an institution lower the barriers of access to the content of modern digital data in a general way *and* empower local communities to take advantage of them for their own purposes? Such a model has been hard to come by. One example that comes close is a project from Georgia Tech, which worked with the Westside Community Alliance in Atlanta, Georgia, to build a map that describes public safety in the neighborhood.[19] They leveraged not only official records but also interviews with the public on the perceived distribution of crime. Though the project was limited to a single neighborhood, the sophisticated technical infrastructure and use of official records offers a potentially scalable model. In contrast, the Boston Area Research Initiative's (BARI) Boston Data Portal (BDP) moves in the other direction, attempting to bring the contents of a generalized portal closer to community members. It publishes its data through the BDP, which has two components: the Data Library, which houses modified, research-ready versions of data from various sources, including administrative records provided by the city of Boston, and BostonMap, where users can explore data visually in conjunction with other tools, including Google StreetView.

The organization and tools of the BDP offer public access to modern digital data in a way that accommodates multiple levels of data literacy. The curated record-level data sets are research-ready resources for data scientists. The ecometric data sets, which distill more complex record-level data into neighborhood-level measures (see Chapter 2), are more immediately useful to those who conduct traditional urban research, and the interactive maps are an important resource for those who are not skilled in data analysis and visualization but would still benefit from knowing about the events, conditions, and dynamics of their community. Our hope was that this structure would not only facilitate collaboration on research and policy but also support community utilization of the information contained in modern digital data. With support from the Herman and Frieda L. Miller Foundation, we have sought to realize this promise through a series of community-based training and conversations about the utility of the BDP and its contents. Much of the work to organize and construct this project was conducted at first by Chelsea Farrell, a PhD student in the School of Criminology and Criminal Justice at Northeastern University, and has since been led by Samantha Levy, BARI's program coordinator. As the subsequent sections describe, we have experienced some success but, more than anything, have learned a lot about the challenges that communities and community organizations face in translating data into public value.

Training Community Organizations in the Boston Data Portal

BARI formally began offering community-based training in the BDP in January 2016. It had previously held annual sessions on the BDP for audiences comprising a mix of faculty and students, public officials, and community leaders, but the new program featured a curriculum that catered to the needs and skill levels of community organizations. The sessions now also allotted time for an open discussion of the public value these tools and content might hold and how we might make them even more useful. The original plan was to have the training follow a two-stage model. First, we would host a training for representatives from a variety of community organizations, whom we would recruit in collaboration with partners who maintained such connections, such as Microsoft's Office for Technology and Civic Engagement and NU Crossing, a unit at Northeastern University that provides programming for the local community. Our vision was that those community organizations that found the BDP particularly useful would help us to establish a direct link to the public by cohosting similar training for their constituents with us.

Our plan turned out to be somewhat naive. Although the community organizations themselves were often enthusiastic about using the BDP in their work, they did not see their constituencies as having the same motivation. Indeed, data could be useful for those trying to better understand, serve, and advocate for a community but would be of less interest to community members themselves. In retrospect, this seemed perfectly obvious. The BDP translates available data into something interpretable, but even then they are still data, and data are traditionally the province of "nerds." Nerdiness has shed much of its stigma and has even become trendy in recent years, but, simply put, not everyone is motivated to analyze data. Put in terms of the digital divide literature, open data creates universal material access, and the BDP lowers the skill level required to utilize it, but the necessary attitudes among the public are often lacking.

The realization that everyday Bostonians have limited interest in utilizing the BDP was not so much a setback to the community-based training but a signal that we would need to reconfigure it. It suggested that our focus should be to empower community organizations to act as a different kind of infomediary: rather than creating new data products, they were uniquely positioned to translate the contents of the BDP into public value, provided they were given the resources and skills necessary to do so. My colleague Michael Johnson from URBAN.Boston has studied the ways that data might support and advance the work of community organizations and has identified three areas of activity.[20] First, an organization might more effectively pursue funding if it has more detailed information about the need it is trying to satisfy or the problem it is trying to solve. Second, accountability is critical to any community organization and can be greatly facilitated by data. Data might be leveraged to assess internal performance, as many public agencies and private corporations already do, or to rigorously evaluate the external impact of programs. As the story of Promise Neighborhoods at the beginning of this chapter illustrated, funders are increasingly requiring such sophistication of community organizations. Third, data can strengthen advocacy efforts by providing clear evidence of need when approaching public officials. Organizations can also use data to advocate locally, communicating to community members how they might understand or grapple with their challenges. Of course, the specific data needs of each community organization will depend on its nature and mission. For example, a community development corporation might focus more on new investment in a neighborhood, whereas a service provider will be concerned with resident outcomes. That said, with the right data sources, any organization would likely be able to benefit in each of these three areas.

Recognizing the potential value of data for community organizations, Johnson conducted in-depth interviews with a set of representatives from such organizations in greater Boston to discover how they do or do not utilize data in their work.[21] His overarching finding was that the organizations were aware of what they needed in terms of information but lacked the capacity to realize those goals. It was apparent that limited material resources within an institution translated into a lack of skills. The average community organization has a staff of only five people, and this modest staff must successfully raise funds and implement, evaluate, and advocate for programming before there is even a need for data.[22] With this in mind, it is unclear where such activity would fit in the budget. Indeed, the average community organization spends only 2 percent of its budget on IT infrastructure, and only 36 percent of organizations include it in their budget at all.[23] As a result, Johnson found that internal expertise was so limited that, even if the requisite resources were available, community organizations did not know what steps they would need to follow to effectively leverage data.

Community organizations represent a crucial but largely ignored player in the civic data ecosystem of a city. They are uniquely positioned to translate information into public value but are severely limited in their ability to do so. Thus, the contribution that organizations like BARI can make is to provide resources and training that lower the skill level necessary to leverage data. This has become increasingly important as data have increased in size and complexity and therefore require considerable processing before they are informative. It is with this mission that we run our community-based training sessions. In order to construct a curriculum that matches this goal, we have conducted a survey of participating community organizations. Beyond informing our pedagogical goals, the responses also provide an additional window into the attitudes that community organizations have toward data, the areas in which they might build their capacity to utilize data, and how they view the societal shift toward "big data."

Survey of Community Organization Representatives

In advance of each community-based training in the BDP in 2016, we invited attendees to complete an online survey regarding their organization's current attitudes and usage of data, including their definition of "big data." The intent was twofold: to enable us to better target the curriculum to the needs and interests of our audience and to learn in a more general sense how such organizations interact with data. The response rate was moderate, with 10 of 21 participating organizations responding to the survey. To be clear, this is by no means a random sample. The organizations attending the training were already sufficiently inclined toward the use of data to choose to attend our training, and those who completed the survey were even further motivated or capable at some level. It might be safe to assume, then, that those represented in the sample are on average more data savvy than the population of community organizations as a whole. Nonetheless, their responses have the potential to reveal certain patterns and dynamics that contribute to or hinder the effective usage of data by such groups.

The majority of respondents to the survey were place-based in that their mission was to serve the residents of a specific geographic area (e.g., a local community development corporation, or CDC). There were also a handful of groups that advocated and intervened on behalf of certain vulnerable populations, such as welfare recipients, or focused on particular societal challenges, such as access to nutrition. One outlying response was from a school of public health at a local university, which has hundreds of employees and a clear understanding of data. For our purposes here, this response does not qualify as a community organization but does offer insights on how community organizations partnering with this university might operate. The nine other community organizations varied broadly in their size, from an all-volunteer staff with no formal employees to 88 employees. The median was four full-time employees.

What follows is a descriptive analysis of a series of Yes-No questions and quotations from the corresponding open-ended responses. In it, I maintain some of the grammatical and syntactical errors made in context. One that will be observed most often is the treatment of "data" as singular, which goes against the convention within this book to treat "data" as plural.

Survey Responses

Of the nine community organizations, seven reported consciously collecting data on their own services, predominantly on the characteristics of service recipients. Though this generally involved information that would be entered during enrollment, making it a community organization's version of administrative data, three organizations also indicated that they conducted surveys of program users. Data sets that required more effort and sophistication, however, were less commonly used. Five of the nine organizations reported using census data to augment their own data collection; two reported using some form of data visualization technology, such as ESRI's online GIS tools or Tableau; and only one reported using any of the local portals that publish data, including the city of Boston's Open Data Portal or CityScore platform, the Metropolitan Area Planning Council's MetroBoston DataCommon, the Massachusetts Budget and Policy Center's Budget Browser, or BARI's Boston Data Portal.

Though these organizations used data from a limited number of sources, they tended to do so purposefully. Six indicated that they used data for funding purposes, and five used data for evaluating effectiveness. Far fewer (three of nine) used data for advocacy. Most stated that they used data primarily to justify the value of programs to foundations and government agencies. In fact, it appeared that many of the respondents conflated the use of data for "funding" and "evaluation" into a single, largely formulaic response to the requirements of funders. One organization did stand out as being more proactive, however, saying that it used data to determine priority areas for which it would then pursue funding. The same organization also generated internal quarterly reports on program activities that were the basis for discussions on how to continue to improve services. This outlier organization, which was rather well staffed, utilized data in a manner similar to that of the municipalities that had seen greater success with Commonwealth Connect in Chapter 7.

In general, the organizations had very little idea of what "big data" was. A few explicitly said they were "unsure" when asked to define it, and others wrote things that had little bearing on the subject. Some of the responses did, however, capture one or more aspects of either the sources, content, or implications of novel digital data. One organization, which had a computer scientist on its staff, had a sophisticated definition of "structured, semi-structured, [or] unstructured data that has the potential to be mined for information." Another described big data as "millions of data points, but I'm not sure what it is. I hear Google and Facebook are collecting big data about their billions of users and can predict what we are interested in and who our 'friends' are or will be." This equation of big data to internet technology was echoed in other responses. One organization did seem to grasp the value of the composite nature of measurement I described in Chapter 1 by noting the value of aggregating record data to achieve fuller insights.

Although the organizations did not fully understand big data, they still believed it to have potential for their own work. Some were optimistic ("I'm sure I could think of applications when I know what it is"), while others were a bit more cautious ("If everyone else is using it, we at least need to know what it is"). All but one of the organizations stated that big data could be more useful than they currently are, the one being an organization that does not currently utilize data in any form. The general consensus was that the value offered by these new informational resources simply was not within reach. One of the more advanced organizations astutely noted that using big data would "[require] a different skill set" than more traditional data resources. The representative from the local school of public health echoed this sentiment, expressing "suspicion that MOST . . . will NOT have the in-house resources or ability (and often not even the understanding to frame the questions)." Another organization went further, identifying the additional hurdle that even when the resources are available "gaining full buy-in from staff continues to be a challenge." This issue may have been obscured by the fact that most organizations do not yet have such conversations in much depth. A proposed solution was that "foundations should get more educated in this field and be open to fund data capacity at the operational level."

Summary: The Limited Capacity for Using Data in Community Organizations

Unsurprisingly, the survey found that community organizations do make use of data, but in a manner limited in both content and range of application. Nonetheless, there were some noteworthy lessons. First, respondents to the survey by and large were not clear on the definition of "big data." This stands to reason in retrospect, but it means that the hurdles to utilization are greater than anticipated. Whereas Johnson noted that community organizations lacked a basic understanding of the skills necessary to make use of data, it turns out that they do not even know what the resources themselves are.[24] Notably, not a single respondent to the survey mentioned administrative data, nor did any indicate using the city of Boston's Open Data portal. Those that referred to social media and internet data did so only in the broadest strokes and with no sense of how they might be informative. Second, there seems to be an initial hint that the same institutional hurdles we saw at the municipal level in Chapter 7 may be lurking in community organizations. Many organizations currently see data and analysis as an unwanted or indifferent requirement of pursuing funding. At the moment, most are still scrambling to gain the capacity to comply with these requirements, but those few that are already there are starting to see resistance to the investments and reorientation necessary for the proactive use of data.

Research Centers and Community Organizations: Complementary Infomediaries

This chapter began with the question of how to place modern digital data in the hands of the broader public. Per some of the early arguments for Open Data, this would empower everyday people to leverage these new resources in ways that address local needs and interests. Though logical enough, it appears that this direct approach, in which the general public accesses data and takes action on its own accord, may not be realistic. The initial problem is that the vast majority of people are not data scientists of any sort and therefore are unequipped to grapple with the complexity of modern digital data resources. This would call for raising data literacy across society, a daunting but not entirely impossible task. However, there is a second, possibly more trenchant issue: very few members of the general public actually *want* to play with data. This situation may change as data become increasingly visible in society and efforts to introduce data literacy during primary and secondary education take hold, but right now few people are motivated to use public data resources.

Instead, the promise that open data holds for public value rests with info-mediaries. Though the term is often used as a general umbrella for institutions that translate data into products that hold public value, I propose a specific solution that requires two types of infomediaries operating in sequence: research-oriented institutions that translate raw data into more accessible forms, and organizations that can identify uses of these resources that reveal and attend to the needs and interests of local communities. This model is distinct from earlier theorizing on infomediaries. First, it outlines a complementarity between two types of infomediaries and argues that coordination between them is necessary to fully unlock the potential of modern digital data. Second, it moves beyond an almost singular emphasis on infomediaries that repackage and publish information for public use. Being that this on its own is not sufficient for empowering the general public, it is also necessary to acknowledge as infomediaries those organizations that work with communities to identify and implement ways to pursue public value through the use of data.

Data to Public Value: A Two-Layer Pipeline

Converting modern digital data directly into public value requires two steps: specifying the needs and interests of the public and identifying, accessing, and analyzing the data that will attend to those needs and interests. The institutions best positioned to do the first are nonprofit community-based organizations, but, as others have shown before and the survey here only served to reinforce, they are unequipped to complete the second part. The average community organization typically has a very small staff, almost none of whom are dedicated to data analysis. When it does utilize data, it tends to be in a formulaic way intended to attract or satisfy funders. Furthermore, our survey suggests that such organizations have very little understanding of the rapidly growing set of data resources that are available and that they still rely almost entirely on a mixture of internal data and census indicators. Few respondents were able to define "big data" and its value, and none referenced the city of Boston's administrative data as being useful. There is also the concern that, without the complete set of skills necessary, they could end up generating conclusions that are not entirely robust and instead conveniently resonate with their goals or impressions.

Even if the limitations in skills were surmounted, there may be additional roadblocks on the horizon for the use of data within community organizations. Just as we saw with municipalities in Chapter 7, the transition to greater use of technology within an institution is not an automatic process. Bureaucracies will vary in their receptivity, with some welcoming the opportunity and others being more intransigent, creating barriers to implementation. This can be reinforced by a negative perception of data-based work as a burden imposed by funders. Most community organizations are motivated by the potential to serve their constituency and to effect social change. They may then see the increased demands of data analysis and reporting as siphoning off time and resources from the organization's "true" mission. Others may simply be resistant to a move toward unfamiliar processes or standards for planning and evaluating programming. In any case, the challenge to incorporating data more strongly into the daily work of community organizations is not a unidimensional problem.

The context here is analogous to that of the Promise Neighborhoods story that began this chapter. Community organizations are aware of a societal push toward data and of the dangers of being left on the wrong side of the emerging institutional digital divide, but the most efficient solution is not to bring data science skills in-house. Instead, they will need to rely on research centers and consortia that can make such data more accessible to them and their level of data literacy. The overall process of empowering communities through data depends heavily on each of these two types of infomediaries: without the research center, the community organization would be ill prepared to leverage modern digital data, and without the community organization, the research center would lack the knowledge necessary to identify and address local concerns.

As is often the case, this two-stage model for infomediaries is far from the clean and tidy solution it might appear to be. It is particularly complicated by the fact that research centers have to provide two different forms of expertise that often sit in different corners of academia. The first is to release data in forms that are interpretable and that can be incorporated into the community organization's work, which is the purview of data scientists, who typically have very little experience talking to community groups. The second is to explore with the organization how such resources might be of value, to educate them in the tools that might be brought to bear on those goals, and to jointly execute the resultant research project. This latter approach is essentially the stated mission of community-based participatory research (CBPR), which is more often based in public health and social scientific disciplines. More pertinent to the point here, CBPR, because of its focus on the interests and needs of localized communities, predominantly works with smaller, more targeted data sets; in many cases, the work is qualitative rather than quantitative.

There are many research centers skilled in data science or in community engagement, but very few are skilled in both. Nevertheless, this combination is necessary if academia is going to partner effectively with community organizations in the localized use of modern digital data. As I have argued repeatedly, ecometrics can be seen as new-age indicators that distill the complex content of modern digital data into accessible information that can be as important as census variables. That said, we saw through the survey that even these rather simple data forms—which amount to a series of interpretable variables for a few dozen recognizable "neighborhoods"—are more than most community organizations can handle on their own. They need thought partners who can help them think through the possible value of these data and offer analytic support. To put a finer point on it, they deserve this. Throughout this book, I have discussed partnerships between researchers and policymakers where the former offer data science skills so that the two can learn novel things about the city together. There is no reason why community organizations should not expect the same level of partnership.

I can foresee two ways that projects might bridge the divide between data science and community engagement on the academic side in order to empower community organizations to use modern digital data effectively. The first and simplest is the combination of public data and training. This is what BARI has done with the Boston Data Portal. This past year, we have expanded the program to have a graduate student as an on-call data consultant available to community organizations. Another success in this vein comes from Michael Gurstein, who recounts a case study in which the people of Zanesville, Ohio, used data skills learned in training by the UCLA Center for Health Policy Research to demonstrate the public health risks of a proposed truck stop.[25] The evidence they presented was sufficiently compelling to halt the construction. In this approach, academia aims to provide the community organizations with as many skills as possible, thereby empowering them to pursue projects on their own.

A second model is more comprehensive and might be thought of as "big data–driven CBPR." Alex Taylor and his colleagues, for example, conducted a year-long, in-depth data project on a single road in Cambridge, United Kingdom, with an approach they called "data-in-place."[26] Through conversations with the community, they identified traffic as a major issue of interest, proceeded to harvest and access sensor data describing traffic volume and air quality, collected new data on the attitudes of residents regarding local traffic, and discussed the results with the community. Returning to Boston, Sandeep Jani, a graduate student under Michael Johnson at the University of Massachusetts Boston (whose work on community-based organizations was summarized earlier in this chapter), collaborated with groups of local businesses that had received "Main Streets grants" to revitalize the commercial areas of residential Boston neighborhoods.[27] Recipients of these grants must report program outcomes, including indicators of economic vitality, a requirement they largely resent. In an effort to reset this negative relationship, Jani has worked with them to identify the kinds of things they would actually want to know and how they might access them through data. What is notable about Johnson and Jani's work is that they offered BARI's ecometrics as a new resource but also found it necessary to consider customized indicators that did not yet exist. These sorts of projects are still few and far between but highlight the value that community organizations can derive from modern digital data when they are invited to the table as equals.

For either of the two models I have described to be realized more consistently, especially the second, there will need to be institutional changes within academia. There are limited incentives for data scientists to participate in highly localized studies, and most proponents of CBPR have limited training in cutting-edge quantitative techniques. These divisions will have to be ameliorated. I will close by noting, however, that a new institution is being piloted that will likely become important in this space. As luck would have it, it also hails from Boston, supported by the

Boston Civic Media Consortium, a group based at Emerson College that I have mentioned previously. They are establishing a community-based institutional review board (IRB). Just as the IRB at a university evaluates the merits and potential risks of a given research study, this body would examine the public value that a research project might provide to the community being studied. It also is intended to act as an arbitrator between the community and the researcher, enabling them to construct a project that is viewed as mutually beneficial. Whereas the previous examples describe the process and goals associated with individual projects, the community IRB is distinctive in that it offers a new institution for negotiating these agreements.

Conclusion: A More Inclusive Civic Data Ecosystem

The earliest proposed solution to the digital divide was for everyone to have access to modern digital resources. Each individual and institution would then make use of them according to their needs and interests. As we have seen, this vision is not only implausible but also only serves to reveal disparities in the skills people have and the choices they make when they do have access. In Chapters 7 and 8, we have seen how the two digital divides of urban informatics clearly embody these lessons. Even when a program like Commonwealth Connect makes a technological policy innovation universally accessible, internal obstacles posed by local bureaucracies can lead to failures in implementation. When it comes to the public and the community organizations that represent it, the level and penetration of data literacy are sufficiently low to suggest that universal utilization is an unreasonable expectation at this time. In each case, the role of institutions is critical: in the former, the realities of institutional change within government agencies are front and center; in the latter, we must consider how multiple institutions with distinct areas of expertise can combine to create public value.

The emphasis on institutional roles brings us back to one of the themes of urban informatics from Chapter 1: the civic data ecosystem, or the network of data sharing and collaboration. If we evaluate a given region's civic data ecosystem on its successes in furthering the understanding of the city and in improving the programs and services that manage that city, then community organizations, which provide many of those programs and services, need to be as active and influential as city agencies. This goal depends on a well-crafted taxonomy of institutions, each with their own role in generating public value from data. In such a context, community organizations would not need to hire data scientists but would more simply need to be able to capitalize on the resources and potential partners within this institutional landscape. My proposal of a two-layer infomediary pipeline that combines the skills of research centers and community organizations is far from comprehensive, but it is a start. The exact form of these institutions will undoubtedly evolve in the coming years. As effective models emerge, they will in turn create a more robust civic data ecosystem that might eventually realize the vision of a city-university-community model of urban informatics.

Conclusion: The Future
of the Urban Commons

IN MARCH 2017, just as I was completing the first full draft of this book, BARI hosted a conference titled "Data-Driven Research, Policy, & Practice: Lessons from Boston, for Boston." This conference, like others hosted by BARI and similar centers around the world, convened members of the local civic data ecosystem, spanning the academic, public, private, and nonprofit sectors. The event was distinctive, however, in that we structured it like a society meeting: rather than impose our own vision for urban informatics, we invited members of the community to submit proposals for talks, thereby crowdsourcing the full span of urban data science and policy work occurring in greater Boston. We received 65 proposals, giving rise to a docket of 13 panels, five participatory workshops, and two keynote panels, featuring speakers from more than a dozen universities, public agencies, and nonprofit organizations.

Thanks in part to the decision to invite proposals for talks, the content of the conference was diverse. Some panels were the usual suspects of urban science and policy, such as "Public Safety & Crime," "Neighborhood Development," and "Strengthening Education through Data." Other sessions reflected recent trends; these included "Driving in Boston," "Human Services and Big Data," and "Government and Accountability." Still others were specific to the field of urban informatics itself, including "Open Data and Data Sharing," "Models for Cross-Sector Collaboration," and the keynote panel on "Data & Society: Boston in the National Context." Overall, the event highlighted not only the potential of data and technology to help us better understand and serve the city but also a wide range of ways in which such work was already occurring in Boston. Whereas five years ago BARI was casting about for a proof of concept, here were dozens of examples of the advances that could be made at the intersection of research, policy, and digital technology.

Throughout the conference, there was an underlying tension surrounding "smart cities," at least in terms of the vision presented by private technology corporations and popularized in the media. It led me to wonder what it means for "a city to be smart." A smart person is someone who can harvest and synthesize information from various sources and generate new ideas and insights from these efforts. In turn, he or she can respond to challenges and opportunities by creatively and dynamically leveraging that information and the deeper understanding of the world that follows from it. In these regards, a city does not necessarily need sensor systems installed throughout the city to be smart, nor does it need predictive algorithms whose operations are largely hidden from the user. Instead, smartness was readily apparent in the more modest efforts featured by the conference's panels: linking data across agencies to gain a comprehensive view of the scourge of opioid addiction in Massachusetts; analyzing field interrogation and observational data to determine whether there are racial disparities in Boston's policing; and using multiple data sources to describe the process of gentrification, enabling local planners to respond to its various components. Each of these examples of "being smart" required attention to local context and collaboration across institutions and sectors, elements that have been lacking from the popular narrative around smart cities. In addition, they illustrate how much can be accomplished with relatively little cost, making it eminently accessible to cities of all sizes.

This book has chronicled an extended example of a city being smart. Boston's 311 program is a technological policy innovation that has reconfigured how city services handle one of the oldest societal challenges: the maintenance of the commons. It has also generated a data resource that provides a novel window into the care of public spaces and infrastructure. The result has been a deeper understanding of when and why people engage in custodianship but also more general insights on the behavioral dynamics of the commons and how communities realize collective efficacy. At this intersection of policy innovation and research, we found an opportunity to examine the operation of coproduction programs and to evaluate the goals of civic tech. Going further, these studies acted as a vehicle for broader lessons about the practice of urban informatics, including the opportunities and challenges presented by naturally occurring data, the institutional structures underpinning the field, and even some of the issues that these institutions have yet to solve.

In closing, I will use this final chapter to conjecture about the future of the urban commons, following the same three levels described in the Introduction. The first level is the physical commons, which will continue to evolve as urban informatics marches forward. Some changes in service delivery and management will be incremental, but other innovations, such as sensors and automated vehicles, promise to reshape urban space. The discoveries and methodologies from this book will be valuable tools for guiding this work. The second level is the more abstract commons of the civic data ecosystem and the data-driven research, policy, and practice that it can generate. While it is one thing to describe a smart person, it is entirely another to determine what makes a city collectively smart. Here I discuss how we build the institutions that facilitate communication and collaboration across sectors that can support this goal. The third level is how these two commons reflect the future of urban informatics, its implementation, and the institutions that will advance it. It is through them that the field will continue to develop, and I will conclude with thoughts about the shape it will take in the coming years.

The Future of Public Spaces and Infrastructure

The 311 database provided a unique opportunity to explore how urbanites care for public spaces. It was so distinctive that it generated multiple contributions via a single line of inquiry. At the outset, we saw that territoriality was the primary motivation for custodianship, providing a framework for understanding when, where, and why people contribute to the maintenance of the commons (see Chapter 3). Emerging from differences in territoriality was a division of labor between typical custodians, who attended particularly to localized, residential spaces; exemplars, who extended their custodianship to "shared" spaces, such as main streets; and city employees, who reported issues more often in institutional and industrial spaces. Each of these three groups contributed in a distinctive way that was necessary for comprehensive maintenance of the commons (see Chapter 4). Furthermore, given the program's clear collaboration between government and the public, we were able to reconceptualize the public as not just a "citizen" with civic and political motivations but also a multifaceted partner who might contribute to coproduction programs in numerous ways (see Chapter 5). We were then able to evaluate how civic tech can best capitalize on these behavioral dynamics through a series of experiments (see Chapter 6).

As the structure and management of urban spaces continue to evolve with the rapid pace of technology, the discoveries from this book have inherent applications. I see this as taking two forms. First is the direct relevance to 311 systems and other programs that seek to leverage custodianship in pursuit of the public weal. We might also extend the lessons herein to the more general efforts to reconfigure the urban commons for a new age, including the introduction of sensor systems, autonomous vehicles, and public kiosks. Let us take each of these in turn.

Custodianship

As I described in Chapter 1, the first 311 systems had the mundane goal of triaging nonemergency issues away from overburdened 911 hotlines. It only gradually became apparent that they also created a natural channel for people's custodianship, empowering them to participate more actively and directly in the upkeep of their communities. Though this success has made 311 the policy innovation du jour that has been implemented in hundreds of municipalities across the United States, administrators are still working to determine how it best engages constituents, in turn making the maintenance of the urban commons even more efficient. The findings here are directly applicable to the continued development of these best practices.

Chapter 6 has already explored some of the practical implications of custodianship's basis in territoriality. Advertisements for the system are most effective if they reference the local neighborhood. We also saw the limitations that these motivations can create. Efforts to construct a "bridge to citizenship" might encourage individuals to report more often but still within a relatively narrow geographic range. I have not, however, fully explored the sorts of interventions that might be informed by a division of labor. For example, a government may describe the strength of custodianship across neighborhoods in terms of two dimensions—

typical custodians and exemplars—and tailor its services accordingly. If a neighborhood is low in exemplars but not in typical custodians, issues in nonresidential spaces might be more likely to go unreported. A city could then develop a marketing campaign that appeals particularly to exemplars or to the care of these "shared" spaces. They could also deploy public works employees more heavily in such spaces to compensate for the community's weaknesses. I also alluded in Chapter 7 to the ways that municipalities might use the division of labor to assess whether their physical organization makes them more or less likely to benefit from a 311 system. The overarching point here is that the public experiments in this book are only a first step and that there is much more that can be accomplished in these regards.

Moving beyond 311, we might apply our fuller understanding of custodianship to other recent innovations in the maintenance of the urban commons. For example, many cities and towns across the country have encouraged local residents and organizations to sponsor or take responsibility for some piece of public infrastructure—from a stretch of highway to the flowers in a public planter. Building on the same logic, the city of Boston and Code for America developed an internet platform where residents can adopt a fire hydrant, thereby committing to shoveling it out during a snowstorm. A similar program has subsequently been implemented by other cities that see lots of snow during the winter, such as Rochester, New York. Similar to 311, the smartphone app Waze invites people to report road-quality issues and traffic jams; in this case, instead of notifying the government, they are proactively sharing these alerts with other drivers who might benefit from them. Other projects have been less explicitly about public spaces but have a similar spirit in their attention to localized social contexts. Nextdoor supports private social networks associated with a given neighborhood. Some neighborhood associations have mimicked this by constructing their own Facebook pages. Neighbor. ly is a clearinghouse for local improvement bonds, thereby encouraging and facilitating financial investments in local communities.

Many of these innovations are likely to capitalize on the same territorial motivations that underpin 311, and their own operations will reflect this. They also almost certainly rely on a division of labor, and the managers of each might consider the typology of actors—some very active, others more episodic in their contributions—that support collective efficacy in the program's main goals. At the same time, Chapter 5's lessons about the public as a multifaceted partner will be essential. Individuals can now contribute to the maintenance and development of their communities through many different programs, and each may call on its own combination of motivations. It would thus be important to conduct case-by-case studies across them to better elucidate how each best engages its users. The true value, however, lies in the combination of these studies, which will offer a panoramic view of the various motivations that govern people's contributions to their local communities. This will not only support refinements to existing apps and programs but will also highlight new areas of opportunity.

Reconfiguring the Urban Commons

There has been a trend in recent years toward ambitious, or even radical, reconfigurations of urban spaces to better support particular types of activities. We might divide these innovations into three groups. First, there has been an interest in reorganizing streets, sidewalks, and adjacent spaces to better integrate walking and biking with automobile usage. Second, as certain manifestations of telecommunication become obsolete, such as the public pay phone or the firebox, some are imagining what the modern version of these public amenities might be. Third, one of the most prominent stories of "smart cities" has been the instrumentation of public spaces and infrastructure—that is, the installation of sensors that track local conditions on various dimensions, including pollution, weather, and volume of pedestrian and vehicular traffic. These three areas of activity vary in how clearly they are a reflection of "urban informatics"; some are ultratechnological, some are data driven, and some are both, but a handful are simply thoughtful ways to reconceptualize the urban commons.

Transportation and the Use of Urban Roadways

In 1997, the Swedish parliament introduced Vision Zero, a policy initiative with a goal of eliminating fatalities to bikers and pedestrians on city streets. The philosophy behind it was that user errors and accidents happen, so roads need to be constructed in ways that minimize the possibility that automobiles will collide with other forms of transportation. In parallel, concerns about climate change have led many cities to encourage a mix of transportation modes that lowers the volume of pollutants emitted. These two trends have supported a series of innovations that prioritize walking and biking on city streets, including separated bike lanes, the closing of certain districts to vehicle traffic (e.g., Times Square in New York City), or the rapid proliferation of bike-sharing systems.

Technology and data have not been the primary drivers of these innovations to urban roadways, but they have proved useful for implementation and evaluation. New York City, for example, has used data to determine the effects of their various initiatives on collisions between cars and bicycles.[1] There have also been numerous data-based reports on bike-sharing systems and their impacts. Interestingly, the most common use is for commuting, though in some cities this means that they act more as an adjunct to public transportation than as a replacement for automobiles.[2] In some cases, cutting-edge technology has proved useful in generating new and useful data. In 2016, Boston's Safest Driver competition encouraged volunteers to download an app that tracked their driving patterns, including average speed, sharp braking, and phone use while behind the wheel. Whereas similar apps had been used by insurance companies to evaluate safe driving in the past, the goal here was to better understand how driving patterns vary across the city.

Alongside projects centered on safer mixed-use roads, companies such as Google and Uber are promising the future of automobile transportation in the form of autonomous vehicles and are piloting the technology in multiple cities. There have been numerous arguments that this will be even safer because the cars will be able to communicate with each other and operate on complementary algorithms—put in simple terms, imagine a world in which no vehicle ever makes an unexpected move and can directly communicate its intentions to the cars around it with complete fidelity. While the focus has been on the technological advances that have made such dreams a reality, there remains an underappreciated question as to how they will transform daily life. For instance, a fleet of public or shared vehicles (à la Zipcar) may obviate the need for personal vehicles in cities, picking up and dropping off passengers on demand. Such a development would radically alter the urban commons in a way that no other technology can match, raising a variety of questions for urban planning: How do we construct streets to accommodate both the autonomous nature of vehicles and the human-directed movement of bikes and pedestrians? Will the most effective arrangements be the same as those we have constructed to manage the interaction between human-driven cars and other modes of transportation? Drop-offs and pickups are quite different from the typical park-and-exit process. Do we need to redesign sidewalks and building fronts to better manage this dynamic? Relatedly, the city will need far fewer parking spaces, and they will likely be concentrated rather than distributed along the sides of all streets. What do we do with this reclaimed space? Do we install new amenities, make larger bike lanes, put in strips of green space, or something completely different? Such changes will not occur overnight or without conscious effort. Again, data can help us evaluate candidate innovations, allowing us to arrive at optimal solutions iteratively and efficiently.

Kiosks, Sensor Systems, and "Smart" Infrastructure

The two other areas of innovation in public spaces—the replacement of obsolete telecommunications infrastructure and the introduction of sensor systems—are emblematic of smart cities. One of the strong attractions of these projects, but also their most prominent weakness, is that they often appear to assume the answer is technology, regardless of the question. In the case of replacing outdated public telecommunications infrastructure, the consensus appears to be kiosks—that is, public tablets that provide wireless internet, access to government services, and related amenities—though there is some debate as to the value they offer. Sensors are even more exaggerated in their combination of cutting-edge technology and underspecified contribution. While technology companies have argued that detailed knowledge of conditions across the city will be able to lower the city services budget in various ways, it is not entirely apparent which specific applications will produce those dividends.

Given the open questions surrounding kiosks and sensor systems, it is ironic that they often overshadow the extensive impact that urban informatics is already having through more modest data analyses and technological innovations. It is not just that this latter set of projects is creating value that deserves attention but also that they are generating lessons about the effective use of modern digital data and civic technology. These lessons, in many cases, provide a road map for turning smart cities innovations into effective tools for helping cities be smart. Starting with the lessons from this book, let us take a closer look at the problem of measurement. Sensor data are deceptively hard to interpret. While they track specific conditions at a place, we have little understanding of the real-world events that are creating these conditions. For example, students in one of my classes used data from a sensor project in Boston called the

Local Sense Lab as the basis for their class projects in fall 2016. Separate projects assumed that the noise sensor was a proxy for vehicular traffic, pedestrian traffic, public performances in the area, and subway cars pulling in and out of the nearby station. The problem is that if a single measure is a proxy for multiple phenomena, it is useless for differentiating between them.

The problem of interpreting sensor data will require their triangulation with other data sources. Administrative data might help us to specify exactly when the trains came and went using transit data, or the days and times when there was a public performance nearby from permit and licensing data. We could use social media check-ins to estimate actual pedestrian activity. We might even conduct in-person audits, as in Chapter 2's streetlight and sidewalk assessments, to relate signatures of one or more sensors to objective observations. In some cases, we may discover that they are picking up information we never anticipated. In the case of the Local Sense Lab, one of my students actually visited one of the noise sensors in question, only to discover that it had been installed right next to the output vent for a local building's HVAC system. Thus, at least some of the temporal "signal" detected by the sensor was merely the building's patterns of heating and cooling. All told, sensors in isolation can tell us relatively basic things about the chemical and ambient composition of the environment but are also vulnerable to microspatial idiosyncrasies. When combined with other data sources, however, they have the potential to be effective proxies for a host of characteristics and events of interest.

The problem of measurement is largely a technical one, meaning it is tractable with some hard work and ingenuity. The potentially greater challenge facing these tools is a philosophical one. What is the definition of "value"? What can a sensor system provide people that they want and need? This is a problem of both definition and social process. If we want to make a comparison, the policy mandates of Vision Zero have embedded in them a clear set of objectives (i.e., no pedestrian or biker fatalities) that acted as the basis of evaluation. The same is true for the Promise Neighborhoods grant program's emphasis on learning environment and student outcomes. But such objectives have not been defined for sensor systems. In some sense, this arises from one of their greatest advantages. They are the epitome of what Tim O'Reilly refers to as a "platform," meaning they can support the vast proliferation of new innovations.[3] That said, they are then by definition unable to preordain the value that these subsequent uses pursue—or what one might call "value-free."

I would advocate for an inclusive approach to defining the public value that might be gained from sensors and kiosks. More than just a negotiation between technology companies and city hall, these conversations need to incorporate the voices of community organizations and their members. This involves more time and cost but is far more likely to achieve the stated goal of developing products that serve the needs and interests of the public. What do people want sensor systems to be able to do? How would they like to interact with the data and have it communicated to them? Are there places they want to be heavily instrumented and others where they would see this as an invasion of privacy? In the case of kiosks, they reflect the natural evolution of the public pay phone, but what form should they take? There are debates about size, with some claiming the Google Sidewalk Labs' LinkNYC "Times-Square-ifies" neighborhoods with its large advertisements. Others might wonder whether, with the increasing ownership of smartphones, we really need to replace pay phones with a new public telecommunications device or instead should reclaim that sidewalk space for pedestrian traffic. Is the kiosk itself worth the investment of capital? Cities should ask these questions of their residents, as their answers will provide guidance for using what are otherwise value-free technologies.

Finally, we need to reconsider whether technology is necessarily the answer to every question. There may be cases where a low-tech solution is as good as, or even better than, the high-tech one. A colleague of mine from the city of Boston illustrated this nicely at a conference of the MetroLab Network a few years ago during a discussion on sensors. He said (and I paraphrase), "These sensors are nice, but I already have this sensor [holds up his iPhone], and it travels around in the pocket of nearly every Bostonian. In a lot of cases this tells me everything I need to know." He went on to tell the story of Street Bump, an app that uses smartphone accelerometers to identify and report potholes while people are driving. When they tested the app in city-owned vehicles, they found that it could identify inconsistencies in pavement, but when they compared the data with 311 records, the app told them nearly nothing that residents had not already reported. In this case, the high-tech solution might make for a compelling story, but it was no more effective than empowering the residents of the city through 311. This is probably true in a lot of cases, as humans are technically sensors for *everything*, not just for pollutants, noise, or bumps in the road. There are, of course, times when a sensor might be valuable. We have seen in this book streetlight outages that languished as pedestrians failed to report them. Research on ShotSpotter, which detects gunshots, has also found that many shootings, especially those occurring at night, would go unreported without the system.[4] Residents may recognize dirty air or water but have no ability to identify particular pollutants. City services, then, will need to identify how humans and sensors complement each other in tracking the conditions of the city.

Tending the Civic Data Ecosystem

How does a city become smart? Unlike a person, a city is not a single entity. It is instead an assemblage of public agencies, universities, corporations, and community organizations, each with their own distinct operations and incentives. With that in mind, we might still borrow from cognitive psychology the concept of *executive functioning*, which is the ability of an individual to coordinate multiple processes in the pursuit of stated goals and outcomes. For a city, the same capacity rests in the organization of the civic data ecosystem. This is not to say there needs to be a central "executive" directing all research and policy efforts but rather that for a city to be smart there must be institutions in place that enable communication, knowledge sharing, collaboration, and even a conscious sense of community among those using data and technology to better understand and serve the city.

In order to describe the roles of different institutions in supporting urban informatics, we first need to define the field and how we think it will operate moving forward, something I first addressed in Chapter 1. At the conference in 2017, we noted something interesting about attendance. A nontrivial number of people joined for only one or two sessions, primarily focusing on those that were strongly associated with their own work. Criminologists and members of the Boston Police Department attended the session on "Public Safety & Crime," community advocates attended the session on "Neighborhood Planning," and so on. From this perspective, the constituency of BARI looked less like the members of a unitary field and more like a pastiche of disciplines, all of which had been energized by the opportunity to ask questions about cities using data of unprecedented scope and detail. The same looseness is visible in the national and international landscape of the field. It does not yet have a canon of foundational theoretical precepts. Nor does it have stand-alone departments, instead operating largely through cross-disciplinary centers that act as conveners. It does not even have its own journal. It is early yet, so it is probably unfair to treat these weaknesses as symptoms of anything more than a nascent field, but there may be a lesson in them nonetheless.

If the institutions that support urban informatics are to be successful, they will need to focus on those themes that are sufficiently unifying to create a field with collective interest. I can think of two. The first is the original basis of the field: modern digital data and technology. In order to capitalize on these new resources, the field has constructed a toolbox of analytic techniques that are applicable across disciplines. On its own, however, this theme would cast urban informatics not so much as its own field but rather as a methodological adjunct for the existing disciplines of sociology, criminology, public health, planning and design, policy, engineering, and computer science. The second unifying theme that I see is a panoramic view of the city itself. It is both natural and convenient to divide society into its components, to study and manage education, public health, crime, transportation, and the other domains independently. But all of these domains intersect. High school students take public transit. Crime in a neighborhood can create stress that leads to mental health issues. Gentrification alters the local context, and thereby the environment experienced by residents, for good and for bad. It is this holistic approach to the city that I believe excites the more ardent practitioners of urban informatics, those individuals who attended our conference from beginning to end, who wanted to understand urban communities in their entirety. If the city is a stage on which all aspects of behavior and society might be observed, then the aspiration of the field, if it is to realize a separate intellectual identity, is to watch the entire performance, not just one set of characters or passage of dialogue.

These two themes—one a methodological toolbox, the other a conceptual vision—create the mandate for the institutions that will support urban informatics moving forward. In the remainder of this section, I describe how each of the sectors—academia, public, private, and nonprofit—contribute to the civic data ecosystem, thereby creating a division of labor in the urban (data) commons. I conclude by discussing the forms that institutions with the goal of facilitating coordination and collaboration might take.

Academia

I start with academia in part because I am an academic and it is easiest to start with oneself. I also start here because, in the end, academics are responsible for many of the cutting-edge breakthroughs that will fuel the field. The opportunity for urban scientists is great, as I have discussed at length. As the world has become increasingly digital, instrumentation and data have followed suit, greatly expanding the breadth and detail of available knowledge. This forces us to develop novel methodologies necessary for analyzing the data, which then instigate new theories that have the potential to transform our basic understanding of cities. These are tangible contributions that will diffuse into the other sectors. The methodologies will eventually become widely available. The theories offer a conceptual foundation for new ideas and innovations. In this way, the work of academia can directly translate into practical advances for the city writ large. This is especially true if researchers choose to partner with policymakers to explore mutually beneficial extensions and applications of their work.

As important as academia's efforts to advance knowledge are its educational programs. The students in these programs are the ones who will carry the new methodologies and theories of urban informatics into the mainstream. Master's programs in urban informatics and related topics have proliferated in recent years, and classical programs in planning or urban studies have incorporated data courses into their curriculum. The students graduating from these programs are the next generation of policymakers, practitioners, and community organizers, and they will be equipped with the new skills and ideas generated by the field. Even those who do not aspire to be data scientists per se can still bring to their future jobs an understanding of what these tools are and how they could be useful.

As I mentioned at the opening of this section, there are currently no departments of urban informatics. The discipline instead lives in centers. Because there is no need for urban informatics to subsume the panoply of existing disciplines that it touches, this strikes me as the right model at this time. If provided with sufficient funding from both internal and external sources, centers have the flexibility and independence to operate as conveners, working across the silos created by disciplines, institutions, and even sectors. Through well-designed programming, a center can stimulate the needed conversations, foster cutting-edge work, and nudge research in new and experimental directions. It can also be a main conduit for communications between the research community and the other sectors, thereby connecting potential collaborators. The one tricky part here is making sure that the centers, which typically are research driven, are sufficiently aligned with the relevant educational programs, which for administrative reasons are typically run by departments.

Public Sector

One might argue that the emergence of urban informatics has had its greatest impact on the public sector. Academia and private corporations have been very much involved, but they were already convinced of the potential of digital data and technology. This same embrace of the future has only recently become popular in city halls around the country, and the transition has been rather rapid. Since New York City introduced the first team dedicated to in-house data-driven projects, other cities have adopted the same model. Similarly, a number of cities have replicated the role of Boston's Mayor's Office of New Urban Mechanics as an "R&D team for the city." We are now beginning to see a second stage in the development of these sorts of teams. As they have provided early evidence of their value, the ensuing demand within city hall is outstripping their capacity. Consequently, a metastasis is on the horizon, with individual agencies and departments implementing their own internal analytics teams. This is already starting to happen in New York City and Boston.

The success and growth of in-house analytic and innovation teams means that cities will conduct more and more of their own analyses and studies. Though it might seem counterintuitive, I think this actually strengthens the future of city-university partnerships. Admittedly, one of the weaknesses of academics is that we are incentivized to do a project only if it contributes to the scholarly literature. If a possible project has applied value to a public agency but lacks a fundamental advance, it is of limited interest to a scientist. This has not been too great a deterrent thus far because the novelty of the data and technology have generated both public value and intellectual contributions. As these initial advances in methodology and knowledge become established, however, their replications and applications will be increasingly derivative, having less impact on scholarship. This does not need to be a dead end for city-university partnerships, though, as two simultaneous shifts are occurring. First, data analytics teams have sufficient talent to enable cities to pursue these applied studies. Second, the initial advances have opened up a new set of cutting-edge questions to which research-policy collaborations can turn their attention. This ability to focus on the new frontier will maintain the field's forward movement while also keeping academics heavily engaged. One of my colleagues describes research-policy collaborations as a beneficial cycle of discovery and application. This is the same dynamic but at an institutional level: discovery across the first stratum of data and urban science has laid the groundwork for new teams within city hall that are trained in those advances, to be followed by another round of scientific advancement, in which the city teams will be trained, and so on.

Public agencies also face new challenges in data infrastructure. As urban informatics moves into more complex problems and more ambitious efforts to forecast events and conditions, there is a need for integration across many different data streams—the records of multiple agencies, the readings of sensors, and the information shared by private corporations might all be utilized in any given project. It is up to public agencies to identify the integrations that would be necessary to inform daily operations and long-term planning. Without this, the elements of the pulse of the city will sit fragmented and limited in their potential, not unlike a hospital where readings of heart rate, blood pressure, body temperature, and x-rays are kept separate and never examined in concert. This enhanced data infrastructure would be a boon for the public sector but also for the broader civic data ecosystem and its productivity. Though the leadership of public agencies is likely to be critical to this process, they will certainly need help. First, academics and private corporations can contribute to the development of the technical infrastructure for integrating disparate data streams. Second, such integrations raise serious questions about the appropriate use of proprietary data provided by private companies, as well as personally identifiable data describing individual constituents. The appropriate models for data storage and sharing in such cases have not yet been determined and will be an important part of this conversation.

Private Corporations

I have spoken little about private corporations in this book and at times have been a bit hard on them. I do not intend this book as a critique of a for-profit model of urban innovation. Rather, city-university partnerships should have more connection with private corporations because there will eventually be a need to develop business models that make the products of urban informatics sustainable. For example, we saw in Chapter 7 how SeeClickFix, a private vendor, was a key player in scaling BOS:311 from Boston to other municipalities statewide. Private corporations have the incentive to perfect and mass-produce a usable product for public consumption, whereas academics do not. This makes private corporations the third leg of a stool of research, development, and deployment, along with academia and government.

Most critiques of the private sector are rooted in a broader concern that technology companies often seem to be trying to go it alone. Many large-scale smart cities implementations are perceived as having little collaboration with academics and limited ability to be customized for the needs of the client city. For those companies that see such openness as a potential threat to proprietary technology, a possible solution is to think of their product as a "platform," as extolled by Tim O'Reilly.[5] He argues that the most influential advances, such as Microsoft Windows or the iPhone, are special because they enable a vast population of bright people to create new tools on top of it, thereby growing its value exponentially. I suggested earlier that this is probably how we should treat citywide sensor systems—as the infrastructure that undergirds widespread innovation on the city's behalf. Corporations that embrace this route will want to work closely with both the public sector and academia in order to ensure that the promised value is realized.

Private Foundations

I have spent even less time speaking about private foundations in this book, but they play an important role as well, in part as a funder but also as an advocate. It almost goes without saying, but foundations do more than make grants. They must decide what issues matter to them, how they want their resources to contribute to society, how these ideals translate into grant programs, and then which projects to support. Given their contribution of capital for service providers and researchers, they are as important as anyone to shaping a city's organizational landscape. This makes them a crucial part of the civic data ecosystem, one that has the opportunity to play a visionary role. They are unique in their ability to articulate the present and future needs of a city without being beholden to political expediencies, expectations of academic originality, or a profit margin. By combining this intellectual independence with their ability to make grants, they are not only positioned to call for research on certain topics but can directly drive work in that direction.

Community Organizations

Because I spent the entirety of Chapter 8 on community organizations and related nonprofits, I have little additional to say about them here. To recap, they can play an essential role as infomediaries that translate data resources into public value. This set of institutions is the furthest behind in terms of their current facility with data, but that can certainly change as partnerships increase, educational programs grow, and the talents needed become more widespread. In many ways, those of us who are skilled in data science need to package and discuss our projects in forms and language that are accessible to this population, because they will be able to do what we cannot: align the content and its implications directly with the needs and interests of local communities. The integration of community organizations more fully into the civic data ecosystem will be largely experimental in the coming years, from training in data portals, to conversations about the implementation of sensor systems, to specific research projects. The necessary next steps will be to build models of interaction that empower community organizations to both speak for the public and bring the implications back to their constituencies.

Managing the Urban (Data) Commons: Cross-Sector Coordination

If each of the sectors—academic, public, private, and nonprofit—succeeds in playing the roles that I have articulated, that still leaves open the question of institutions that create the connections between them. That is to say, *someone* must bring together these various talents and capacities to form a functional civic data ecosystem, an urban commons that generates a collective "smartness" that broadly benefits the city. Numerous models for solving this problem of coordination have arisen. In many, a partnership between the city's department of innovation and technology (or similar agency) and a single academic center forms the foundation for all local research-policy collaboration. In places with a larger, more complex ecosystem, one or more institutions work together to convene the many entities that might contribute to the conversation. In Boston, BARI and the Mayor's Office of New Urban Mechanics have accepted this responsibility, a job we share with a variety of other partners. Distinctively, the Los Angeles Housing Library has assumed this role with the public libraries. Other cities have seen the creation of independent nonprofits, such as Chicago's UI Labs and Envision Charlotte, that help to broker cross-sector, data- and technology-driven collaborations. Often referred to as "test beds," they are more accurately described as social infrastructure for identifying local needs, connecting partners who might attend to them, and mediating access to the necessary resources. At this point in time, there is no clear "best" model, though we may learn more in the coming years. What stands out as important is that there be intentional engagement from at least one institution in each sector, with the public and academic sectors being the most critical, followed closely by private corporations and community organizations.

There are three functions that these leading institutions must fulfill. The first and most apparent is to convene. How this is best achieved— through events and conferences, creating "affiliates" of various sorts, or seed grant programs—has been explored extensively, and cities across the country will continue to do so. Of particular interest is how to develop an agenda in a collaborative way that imparts coherence to the work while not stifling the independence of the many members. The second essential function is to facilitate education. As scientists advance what we can do with data, these skills need to be transferred to the other sectors. Various models of this are being tested, from traditional partnerships around master's programs and certificates to specialized fellowships for policymakers. On the other hand, academics often could use a greater understanding of the practical challenges that members of the other sectors face on a day-to-day basis. The potential for multiway learning of this sort between the sectors is broad and is ripe for innovation.

The last function for leading institutions of this sort, and one for which I do not yet have a good answer, is governance. At the moment, urban informatics runs on the enthusiasm of its early adopters and their zeal for collaboration. In a sense, we are both the constructors and custodians of this particular urban commons. But it is important to recall the lessons of Elinor Ostrom, who wrote more than one book describing the need for norms that set the ground rules for participating in a community and for institutions that ensure that those norms are followed.[6] How do we require that people share their findings with the original data producer or with the community as a whole? How do we confirm that a given analysis and its implications are sound before a policymaker makes a decision based on them? What are the expectations for reporting in a publicly accessible way? These are the questions that sit before us now, but their number and urgency will only increase as the field continues to grow. This book has chronicled a series of projects on custodianship, but they are just the tip of the iceberg—one line of inquiry inspired by one technological innovation and one data set among many. As these opportunities proliferate, we will need to think seriously about how we maintain this particular urban common.

Neighborhood Audits

Streetlight Outages and Garbage

Neighborhood audits identifying streetlight outages and assessing levels of street garbage were conducted in 72 of Boston's 156 census tracts (46 percent) between June 1 and August 31, 2011, as part of an undergraduate seminar. The sample was constructed in a multistep process, intended to cover about half of the city, while capturing its full range of demographic, socioeconomic, and geographic diversity.

First, tracts were attributed to one of Boston's 16 planning districts, contiguous regions with characteristic demographic and socioeconomic profiles.[1] The population-weighted mean for tract-level median income was calculated for each planning district. A stratified sample of three or four tracts was then created for each planning district (depending on the size), including one tract more than a standard deviation above the local weighted mean for median income, one more than a standard deviation below the weighted mean, and either one or two within a standard deviation of the weighted mean. Because planning districts vary in the number of tracts they contain (*min* = 1, *max* = 24), the sample was completed by random selection from planning districts with a high number of tracts. The final sample was representative of the diversity across all Boston tracts, both in terms of its central tendency and range (see Table A.1).

TABLE A.1 Comparison of demographic characteristics between all census tracts in Boston and those sampled in streetlight outage and garbage audits

	All tracts		Sampled tracts	
	Mean (SD)	Range	Mean (SD)	Range
Median income	$52,572 ($23,607)	$10,250–$143,819	$55,256 ($27,436)	$10,250–$143,819
Population density[a]	22.83 (16.24)	1.36–93.07	23.96 (17.55)	3.18–93.07
% Homeowners	.36 (.19)	.00–.88	.38 (.21)	.00–.88
% White	.51 (.31)	.00–.99	.52 (.33)	.00–.98
% Black	.21 (.25)	.00–.92	.22 (.26)	.00–.92
% Hispanic	.17 (.16)	.00–.84	.15 (.1f)	.00–.62

a. Thousands per square mile.

During each audit, teams of two walked the streets of a particular tract. Highways, service roads, and other roads rarely used by pedestrians were omitted. The goal was to cover all other roads, though sometimes this was not possible given time constraints on audits. One person walked each side of the street. On each street segment (intersection to intersection or intersection to dead end), each person recorded the level of garbage and the presence of any streetlight outages on his or her side of the street. In total, 4,239 street segments were assessed. Garbage was rated on a five-point scale, with higher scores indicating larger piles of garbage and more of them, for both the street and the sidewalk (if present). These observations were then processed to create measures that were more informative.

REPORTING STREETLIGHT OUTAGES. We identified the date on which each streetlight outage was reported, defined as the earliest case of an outage reported on the street segment in question that was fixed by the city after the date an auditor noted the outage. Note that this means a streetlight might have been reported before the audit, as long as the city had not completed the job until after the audit. It was possible to distinguish whether a report was made by a constituent or a city employee. Thus, a continuous measure of the time before reporting would not necessarily reflect the strength of constituent response. Instead, we created a series of dichotomous measures for whether a streetlight had been reported after a given amount of time (e.g., one week, one month, three months, etc.) so that employee-reported outages could be considered not reported until the date the employee report appeared. Thereafter they were omitted from the data, as it is not possible to know whether a constituent would have reported up to that point. For example, a streetlight outage reported 16 days later by a city employee takes the value "0" for the measure of being reported within two weeks but would take no value (omitted) for the measure one month.

GARBAGE. The date of data collection was used in conjunction with the city's street-sweeping schedule to fit a linear model that used the number of days since that side of the street was swept to predict the level of garbage. The linear model indicated that streets swept within the past three days had lower-than-expected litter at the rate of .06/day on our scale. After three days had passed, there was no substantial difference in garbage ratings. Sidewalks were not adjusted in this fashion, as they are not swept. Following this, an average of the adjusted street measure and the sidewalk measure on each side of the street was calculated as the total garbage rating for the street segment. Before data collection, interrater reliability was established through PowerPoint training slides and neighborhood walks.

Sidewalk Quality Audit

A consulting group hired by the city of Boston's Public Works Department assessed the quality of all of the city's sidewalks between November 2009 and April 2012. For each sidewalk, the assessors noted the proportion of panels that required replacement (i.e., cracked, broken) and subtracted this from the total, creating a measure of sidewalk quality. The unit of analysis was each continuous stretch of sidewalk that ran from intersection to intersection ($N = 27{,}388$). The 311 reports were then joined to the nearest sidewalk polygon from the same road. We were able to exclude those created by city employees, as an additional code was included with such cases. This then enabled us to create counts of reports for every sidewalk polygon in the city.

Constructing Neighborhood-Level Measures

The streetlight outages, sidewalk reports, and garbage assessments all describe events or conditions on a single street segment within a census block group (CBG). To create CBG-level measures that controlled for the microspatial effects of street characteristics, multilevel models[2] were developed in which two simultaneous equations were estimated, the first at the level of streets (first level), the second at the level of CBGs (second level). The street-level equation was defined as

$$Y_{jk} = \beta_{0k} + \sum_i \beta_i X_{ijk} + r_{jk}$$
$$r_{jk} \sim N(0, \sigma^2),$$

where Y_{jk} represents the jth street in CBG k, and β_{0k} is the estimated mean for neighborhood k. Each X_i is a first-level predictor, and each β_i is the corresponding regression parameter, explaining differences between streets within the same CBG. The errors of measurement r_{ij} for street j in neighborhood k are assumed to be normally distributed with variance σ^2. The estimated mean for neighborhood k is modeled as

$$\beta_{0k} = \gamma_{00} + \mu_{0k}$$
$$\mu_{0k} \sim N(0, \tau),$$

where γ_{00} is the estimated mean value for the neighborhood-level measure across neighborhoods, and μ_{0k} is the random neighborhood effect for neighborhood k. The latter can also be described as the deviation of the average value in neighborhood k from the cross-neighborhood mean. These random neighborhood effects are assumed to be normally distributed with variance τ and are the values extracted for the desired CBG-level measure. For example, in the case of garbage, μ_{0k} indicates the extent to which the average street in CBG k has more or less loose garbage than the average street in the average neighborhood. In addition, the magnitude of τ in relation to σ^2 is valuable in determining how well Y captures differences between neighborhoods. This is evaluated with a χ^2 test.

There were slight variations between the models for streetlight outages, sidewalks, and garbage, including in first-level predictors and the link function used. For sidewalks, the sidewalk care index was the lone first-level predictor. The binary outcome (whether a sidewalk generated any reports) used a logit link, and the continuous outcome (how many reports a sidewalk generated) used a zero-inflated Poisson link. The models for both garbage and streetlight outages incorporated dichotomous variables distinguishing between main and side streets, and between streets with different types of zoning. For garbage, dichotomous variables for all nonresidential zonings were included (i.e., commercial, industrial, exempt, and unzoned). To conserve degrees of freedom for the analysis of streetlight outages, this was simplified to a single dichotomous variable distinguishing between residential and nonresidential zonings. The garbage model used a standard regression, as garbage was a continuous, normal variable. The streetlight outage outcomes were dichotomous, necessitating a logit link.

In determining the proper event-level outcome to use as the basis for the CBG-level measure, there were multiple options for the streetlight outages and sidewalk reports. Multilevel models were run using each option, and their results were compared. For sidewalks, there were two candidate measures: whether a sidewalk polygon generated one or more reports (binary model), and if a polygon had generated any reports, how many it had generated (continuous model). Since not all CBGs contained a sidewalk that generated a request for repair, the continuous model only analyzed 416 CBGs. In each model, in order to control for the objective need for repair, the sidewalk care index was entered as the sole first-level predictor. Both models indicated significant CBG-level variation, with the binary measure appearing to do so more effectively (binary: $\chi^2_{df=541} = 940.47$, $p < .001$; continuous: $\chi^2_{df=415} = 505.11$, $p < .01$). In addition, the binary measure was predicted by the sidewalk care index in the expected direction (i.e., a higher index predicts a lower likelihood of requests for repair), while the continuous measure was not (binary: $\beta = -0.003$, $p < .01$; continuous: $\beta = 0.001$, $p = ns$), suggesting it as the superior measure for the subsequent analyses. Neighborhood-level residuals for this measure were extracted, with higher values indicating a CBG with a greater likelihood of requesting a sidewalk repair, controlling for quality of the sidewalk.

For streetlight outages, it was necessary to run the models at the tract level, owing to the low number of streetlight outages per CBG (244 in 127 CBGs and 56 tracts with outages.)[3] The model was used to predict the likelihood of an outage being reported by a constituent at six time points after being identified: one week, two weeks, one month, two months, three months, and four months. Of these, the one-month ($\chi^2_{df=54} = 78.39, p < .05$), two-month ($\chi^2_{df=53} = 80.80, p < .01$), three-month ($\chi^2_{df=53} = 73.95, p < .05$), and four-month ($\chi^2_{df=53} = 73.30, p < .05$) models identified significant differences between tracts. We use two-month windows in the main analyses because they uncovered the greatest amount of variance.

The continuous measure of garbage was also assessed for neighborhood-level variation. The model indicated significant CBG-level variation ($\chi^2_{df=350} = 4,765.56, p < .001$). The neighborhood-level residual was extracted as the measurement of garbage.

Reliability Estimates
for 311-Based Indicators

Chapter 2 presented a methodology for measuring multiple dimensions of physical disorder through 311. This appendix reports reliability estimates for the components of these measures at different time windows (from one week to six months) for census block groups (Table B.1) and census tracts (Table B.2).

TABLE B.1 Intraclass correlations (ICC) and reliabilities (λ) for level (intercept) and cross-time change (slope) in measures used to calculate public denigration and private neglect across census block groups for various time windows

	Housing			Uncivil use			Big buildings		
	Intercept		Slope	Intercept		Slope	Intercept		Slope
	ICC	λ	λ	ICC	λ	λ	ICC	λ	λ
2 weeks	.23	.91	.36	.03	.78	.30	.02	.46	.10
1 month	.39	.91	.36	.07	.78	.30	.03	.46	.11
2 months	.56	.91	.37	.13	.78	.29	.04	.46	.10
3 months	.65	.91	.37	.19	.77	.30	.10	.46	.09
4 months	.72	.91	.37	.25	.78	.29	.19	.46	.12
6 months	.77	.90	.33	.39	.74	.25	.31	.48	.01

	Graffiti			Trash			Public reporters		
	Intercept		Slope	Intercept		Slope	Intercept		Slope
	ICC	λ	λ	ICC	λ	λ	ICC	λ	λ
2 weeks	.13	.87	.51	.09	.88	.48	.32	.96	.40
1 month	.24	.87	.51	.17	.88	.48	.47	.96	.30
2 months	.38	.87	.51	.30	.88	.48	.63	.95	.21
3 months	.47	.86	.51	.41	.88	.45	.68	.95	.03
4 months	.56	.87	.51	.47	.88	.47	.75	.95	.04
6 months	.60	.84	.56	.63	.86	.39	.80	.93	.01

Note: N varies based on the number of time intervals possible for the 28-month period in the database, nested in 541 census block groups. All ICCs are significant at $p < .001$.

TABLE B.2 Intraclass correlations (ICC) and reliabilities (λ) for level (intercept) and cross-time change (slope) in measures of public denigration and private neglect across census tracts for various time windows

	Housing			Uncivil use			Big buildings		
	Intercept		Slope	Intercept		Slope	Intercept		Slope
	ICC	λ	λ	ICC	λ	λ	ICC	λ	λ
2 weeks	.46	.97	.45	.12	.92	.37	.04	.68	.27
1 month	.64	.97	.46	.22	.92	.37	.09	.68	.27
2 months	.78	.97	.46	.35	.92	.36	.12	.68	.27
3 months	.84	.97	.44	.46	.91	.40	.24	.68	.24
4 months	.88	.97	.45	.55	.92	.37	.40	.68	.29
6 months	.90	.96	.36	.75	.90	.31	.41	.70	.01
Composite[a]	.78	.92	—	.64	.84	—	.20	.43	—

	Graffiti			Trash			Public reporters		
	Intercept		Slope	Intercept		Slope	Intercept		Slope
	ICC	λ	λ	ICC	λ	λ	ICC	λ	λ
2 weeks	.31	.95	.71	.25	.96	.67	.59	.99	.39
1 month	.49	.95	.71	.40	.96	.67	.73	.98	.28
2 months	.64	.95	.72	.59	.96	.67	.84	.98	.06
3 months	.73	.95	.72	.67	.96	.62	.88	.98	.07
4 months	.79	.95	.71	.74	.96	.66	.90	.98	.05
6 months	.86	.94	.77	.86	.95	.55	.93	.98	.00
Composite[a]	.53	.77	—	.59	.82	—	—	—	—

Note: N varies based on the number of time intervals possible for the 28-month period in the database, nested in 156 census tracts. All ICCs are significant at $p < .001$.

a. A combination of the raw count and the measures of concern for the public space, calculated for six-month windows only. See the text for more details on construction.

Models Using Survey Variables to Predict Custodianship

A series of models were run using demographic characteristics, self-reported attitudes and behaviors, and officially recorded voting activity to predict patterns of custodianship. The first two sets of information come from the survey of 311 users (see Chapters 3 and 5), voting activity was accessed from public voter records (see Chapter 5), and custodianship was measured using 311 records (see Chapter 3). Table C.1 uses territoriality to predict custodianship behavior, Table C.2 divides custodianship into reports of man-made incivilities and natural deterioration, and Table C.3 incorporates civic and political activities into the models in Table C.1.

The models run were multilevel models that nested individuals in their tract of residence, thereby controlling for neighborhood-level factors that might influence individual patterns of custodianship. This makes the interpretation of individual-level predictors more robust. To conduct such analyses, it was necessary to limit the analysis to survey respondents who had a home address associated with their account and living in a census tract from which at least three residents participated in the survey (final $N = 427$ individuals in 81 tracts). Because all outcome variables are either dichotomous (i.e., $0/1$) or heavily skew (i.e., Poisson distributed, with a long tail of high values), the models used a logit link, and odds ratios are reported.

TABLE C.1 Parameter estimates from multilevel models predicting reporting patterns among custodians using demographic and behavioral predictors, while controlling for neighborhood effects

	Custodian?		Calls in neighborhood		Size of home ra
	Beta (std. error)	Odds ratio	Beta (std. error)	Odds ratio	Beta (std. error)
Demographic predictors					
Female[a]	−0.22 (0.21)	0.80	−0.57*** (0.09)	0.56	−0.67* (0.26)
Black[a]	−0.37 (0.34)	0.69	0.58** (0.17)	1.79	−0.94 (0.76)
Hispanic[a]	0.46 (0.55)	1.59	−0.30 (0.30)	0.74	−1.31 (1.10)
Age	0.17 (0.08)	1.18	0.05 (0.03)	1.05	−0.12 (0.09)
Education	0.01 (0.06)	1.01	−0.11 (0.02)	0.90	−0.20** (0.07)
Behavioral predictors					
Property value	−0.02 (0.08)	0.98	−0.06 (0.03)	0.95	−0.08 (0.09)
Benefit community	0.27* (0.13)	1.32	0.23** (0.07)	1.26	0.87** (0.25)
Enforce norms	0.06 (0.10)	1.06	0.19*** (0.05)	1.20	0.31** (0.12)
Model details					
Second-level variance	.08		.40***		.49***
N (tracts)	427 (81)		211 (48)		197 (48)

Note: The most comprehensive model includes all respondents living in census tracts with three or more respondents who completed all items regarding demographics, political participation, territoriality, and where they use 311. Other models were limited to custodians living in census tracts with three or more custodians who fit the same inclusion criteria. The model predicting home range size is limited to those who had reports within the home range.

a. Dichotomous variable with 1 equal to the variable's name.

* $p < .05$, ** $p < .01$, *** $p < .001$.

n neighborhood of work?		On commute?		From neighborhood of family/friends?	
eta error)	Odds ratio	Beta (std. error)	Odds ratio	Beta (std. error)	Odds ratio
(0.40)	0.47	−0.48 (0.36)	0.62	−0.53 (0.49)	0.59
(0.74)	1.81	−0.02 (0.83)	0.98	1.29 (0.72)	3.63
(0.82)	3.34	−1.29 (1.13)	0.28	−0.10 (1.14)	0.90
(0.15)	0.78	−0.33* (0.14)	0.72	−0.22 (0.18)	0.80
(0.11)	0.90	0.12 (0.12)	1.13	−0.22 (0.13)	0.80
(0.15)	1.06	−0.18 (0.12)	0.84	0.05 (0.19)	1.05
(0.31)	1.10	0.86** (0.32)	2.37	−0.20 (0.34)	0.82
(0.20)	0.97	−0.22 (0.19)	0.80	−0.19 (0.26)	0.82
.53		~.00		~.00	
211 (48)		211 (48)		211 (48)	

TABLE C.2 Parameter estimates from regressions modeling both the likelihood of zeros and the total count for reports of incivilities and natural deterioration, using demographic and behavioral predictors, while controlling for neighborhood effects

| | Reports of incivilities | | | |
| | Zero model | | Total count | |
	Beta (std. error)	Odds ratio	Beta (std. error)	Oc ra
Reports of incivilities[a]	—	—	—	-
Reports of natural deterioration[a]	—	—	0.35* (0.14)	1.
Demographic predictors				
Female[b]	0.36 (0.26)	1.43	−0.72* (0.28)	0.
Black[b]	2.36* (1.03)	11.11	−1.04 (1.49)	0.
Hispanic[b]	0.37 (0.69)	1.45	−0.77 (0.92)	0.
Age	0.03 (0.09)	1.03	0.07 (0.09)	1.
Education	−0.10 (0.08)	0.90	−0.04 (0.08)	0.
Territorial motivations				
Benefit community	−0.35 (0.19)	0.70	0.83** (0.29)	2.
Enforce norms	−0.24* (0.12)	0.79	0.40* (0.16)	1.
N/Nonzeros			427/70	

a. Log-transformed.
b. Dichotomous variable with 1 equal to the variable's name.
* $p < .05$, ** $p < .01$, *** $p < .001$.

| Reports of natural deterioration | | | |
| Zero model | | Total count | |
Beta (std. error)	Odds ratio	Beta (std. error)	Odds ratio
—	—	0.36** (0.11)	1.44
—	—	—	—
0.04 (0.20)	0.96	−0.45** (0.14)	0.64
0.11 (0.33)	1.11	0.90*** (0.24)	2.45
0.04 (0.50)	0.96	−0.11 (0.42)	0.89
−0.17 (0.07)	0.85	−0.08 (0.05)	0.93
−0.03 (0.06)	0.98	−0.08 (0.04)	0.93
0.26* (0.13)	0.77	0.12 (0.10)	1.13
−0.03 (0.10)	0.97	−0.02 (0.07)	0.99
	427 / 187		

TABLE C.3 Parameter estimates from multilevel models predicting reporting patterns among custodians using demographic predictors, territoriality, and civic and political activities, while controlling for neighborhood effects

	Custodian?		Calls in neighborhood		Size of home ran	
	Beta (std. error)	Odds ratio	Beta (std. error)	Odds ratio	Beta (std. error)	Od
Demographic predictors						
Female[a]	−0.22 (0.21)	0.79	−0.67*** (0.09)	0.51	−0.71** (0.26)	
Black[a]	−0.37 (0.34)	0.60	0.43* (0.19)	1.54	−0.88 (0.77)	
Hispanic[a]	0.46 (0.55)	1.58	−0.20 (0.32)	0.82	−1.22 (1.09)	
Age	0.17 (0.08)	1.16	0.05 (0.03)	1.06	−0.12 (0.09)	
Education	0.01 (0.06)	1.01	−0.03 (0.03)	0.97	−0.20** (0.07)	
Behavioral predictors						
Civic activities	−0.04 (0.06)	0.96	−0.14*** (0.02)	0.87	0.08 (0.07)	
Voted in municipal election[a]	0.19 (0.22)	1.21	−0.01 (0.09)	0.99	−0.08 (0.25)	
Benefit community	0.29* (0.13)	1.33	0.19** (0.06)	1.21	0.86** (0.24)	2
Enforce norms	0.04 (0.10)	1.04	0.18*** (0.04)	1.19	0.28* (0.11)	1
Model details						
Second-level variance	.09		.36***		.51***	
N (tracts)	439 (82)		220 (50)		206 (50)	

Note: The most comprehensive model includes all respondents living in census tracts with three or more respondents who completed all items regarding demographics, political participation, territoriality, and where they use 311. Other models were limited to custodians living in census tracts with three or more custodians who fit the same inclusion criteria. The model predict home range size is limited to those who had reports within the home range.

a. Dichotomous variable with 1 equal to the variable's name.

* *p* < .05, ** *p* < .01, *** *p* < .001.

neighborhood of work?		On commute?		From neighborhood of family/friends?	
a rror)	Odds ratio	Beta (std. error)	Odds ratio	Beta (std. error)	Odds ratio
).39)	0.54	−0.45 (0.37)	0.64	−0.56 (0.51)	0.57
).76)	1.94	0.04 (0.87)	1.04	1.29 (0.77)	3.62
0.82)	2.79	−1.77 (1.20)	0.17	0.23 (1.15)	1.25
0.15)	0.80	−0.40** (0.15)	0.66	−0.35 (0.20)	0.71
).12)	0.85	0.09 (0.13)	1.10	−0.33* (0.15)	0.72
(0.12)	1.34	0.45*** (0.12)	1.57	0.19 (0.14)	1.21
0.42)	0.79	0.26 (0.40)	1.29	1.38* (0.56)	3.98
0.31)	1.37	0.80* (0.32)	2.23	−0.28 (0.35)	0.76
0.19)	0.95	−0.33 (0.19)	0.72	−0.22 (0.26)	0.80
.49		~.00		~.00	
220 (50)		220 (50)		220 (50)	

Models Testing Division of Labor

Chapter 4 evaluated the presence of a division of labor in the maintenance of the urban commons through two tests. The first set of analyses found that both typical and exemplar custodians contributed to the likelihood of a neighborhood reporting a broken sidewalk (Table D.1) or streetlight outage (Table D.2). The second set of analyses revealed distinctions in the types of situations and contexts in which typical and exemplar custodians reported issues in the public space. They also found that city employees and constituents differed in their patterns of reporting (Table D.3).

TABLE D.1 Parameter estimates from models using the relative prevalence of typical and exemplar custodians and demographic characteristics to predict a census tract's likelihood to report a broken sidewalk

	Model 1		Model 2		Model 3	
	Beta (SE)	Stand. Beta	Beta (SE)	Stand. Beta	Beta (SE)	Stand. Bet.
Typical custodians/mi² [a]	0.21*** (0.03)	.47	—	—	0.17*** (0.04)	.38
Exemplars[a]	—	—	0.24*** (0.04)	.41	0.17*** (0.04)	.29
Typical * exemplars	—	—	—	—	—	—
Total custodians/mi²	—	—	—	—	—	—
Total custodians	—	—	—	—	—	—
% Immigrant	—	—	—	—	—	—
% Hispanic[a]	—	—	—	—	—	—
% Black[a]	—	—	—	—	—	—
Median income	—	—	—	—	—	—
Adjusted R^2	.21		.16		.29	

Note: $n = 155$ census tracts.
a. log-transformed to adjust for skew.
* $p < .05$, ** $p < .01$, *** $p < .001$.

Model 4		Model 5		Model 6		Model 7	
ta (SE)	Stand. Beta	Beta (SE)	Stand. Beta	Beta (SE)	Stand. Beta	Beta (SE)	Stand. Beta
.17*** (0.03)	.38	—	—	—	—	0.17*** (0.03)	.38
.17*** (0.04)	.29	—	—	—	—	0.17*** (0.05)	.30
5* (0.03)	.13	—	—	—	—	0.05* (0.03)	.14
—	—	0.22*** (0.03)	.48	—	—	—	—
—	—	—	—	0.20*** (0.04)	.35	—	—
—	—	—	—	—	—	0.16 (0.03)	.06
—	—	—	—	—	—	0.52 (0.03)	.16
—	—	—	—	—	—	0.02 (0.01)	.13
—	—	—	—	—	—	0.03 (0.15)	.02
.30		.22		.12		.31	

TABLE D.2 Parameter estimates from models using the relative prevalence of typical and exemplar custodians and demographic characteristics to predict a census tract's likelihood to report a streetlight outage

	Model 1		Model 2		Model 3		Model 4		Model 5		Model 6	
	Beta (SE)	Stand. Beta	Beta (SE)	Stand. Beta	Beta (SE)	Stand. Beta	Beta (SE)	Stand. Beta	Beta (SE)	Stand. Beta	Beta (SE)	Stand. Beta
Typical custodians/mi² [a,b]	0.17* (0.08)	.28	—	—	0.14+ (0.08)	.23	—	—	—	—	—	—
Exemplars [a]	—	—	0.27* (0.12)	.30	0.23+ (0.12)	.26	—	—	—	—	—	—
Typical * exemplars	—	—	—	—	—	—	0.21** (0.08)	.36	—	—	—	—
Total custodians/mi²	—	—	—	—	—	—	—	—	0.17* (0.08)	.29	—	—
Total custodians	—	—	—	—	—	—	—	—	—	—	0.26* (0.12)	.28
% Immigrant	—	—	—	—	—	—	—	—	—	—	—	—
% Hispanic [a]	—	—	—	—	—	—	—	—	—	—	—	—
% Black [a]	—	—	—	—	—	—	—	—	—	—	—	—
Median income	—	—	—	—	—	—	—	—	—	—	—	—
Adjusted R²	.08		.08		.11		.12		.06		.06	

Note: $n = 53$ census tracts with streetlight outages. A final model found no demographic factors to be significant for which reason they are not reported.

a. log-transformed to adjust for skew.

b. During the three months in advance of the streetlight outage audits.

* $p < .05$, ** $p < .01$, *** $p < .001$.

ABLE D.3 Parameter estimates from multilevel models predicting whether a report was made / an exemplar or typical custodian or by an employee or constituent based on characteristics of ie report, street, and census tract

	Exemplar vs. typical		City employee vs. constituent	
	Beta (std. error)	Odds ratio	Beta (std. error)	Odds ratio
port characteristics				
Man-made incivility[a]	0.54*** (0.01)	1.72	−1.10*** (0.01)	0.33
Weekend[a]	0.09*** (0.02)	1.10	−0.33*** (0.02)	0.72
Spring[a]	0.05** (0.02)	1.05	−0.11*** (0.01)	0.90
Summer[a]	−0.06*** (0.02)	0.94	−0.10*** (0.01)	0.90
Fall[a]	−0.18*** (0.02)	0.83	0.17*** (0.01)	1.18
Snow removal[a]	−0.03 (0.02)	0.97	−2.31*** (0.03)	0.10
reet characteristics				
Length[b]	−0.06*** (0.01)	0.94	−0.06*** (0.01)	0.94
Main street	0.26*** (0.02)	1.29	0.33*** (0.02)	1.39
Commercial	0.22*** (0.04)	1.25	0.42*** (0.03)	1.52
Industrial	0.34*** (0.06)	1.40	0.57*** (0.05)	1.77
Exempt	0.33*** (0.04)	1.39	0.46*** (0.04)	1.58
No zoning	0.50*** (0.04)	1.65	0.46*** (0.03)	1.59
eighborhood characteristics				
Population density[c]	0.01*** (0.001)	1.01	−0.01** (0.002)	0.99
Downtown	0.14 (0.10)	1.15	−0.42** (0.15)	0.66
Institutional	0.20** (0.06)	1.22	−0.29** (0.10)	0.75
Park	−0.03 (0.10)	0.97	−0.09 (0.15)	0.92
*cond-level variance	.60***		.52***	
hird-level variance	.07***		.21***	
(roads / tracts)	152,556 (13,163 / 178)		265,243 (12,124 / 178)	

a. Dichotomous variable with 1 equal to the variable's name.
b. 100s of meters.
c. 1,000s / mile^2.
** $p < .01$, *** $p < .001$.

Models Testing Transparency Messages in BOS:311

Chapter 6 evaluated an effort by the city of Boston to have government service workers take pictures of completed work orders and send them to the BOS:311 user who made the original request. This was treated as an instance of operational transparency, and the evaluation tested whether this led BOS:311 users to make more reports over a greater geographical range in the following months. The study analyzed each individual's behavior in each month following their initial installation of the app through panel models that included fixed effects for each user. Full results are reported in Table E.1.

TABLE E.1 Parameter estimates from panel models testing the effect of transparency messages on reporting behavior of BOS:311 users

	Number of reports		Range of reporting (100 m)[a]		Reports outside home cluster[a]	
	Beta (std. error)	Beta (std. error)	Beta (std. error)	Beta (std. error)	Beta (std. error)	Beta (std. error)
Transparency	0.81*** (0.01)	-6.98*** (0.29)	-0.25*** (0.03)	-0.33*** (0.04)	-0.17 (0.17)	-0.05 (0.20)
First month of transparency	—	1.66*** (0.02)	—	0.18*** (0.03)	—	-0.33 (0.28)
% of requests closed	—	1.60*** (0.07)	—	—	—	—
% of requests closed[2]	—	-1.16*** (0.05)	—	—	—	—
Transparency × % closed	—	18.07*** (0.74)	—	—	—	—
Transparency × % closed[2]	—	-10.76*** (0.45)	—	—	—	—

Note: 371,992 user-months nested within 21,786 users. Models control for length of time with BOS:311 installed (both as linear and quadratic predictors), the total number of requests fulfilled, and reporter-level fixed effects. The latter two models were limited to 1,651 users who had home addresses on file.

a. Because there were no interesting initial results, we did not further examine the effects of percentage of cases closed and their interaction with transparency.

*** $p < .001$.

Models for Evaluation of Commonwealth Connect

Chapter 7 evaluated the implementation of Commonwealth Connect, a smartphone app modeled on BOS:311 and subsidized by the Commonwealth of Massachusetts, across municipalities. An initial analysis attempted to explain variations in the adoption of Commonwealth Connect by the public using demographic composition and the extent to which the municipality embraced the program (Table F.1). A later analysis used variables suggested by the coproduction, administrative culture, and imitation models to examine which municipalities joined, promoted, and internally utilized Commonwealth Connect (Table F.2).

TABLE F.1 Parameter estimates from models using demographic composition and government adoption of Commonwealth Connect to predict custodians per capita in a municipality

	Model 1		Model 2	
	Beta (SE)	Stand. Beta	Beta (SE)	Stand. Beta
Median income (in $1,000s)	−0.01 (0.02)	−.13	−0.01 (0.02)	−.11
Home ownership	0.57 (4.43)	.04	−0.30 (4.07)	−.02
% Black[a]	2.11 (5.11)	.07	−1.56 (4.80)	−.05
% Hispanic[a]	−0.23 (3.95)	−.01	−1.69 (3.69)	−.07
% Immigrant	7.58 (5.39)	.32	5.01 (5.39)	.21
Median age	0.03 (0.10)	.05	0.01 (0.09)	−.02
Public promotion[b]	—	—	1.30** (0.58)	.27
City official reports (per 1,000 residents)	—	—	81.72** (35.10)	.29
Adjusted R^2		.04		.19

Note: $n = 64$ municipalities.
a. log-transformed to adjust for skew.
b. Dichotomous variable with 1 equal to the variable's name.
* $p < .05$, ** $p < .01$, *** $p < .001$.

TABLE F.2 Parameter estimates from models testing the effects of coproduction, administrative culture, and imitation on a municipality's decision to join, promote, and internally utilize Commonwealth Connect

	Joined Commonwealth Connect?					
	Model 1		**Model 2**		**Model 3**	
	Beta (std. error)	Odds ratio	Beta (std. error)	Odds ratio	Beta (std. error)	Odd...
Coproduction						
Total population (in 10,000s)	0.33** (0.12)	1.39	0.38** (0.13)	1.46	0.35** (0.13)	1.
Population density	0.24 (0.22)	1.27	0.36 (0.24)	1.43	0.26 (0.23)	1.
Road length (millions of meters)	−0.04 (0.12)	0.96	−0.03 (0.13)	0.97	−0.04 (0.13)	0.
% Road length residential (0–100)	0.03 (0.02)	1.03	0.03 (0.03)	1.03	0.02 (0.03)	1.
Administrative culture						
Expenditures per capita (in $1,000s)	—	—	0.15 (0.13)	1.16	0.14 (0.14)	1.
Imitation						
Free cash (in $1,000s)	—	—	−0.49 (0.28)	0.61	−0.48 (0.28)	0.
Neighboring members of CC	—	—	—	—	0.31 (0.13)	1.
Adjusted R^2	N/A		N/A		N/A	
N			351 municipalities			

	City official reports (per 10,000 residents)					
	Model 1		**Model 2**		**Model 3**	
	Beta (SE)	Stand. Beta	Beta (SE)	Stand. Beta	Beta (SE)	Sta... Be...
Coproduction						
Total population (in 10,000s)	0.01 (0.02)	.08	0.01 (0.06)	.09	0.01 (0.06)	.
Population density	−0.04 (0.09)	−.06	−0.05 (0.10)	−.09	−0.06 (0.10)	−.
Road length (millions of meters)	−0.05 (0.06)	−.17	−0.06 (0.08)	−.21	−0.06 (0.08)	−.
% Road length residential (0–100)	0.04 (0.03)	.19	0.04 (0.03)	.19	0.04 (0.03)	
Administrative culture						
Expenditures per capita (in $1,000s)	—	—	−0.12 (0.15)	−.11	−0.12 (0.15)	−.
Free cash (in $1,000s)	—	—	−0.01 (0.14)	.03	−0.01 (0.14)	.
Imitation						
Neighboring members of CC	—	—	—	—	0.04 (0.09)	
Adjusted R^2	~.00		~.00		~.00	
N			64 municipalities			

a. log-transformed to adjust for skew.
b. During the three months in advance of the streetlight outage audits.
* $p < .05$, ** $p < .01$, *** $p < .001$.

		Promoted Commonwealth Connect?			
Model 1		Model 2		Model 3	
ta ·rror)	Odds ratio	Beta (std. error)	Odds ratio	Beta (std. error)	Odds ratio
0.08)	1.03	−0.12 (0.16)	0.87	−0.11 (0.17)	0.90
0.22)	1.27	−0.23 (0.27)	0.79	0.02 (0.28)	1.02
0.18)	0.96	0.16 (0.20)	1.17	0.16 (0.21)	1.17
0.06)	1.06	0.07 (0.06)	1.07	0.08 (0.06)	1.08
-	—	−0.02 (0.37)	0.98	−0.01 (0.37)	1.00
-	—	1.83 (1.07)	6.23	1.76 (1.06)	5.81
-	—	—	—	−0.12 (0.19)	0.89
N/A		N/A		N/A	
		64 municipalities			

Notes

Introduction

1. See the video at https://vimeo.com/41535798.
2. All quotations that follow are taken directly from the source, including any grammatical or typographical errors.
3. S. Goldsmith and S. Crawford, *The Responsive City: Engaging Communities through Data-Smart Governance* (San Francisco: Jossey-Bass, 2014); T. Newcombe, "Is the Cost of 311 Systems Worth the Price of Knowing?," *Governing*, March 2014.
4. E. Ostrom, "Crossing the Great Divide: Coproduction, Synergy, and Development," *World Development* 24 (1996):1073–1087; G. P. Whitaker, "Coproduction: Citizen Participation in Service Delivery," *Public Administration Review* 40 (1980): 240–246.
5. Pew Research Center, *The Web at 25 in the U. S.,* February 27, 2014.
6. United Nations, *2014 Revision of the World Urbanization Prospects,* July 10, 2014.
7. L. Bettencourt and G. B. West, "A Unified Theory of Urban Living," *Nature* 467, no. 7318 (2010): 912–913.
8. Goldsmith and Crawford, *The Responsive City.*
9. A. M. Townsend, *Smart Cities* (New York: W. W. Norton, 2013).
10. A. M. Townsend, *Making Sense of the New Urban Science* (New York: NYU Wagner Rudin Center for Transportation Policy and Management, 2015).
11. P. Szanton, *Not Well Advised* (New York: Russell Sage Foundation and the Ford Foundation, 1981).
12. M. Batty, "The Pulse of the City," *Environment and Planning B: Planning and Design* 37 (2010): 575–577.

13. D. Boyd and K. Crawford, "Critical Questions for Big Data: Provocations for a Cultural, Technological, and Scholarly Phenomenon," *Information, Communication and Society* 15, no. 5 (2012): 662–679; D. Lazer R. Kennedy, G. King, and A. Vespignani, "The Parable of Google Flu: Traps in Big Data Analysis," *Science* 343, no. 6176 (2014): 1203–1205; R. Wagner-Pacifici, J. W. Mohr, and R. L. Breiger, "Ontologies, Methodologies, and New Uses of Big Data in the Social and Cultural Sciences," *Big Data and Society*, July–December 2015, 1–11.

14. Newcombe, "Is the Cost of 311 Systems Worth the Price of Knowing?"

15. J. Legewie and M. Schaeffer, "Contested Boundaries: Explaining Where Ethnoracial Diversity Provokes Neighborhood Conflict," *American Journal of Sociology* 122, no 1 (2016): 125–161.

16. A. E. Lerman and V. Weaver, "Staying Out of Sight? Concentrated Policing and Local Political Action," *Annals of the American Academy of Political and Social Science* 651 (2014): 202–219.

17. J. R. Levine and C. Gershenson, "From Political to Material Inequality: Race, Immigration, and Request for Public Goods," *Sociological Forum* 29 (2014): 607–627.

18. D. Offenhuber, "Infrastructure Legibility—A Comparative Analysis of Open311-Based Citizen Feedback Systems," *Cambridge Journal of Regions, Economy and Society* 8, no. 1 (2015): 93–112.

19. S. L. Minkoff, "NYC 311: A Tract-Level Analysis of Citizen-Government Contacting in New York City," *Urban Affairs Review* 52, no. 2 (2016): 211–246.

20. City of Boston, *CityScore 2016,* April 20, 2016, http://www.cityofboston.gov/cityscore/.

21. T. Trenkner, "Public Officials of the Year: Nigel Jacob and Chris Osgood, Co-chairs, Mayor's Office of New Urban Mechanics, City of Boston," *Governing,* October 27, 2011.

22. M. Reis, "5 U.S. Cities Using Technology to Become Smart and Connected," *Forbes,* August 15, 2014; B. Cohen, "The 10 Smartest Cities in North America," *Co.Design,* December 3, 2012.

23. G. Hardin, "The Tragedy of the Commons," *Science* 162, no. 3859 (1968): 1243–1248.

24. C. Booth, *Life and Labour of the People in London* (London: Macmillan, 1903); J. Jacobs, *The Death and Life of Great American Cities* (New York: Random House, 1961).

25. J. Q. Wilson and G. L. Kelling, "Broken Windows: The Police and Neighborhood Safety," *Atlantic Monthly* 127 (March 1982): 29–38.

26. R. J. Sampson, *Great American City: Chicago and the Enduring Neighborhood Effect* (Chicago: University of Chicago Press, 2012).

27. E. Ostrom, J. Burger, C. B. Field, R. B. Norgaard, and D. Policansky, "Revisiting the Commons: Local Lessons, Global Challenges," *Science* 284, no. 5412 (1999): 278–282; E. Ostrom, *Understanding Institutional Diversity* (Princeton, NJ: Princeton University Press, 2005); E. Ostrom, *Governing the Commons: The Evolution of Institutions for Collective Action* (Cambridge, MA: Harvard University Press, 1990).

28. R. J. Sampson and W. B. Groves, "Community Structure and Crime: Testing Social Disorganization Theory," *American Journal of Sociology* 94, no. 4 (1989): 774–802; R. Bursik and H. G. Grasmick, *Neighborhoods and Crime: The Dimensions of Effective Community Control* (New York: Lexington Books, 1993); E. Silver and L. L. Miller, "Sources of Informal Social Control in Chicago Neighborhoods," *Criminology* 42, no. 3 (2004): 551–583.

29. R. B. Taylor, *Human Territorial Functioning: An Empirical, Evolutionary Perspective on Individual and Small Group Territorial Cognitions, Behaviors and Consequences* (Cambridge: Cambridge University Press, 1988); B. B. Brown and I. Altman, "Territoriality and Residential Crime," in *Environmental Criminology*, ed. P. J. Brantingham and P. L. Brantingham (Beverly Hills, CA: Sage, 1981), 56–76; B. B. Brown, "Territoriality," in *Handbook of Environmental Psychology*, ed. D. Stokols and I. Altman (New York: Wiley, 1987), 505–531.

30. R. Ardrey, *The Territorial Imperative* (New York: Atheneum, 1966).

31. Taylor, *Human Territorial Functioning;* Brown, "Territoriality"; J. J. Edney, "Human Territoriality," *Psychological Bulletin* 81, no. 12 (1974): 959–975; I. Altman, "Territorial Behavior in Humans: An Analysis of the Concept," in *Spatial Behavior of Older People*, ed. L. A. Pastalan and D. A. Carson (Ann Arbor: University of Michigan Press, 1970), 1–24.

32. B. B. Brown and C. M. Werner, "Social Cohesiveness, Territoriality and Holiday Decorations: The Influence of Cul-de-Sacs," *Environment and Behavior* 17 (1985): 539–565; C. M. Werner, S. Peterson-Lewis, and B. B. Brown, "Inferences about Homeowners' Sociability: Impact of Christmas Decorations and Other Cues," *Journal of Environmental Psychology* 9, no. 4 (1989): 279–296; M. O. Caughy, P. J. O'Campo, and J. Patterson, "A Brief Observational Measure for Urban Neighborhoods," *Health and Place* 7 (2001): 225–236; P. B. Harris and B. B. Brown, "The Home and Identity Display: Interpreting Resident Territoriality from Home Exteriors," *Journal of Environmental Psychology* 16 (1996): 187–203.

33. R. B. Parks, P. C. Baker, L. Kiser, R. Oakerson, E. Ostrom, V. Ostrom, S. L. Percy, M. B. Vandivort, G. P. Whitaker, and R. Wilson, "Consumers as Coproducers of Public Services: Some Economic and Institutional Considerations," *Policy Studies Journal* 9 (1982): 1001–1011; E. Ostrom,

"Metropolitan Reform: Propositions Derived from Two Traditions," *Social Science Quarterly* 53 (1972): 474–493.

34. Ostrom, "Crossing the Great Divide."

35. A. L. Schneider, "Coproduction of Public and Private Safety: An Analysis of Bystander Intervention, 'Protective Neighboring,' and Personal Protection," *Western Political Quarterly* 40 (1987): 611–630; D. H. Folz, "Recycling Solid Waste: Citizen Participation in the Design of a Coproduced Program," *State and Local Government Review* 23 (1991): 92–102; M. J. Marschall, "Parent Involvement and Educational Outcomes for Latino Students," *Review of Policy Research* 23 (2006): 1053–1076; K. J. Powers and F. Thompson, "Managing Coprovision: Using Expectancy Theory to Overcome the Free-Rider Problem," *Journal of Public Administration Research and Theory* 4, no. 2 (1994): 179–196.

36. C. H. Levine, "Citizenship and Service Delivery: The Promise of Coproduction," *Public Administration Review* 44 (1984): 178–187; T. Bovaird, "Beyond Engagement and Participation: User and Community Coproduction of Public Services," *Public Administration Review* 67, no. 5 (2007): 846–860.

37. J. A. Fodor, *Modularity of Mind: An Essay on Faculty Psychology* (Cambridge, MA: MIT Press, 1983); J. Tooby and L. Cosmides, "The Psychological Foundations of Culture," in *The Adapted Mind: Evolutionary Psychology and the Generation of Culture,* ed. J. H. Barkow, L. Cosmides, and J. Tooby (New York: Oxford University Press, 1992), 19–136.

38. S. P. Osborne and K. Strokosch, "It Takes Two to Tango? Understanding the Co-production of Public Services by Integrating the Services Management and Public Administration Perspectives," *British Journal of Management* 24 (2013): S31–S47; S. P. Osborne, "Delivering Public Services: Time for a New Theory?," *Public Management Review* 12 (2010): 1–10.

39. Lerman and Weaver, "Staying Out of Sight?"; Levine and Gershenson, "From Political to Material Inequality"; Minkoff, "NYC 311"; B. Y. Clark, J. L. Brudney, and S. G. Jang, "Coproduction of Government Services and the New Information Technology: Investigating the Distributional Biases," *Public Administration Review* 73 (2013): 687–701; J. Fountain, "Connecting Technologies to Citizenship," in *Technology and the Resilience of Metropolitan Regions,* ed. M. A. Pagano (Champaign: University of Illinois Press, 2014), 25–51.

1. A Data-Driven Approach to Urban Science and Policy

1. Then mayor Martin O'Malley (later governor of the state of Maryland) claims he borrowed the idea from Chicago, but Baltimore was the first to

fully adopt the 311 system as we know it now, and the one that has been in continuous operation longest.

2. Based on a research project conducted by a graduate student in Northeastern University's master of urban informatics program. Data available upon request.

3. S. Johnson, "What a Hundred Million Calls to 311 Reveal about New York," *Wired*, November 1, 2010.

4. T. Newcombe, "Is the Cost of 311 Systems Worth the Price of Knowing?," *Governing*, March 2014.

5. Because the list is not exhaustive, to those who would like such a treatment, I recommend Anthony Townsend's report on "the new urban science" in A. M. Townsend, *Making Sense of the New Urban Science* (New York: NYU Wagner Rudin Center for Transportation Policy and Management, 2015). That said, given the rapid growth of the field, even this work might now be considered outdated.

6. R. J. Sampson, S. W. Raudenbush, and F. Earls, "Neighborhoods and Violent Crime: A Multilevel Study of Collective Efficacy," *Science* 277 (1997): 918–924.

7. A. A. Braga, A. V. Papachristos, and D. M. Hureau, "The Concentration and Stability of Gun Violence at Micro Places in Boston, 1980–2008," *Journal of Quantitative Criminology* 26 (2010): 33–53.

8. J. Patinkin, "These Digital Maps Could Revolutionize Nairobi's Minibus Taxi System," *Next City*, February 11, 2014.

9. M. Batty, "The Pulse of the City," *Environment and Planning B: Planning and Design* 37 (2010): 575–577.

10. S. Grauwin, S. Sobolevsky, S. Moritz, I. Gódor, and C. Ratti, "Towards a Comparative Science of Cities: Using Mobile Traffic Records in New York, London and Hong Kong." arXiv, 2014. 1406.440 [physics.soc-ph].

11. K. Batygin and M. E. Brown, "Evidence for a Distant Giant Planet in the Solar System." *Astronomical Journal* 151, no. 2 (2016).

12. D. Lazer et al., "Computational Social Science," *Nature* 323 (2009): 721–723.

13. A. P. Masucci, K. Stanilov, and M. Batty, "Limited Urban Growth: London's Street Network Dynamics since the 18th Century," *Public Library of Science* 8, no. 8 (2013): e69469.

14. A. Mavrogianni, A., et al., "The Comfort, Energy and Health Implications of London's Urban Heat Island," *Building Services Engineering Research and Technology* 32, no. 1 (2011): 35–52.

15. D. Offenhuber, D. Lee, M. I. Wolf, S. Phithakkitnukoon, A. Biderman, and C. Ratti, "Putting Matter in Place," *Journal of the American Planning Association* 78, no. 2 (2012): 173–196; D. Offenhuber, *Waste Is Information* (Cambridge, MA: MIT Press, 2017).

16. P. Santi, G. Resta, M. Szell, S. Sobolevsky, S. H. Strogatz, and C. Ratti, "Quantifying the Benefits of Vehicle Pooling with Shareability Networks," *Proceedings of the National Academy of Sciences* 111 (2014): 13290–13294.

17. https://www.youtube.com/watch?v=MqEXDzlCltw.

18. A. A. Braga, D. M. Hureau, and A. V. Papachristos, "The Relevance of Micro Places to Citywide Robbery Trends: A Longitudinal Analysis of Robbery Incidents at Street Corners and Block Faces in Boston," *Journal of Research in Crime and Delinquency* 48, no. 1 (2011): 7–32.

19. F. J. Odling-Smee, K. N. Laland, and M. W. Feldman, *Niche Construction: The Neglected Process in Evolution* (Princeton, NJ: Princeton University Press, 2003).

20. https://www.northeastern.edu/csshresearch/bostonarearesearchinitiative/baris-spring-conference-2018/.

21. S. Goldsmith and S. Crawford, *The Responsive City: Engaging Communities through Data-Smart Governance* (San Francisco: Jossey-Bass, 2014).

22. http://opengrid.io/.

23. https://www.boston.gov/cityscore.

24. T. Small, "South Bend Saves Millions with Smart Sewers," *ABC57 News,* 2016.

25. Z. Friend, "Predictive Policing: Using Technology to Reduce Crime," *FBI Law Enforcement Bulletin,* April 9, 2013.

26. City of Boston, "Ordinance to Eliminate Public Nuisance Precipitated by Problem Properties in the City," in *Ordinances,* ed. Boston City Council (Boston: City of Boston, 2011), Chapter 16–55.

27. City of Minneapolis, MN, *Problem Properties Unit,* 2015, http://www.minneapolismn.gov/ppu/.

28. Though the benefits from these changes are mixed. See New York City Department of Transportation, *Making Safer Streets* (New York: New York City Department of Transportation, 2013).

29. For example, the effects of homelessness on school success. See J. Fantuzzo and S. Perlman, "The Unique Impact of Out-of-Home Placement and the Mediating Effects of Child Maltreatment and Homelessness on Early School Success," *Children and Youth Services Review* 29 (2007): 941–960.

30. J. Lin, "Center in Phila. Helps Battle Veteran Homelessness," *Philadelphia Inquirer,* January 2, 2014.

31. E. M. Kitzmiller, "The Circle of Love: South Carolina's Integrated Data System," IDS Case Study (Philadelphia: Actionable Intelligence for Social Policy, University of Pennsylvania, 2014).

32. K. Giammarise, "Allegheny County DHS Using Algorithm to Assist in Child Welfare Screening," *Pittsburgh Post-Gazette,* April 9, 2017.

33. A. M. Townsend, *Smart Cities* (New York: Norton, 2013).

34. E. Gordon and J. Baldwin-Philippi, "Playful Civic Learning: Enabling Lateral Trust and Reflection in Game-Based Public Participation," *International Journal of Communication* 8 (2014): 759–786.

35. Y. Cabannes, "Participatory Budgeting: A Significant Contribution to Participatory Democracy," *Environment and Urbanization* 16 (2004): 27–46.

36. T. Kuhn, *The Structure of Scientific Revolutions* (Chicago: University of Chicago Press, 1962, reprinted 1996).

37. R. E. Park and E. W. Burgess, *The City* (Chicago: University of Chicago Press, 1925).

38. L. Bettencourt, "The Kind of Problem a City Is: New Perspectives on the Nature of Cities from Complex Systems Theory," in *Decoding the City*, ed. D. Offenhuber and C. Ratti (Basel: Birkhauser, 2014), 168–179; L. Bettencourt and G. B. West, "A Unified Theory of Urban Living," *Nature* 467, no. 7318 (2010): 912–913.

39. Park and Burgess, *The City*.

40. Sampson, Raudenbush, and Earls, "Neighborhoods and Violent Crime"; T. Leventhal and J. Brooks-Gunn, "The Neighborhoods They Live In: The Effect of Neighborhood Residence on Child and Adolescent Outcomes," *Psychological Bulletin* 126, no. 2 (2000): 309–337; R. J. Sampson, *Great American City: Chicago and the Enduring Neighborhood Effect* (Chicago: University of Chicago Press, 2012); A. V. Diez Roux and C. Mair, "Neighborhoods and Health," *Annals of the New York Academy of Sciences* 1186 (2010): 125–145.

41. M. Schlapfer, L. M. A. Bettencourt, S. Grauwin, M. Raschke, R. Claxton, Z. Smoreda, G. B. West, and C. Ratti, "The Scaling of Human Interactions with City Size," *Journal of the Royal Society Interface* 11 (2014); L. Bettencourt, J. Lobo, D. Helbing, C. Kühnert, and G. B. West, "Growth, Innovation, Scaling, and the Pace of Life in Cities," *Proceedings of the National Academy of Sciences* 104 (2007): 7301–7306.

42. Lazer et al., "Computational Social Science."

43. A. E. Lerman and V. Weaver, "Staying Out of Sight? Concentrated Policing and Local Political Action," *Annals of the American Academy of Political and Social Science* 651 (2014): 202–219.

2. "Seeing" the City through "Big Data"

1. This has been presented with greater technical detail in D. T. O'Brien, R. J. Sampson, and C. Winship, "Ecometrics in the Age of Big Data: Measuring and Assessing 'Broken Windows' Using Administrative Records," *Sociological Methodology* 45 (2015): 101–147.

2. D. Boyd and K. Crawford, "Critical Questions for Big Data: Provocations for a Cultural, Technological, and Scholarly Phenomenon," *Information, Communication and Society* 15, no. 5 (2012): 662–679; N. M. Richards and J. H. King, "Big Data Ethics," *Wake Forest Law Review* 49 (2014): 393–432; R. Kitchin, *The Data Revolution* (Woburn, MA: SAGE Publications, 2014); O. Tene and J. Polonetsky, "Big Data for All: Privacy and User Control in the Age of Analytics," *Northwestern Journal of Technology and Intellectual Property* 11, no. 5 (2013): 240–273.

3. R. Kitchin and G. McArdle, "What Makes Big Data, Big Data? Exploring the Ontological Characteristics of 26 Datasets," *Big Data and Society* 3, no. 1 (January–June 2016):1–10.

4. C. Anderson, "The End of Theory: The Data Deluge Makes the Scientific Method Obsolete," *Wired,* June 23, 2008.

5. M. Pigliucci, "The End of Theory in Science?" *EMBO Reports* 10, no. 6 (2009): 534.

6. D. Lazer, R. Kennedy, G. King, and A. Vespignani, "The Parable of Google Flu: Traps in Big Data Analysis," *Science* 343, no. 6176 (2014): 1203–1205.

7. C. Booth, *Life and Labour of the People in London* (London: Macmillan, 1903); H. Mayhew, *London Labor and the London Poor* (London: Griffin, Bohn, 1862); R. E. Park and E. W. Burgess, *The City* (Chicago: University of Chicago Press, 1925).

8. But see R. B. Taylor, *Breaking Away from Broken Windows: Baltimore Neighborhoods and the Nationwide Fight against Crime, Grime, Fear, and Decline* (Boulder, CO: Westview Press, 2001).

9. S. W. Raudenbush and R. J. Sampson, "Ecometrics: Toward a Science of Assessing Ecological Settings, with Application to the Systematic Social Observation of Neighborhoods," *Sociological Methodology* 29, no. 1 (1999): 1–41; R. J. Sampson and S. W. Raudenbush, "Systematic Social Observation of Public Spaces: A New Look at Disorder in Urban Neighbor-hoods," *American Journal of Sociology* 105, no. 3 (1999): 603–651; R. J. Sampson, S. W. Raudenbush, and F. Earls, "Neighborhoods and Violent Crime: A Multilevel Study of Collective Efficacy," *Science* 277, no. 5328 (1997): 918–924.

10. D. Cohen, S. Spear, R. Scribner, P. Kissinger, K. Mason, and J. Wildgren, "'Broken windows' and the Risk of Gonorrhea," *American Journal of Public Health* 90, no. 2 (2000): 230–236; T. Leventhal and J. Brooks-Gunn, "The Neighborhoods They Live In: The Effect of Neighborhood Residence on Child and Adolescent Outcomes," *Psychological Bulletin* 126, no. 2 (2000): 309–337; C. R. Browning, B. Soller, and A. L. Jackson, "Neighborhoods and Adolescent Health-Risk Behavior: An Ecological Network Approach," *Social Science and Medicine* 125 (2015): 163–172; I. Kawachi and L. F.

Berkman, eds., *Neighborhoods and Health* (Oxford: Oxford University Press, 2003); C. L. Gibson, C. J. Sullivan, S. Jones, and A. R. Piquero, "'Does It Take a Village?' Assessing Neighborhood Influences on Children's Self-Control," *Journal of Research in Crime and Delinquency* 47, no. 1 (2010): 31–62.

11. The full analysis is presented in greater detail in O'Brien, Sampson, and Winship, "Ecometrics in the Age of Big Data."

12. https://dataverse.harvard.edu/dataset.xhtml?persistentId=hdl:1902.1/18907.

13. Boyd and Crawford, "Critical Questions for Big Data"; W. G. Skogan, *Disorder and Decline* (Berkeley: University of California Press, 1992).

14. J. Q. Wilson and G. L. Kelling, "Broken Windows: The Police and Neighborhood Safety," *Atlantic Monthly* 127 (March 1982): 29–38.

15. M. Wen, L. C. Hawkley, and J. T. Cacioppo, "Objective and Perceived Neighborhood Environment, Individual SES and Psychosocial Factors, and Self-Rated Health: An Analysis of Older Adults in Cook County, Illinois," *Social Science and Medicine* 63 (2006): 2575–2590; T. J. Haney, "'Broken Windows' and Self-Esteem: Subjective Understandings of Neighborhood Poverty and Disorder," *Social Science Research* 36, no. 3 (2007): 968–994; K. P. Theall, Z. H. Brett, E. A. Shirtcliff, E. C. Dunn, and S. S. Drury, "Neighborhood Disorder and Telomeres: Connecting Children's Exposure to Community Level Stress and Cellular Response," *Social Science and Medicine* 85 (2013): 50–58; M. S. Mujahid, M. Shen, D. Gowda, S. A. Jackson, B. Sanchez, A. V. Diez Roux, S. Shea, and D. R. Jacobs, "Relation between Neighborhood Environments and Obesity in the Multi-ethnic Study of Atherosclerosis," *American Journal of Epidemiology* 167, no. 11 (2008): 1349–1357; A. Dulin-Keita, K. Casazza, J. R. Fernandez, M. I. Goran, and B. Gower, "Do Neighbourhoods Matter? Neighbourhood Disorder and Long-term Trends in Serum Cortisol Levels," *Journal of Epidemiology and Community Health* 66, no. 1 (2012): 24–29.

16. Cohen et al., "'Broken Windows' and the Risk of Gonorrhea."

17. H. Meltzer, L. Doos, P. Vostanis, T. J. Ford, and R. Goodman, "The Mental Health of Children Who Witness Domestic Violence," *Child and Family Social Work* 14 (2009): 491–501.

18. Sampson and Raudenbush, "Systematic Social Observation of Public Spaces."

19. D. S. Massey, "Segregation and Stratification: A Biosocial Perspective," *Du Bois Review* 1 (2004): 7–25.

20. Raudenbush and Sampson, "Ecometrics."

21. Taylor, *Breaking Away from Broken Windows*, 5.

22. Taylor, *Breaking Away from Broken Windows*; Cohen et al., "'Broken Windows' and the Risk of Gonorrhea"; Skogan, *Disorder and Decline;* D. T. O'Brien and D. S. Wilson, "Community Perception: The Ability to Assess the Safety of Unfamiliar Neighborhoods and Respond Adaptively," *Journal of Personality and Social Psychology* 100, no. 4 (2011): 606–620; C. E. Ross and J. Mirowsky, "Disorder and Decay: The Concept and Measurement of Perceived Neighborhood Disorder," *Urban Affairs Review* 34 (1999): 412–432; M. O. Caughy, P. J. O'Campo, and J. Patterson, "A Brief Observational Measure for Urban Neighborhoods," *Health and Place* 7 (2001): 225–236; C. D. M. Furr-Holden, M. J. Smart, J. L. Pokorni, N. S. Ialongo, P. J. Leaf, H. D. Holder, and J. C. Anthony, "The NIfETy Method for Environmental Assessment of Neighborhood-Level Indicators of Violence, Alcohol, and Other Drug Exposure," *Prevention Science* 9, no. 4 (2008): 245–255; A. G. Rundle, M. D. M. Bader, C. A. Richards, K. M. Neckerman, and J. Teitler, "Using Google Street View to Audit Neighborhood Environments," *American Journal of Preventive Medicine* 40, no. 1 (2011): 94–100.

23. All cases that had geographic reference and were received between March 1, 2010, when a standardized data entry form was implemented, and June 29, 2012. An additional 30,855 cases had no geographic reference.

24. https://dataverse.harvard.edu/dataset.xhtml?persistentId=hdl:1902.1 /18907.

25. Ross and Mirowsky, "Disorder and Decay."

26. All items loaded on the given factor at .4 or greater, except for four exceptions that were maintained based on conceptual similarity: abandoned buildings loaded at .36 on the factor of uncivil use; requests to empty a litter basket loaded >.3 on both trash and graffiti, and was maintained on the former factor based on its substantive content; two items were added to the housing factor, as they were conceptually identical to the definition of the factor and likely did not load in the factor analysis because of their low frequency.

27. We summed counts for all case types within each of the five factors for each neighborhood. These measures had substantial outliers and were all log-transformed before analysis. We then conducted a pair of confirmatory factor analyses that compared a one-factor structure in which all five measures loaded together to the two-factor structure. The two-factor model was superior by all measures. It had better fit (CFI = .82 vs. 61; SRMR = .07 vs. 10; $\Delta\chi^2_{df=1} = 89.27, p < .001$), and accounted for 42 percent of the variation across factors, as opposed to 26 percent. One will note that although the two-factor model was stronger, it still had a

poor fit. Because the hypothesis in question was the efficacy of a one- or two-factor model, there were no assumptions that the components of each were completely independent. Thus, we took the exploratory step of examining modification indices, leading to the addition of a covariance between uncivil use and trash, greatly improving fit (CFI = .95, SRMR = .05, $\chi^2_{df=5}$ = 24.26, $p < .001$). The parameter estimates presented in Figure 2.1 are from this final model.

28. J. McCorriston, D. Jurgens, and D. Ruths, "Organizations Are Users Too: Characterizing and Detecting the Presence of Organizations on Twitter," in *Proceedings of the 9th International AAAI Conference on Web and Social Media*, ed. D. Quercia and B. Hogan (Palo Alto, CA: Association for the Advancement of Artificial Intelligence, 2015), 650–653.

29. S. Messick, "Validity of Psychological Assessment: Validation of Inferences from Persons' Responses and Performances as Scientific Inquiry into Score Meaning," *American Psychologist* 50, no. 9 (1995): 741–749.

30. Defined as intersection to intersection or intersection to dead end.

31. Our audits covered all streets in a neighborhood, leading us to observe streetlight outages and garbage in many different contexts, from residential streets, to commercial streets, to isolated industrial areas, that might be more or less likely to elicit 311 reports, independent of the local community's generalized tendency to do so. For the sidewalk audits, it was also necessary to control for the quality of each sidewalk: three reports of a sidewalk with a score of 50 is a different reflection of a community's responsiveness to public issues than three reports of a sidewalk with a score of 10. To address these issues, we utilized multilevel models that nested streets within neighborhoods (tracts for sidewalks and census block groups for streetlight outages) and could accommodate predictors at both levels. See S. W. Raudenbush, A. S. Bryk, Y. F. Cheong, and R. T. Congdon Jr., *HLM 6: Hierarchical Linear and Nonlinear Modeling* (Lincolnwood, IL: Scientific Software International, 2004). The second-level residuals (i.e., the expected score for each neighborhood after controlling for street-level characteristics) were then used as the neighborhood-level estimates of civic response rate.

32. A test of the variance component for two-month intervals of the second level was significant ($\chi^2_{df=53}$ = 80.80, $p < .01$) and was greater than the two other intervals that also featured significant or nearly significant variation (one month: $\chi^2_{df=54}$ = 78.39, $p < .05$; two weeks: $\chi^2_{df=54}$ = 68.61, $p < .10$).

33. Because most sidewalks elicited zero reports, we compared two models, each controlling for sidewalk quality, one predicting the likelihood of generating any requests (a logit model) and the other predicting the

number of requests across those with one or more (a log-link model). There was significant variation between tracts in a sidewalk generating any reports, controlling for the sidewalk quality index ($\chi^2_{df=155}$ = 425.16, $p < .001$), but not in the number of reports per sidewalk ($\chi^2_{df=152}$ = 179.58, $p < .10$), making the former the preferable measure. In addition, sidewalk quality did not significantly predict more reports for a sidewalk, suggesting it is a less effective measure for the purposes here ($\beta = .001$, $p = ns$, odds ratio = 1.001).

34. S. Verba, K. L. Schlozman, and H. E. Brady, *Voice and Equality: Civic Volunteerism in American Politics* (Cambridge, MA: Harvard University Press, 1995); R. Putnam, *Making Democracy Work: Civic Traditions in Modern Italy* (Princeton, NJ: Princeton University Press, 1993).

35. For example, total road length, dead ends. This idea was developed with my colleague Jeremy Levine. See also J. R. Levine and C. Gershenson, "From Political to Material Inequality: Race, Immigration, and Request for Public Goods," *Sociological Forum* 29 (2014): 607–627.

36. This list was expanded to 77 case types in later studies of custodianship that covered a longer time period of the data. See Chapter 3 for a full list.

37. We regressed the number of snowplow requests (log-transformed to adjust for a skewed distribution) on the total population, road length, and the length of dead end roads and extracted the residuals as an adjusted measure of snowplow requests.

38. To be concurrent with the audits, the 311 indicators are calculated using only reports from 2011, comprising 161,703 cases with geographic reference across 154 case types. In this time, there were 29,439 constituent users, accounting for 38 percent of all requests for service. Users who made one or more reports as a department member at any time (including 2010 or 2012) were removed because city employees differ from other constituents in their motivation for making reports. This excluded five individuals, a number that is low because for many employee-specific case types user IDs were stripped before data sharing. Two CBGs were excluded from analysis because there were concerns that calls from there might not reflect usage of the CRM system by actual residents: (1) the CBG that contains City Hall, because many reports without an address are attributed to that location, and (2) the CBG that contains a large park, zoo, and golf course but includes the houses that ring the park.

39. The model analyzed those 195 CBGs with a measure for propensity to report streetlight outages and had good fit (CFI = .95, SRMR = .06, $\chi^2_{df=9}$ = 25.44, $p < .01$).

40. We again used multilevel models to nest observations in neighborhoods and account for street characteristics (see note 31 for more details).

Because sampling for the garbage audit occurred at the tract level, CBGs varied in the number of street segments that were rated. In order to be certain that neighborhood-level measures were reliable, the ensuing analysis was limited to the 196 CBGs with ten or more street segment measures. See also Sampson and Raudenbush, "Systematic Social Observation of Public Spaces."

41. These measures were log-transformed to better approximate normality.
42. $n = 135$ residential CBGs.
43. The response rate was standardized and centered before the interaction was calculated. The physical disorder measures were left uncentered, with a minimum of zero, so that the response rate would adjust up or down in proportion to the total number of actual reports.
44. Because the time points of these data sources vary, we analyzed their relationship to the CRM-based measure for the most concurrent year: 2010 for the American Community Survey and Boston Neighborhood Survey, and 2011 for 911. Models were run for $N = 121$ residential census tracts.
45. Raudenbush and Sampson, "Ecometrics."
46. Taylor, *Breaking Away from Broken Windows;* R. J. Sampson and S. W. Raudenbush, "Seeing Disorder: Neighborhood Stigma and the Social Construction of 'Broken Windows,'" *Social Psychology Quarterly* 67, no. 4 (2004): 317–342; L. Franzini, M. O. Caughy, S. M. Nettles, and P. O'Campo, "Perceptions of Disorder: Contributions of Neighborhood Characteristics to Subjective Perceptions of Disorder," *Journal of Environmental Psychology* 28, no. 1 (2008): 83–93; B. B. Brown, D. D. Perkins, and G. Brown, "Incivilities, Place Attachment and Crime: Block and Individual Effects," *Journal of Environmental Psychology* 24 (2004): 359–371.
47. O'Brien, Sampson, and Winship, "Ecometrics in the Age of Big Data."
48. For each interval setting, the original database was split into intervals of the given size, starting with March 1, 2010, and ending with the last complete interval. Exemplars were always measured for a given time interval as the number of public reports in a region obtaining exemplar status over the course of the 365 days preceding the end of the interval.
49. One will note that these require the incorporation of the number of exemplars, measured for the full year preceding the last day of the given time window. Consequently, the first time window analyzed must be that which ends at or after the end of the twelfth month of the available database, diminishing the number of measurements per tract. For this reason, this analysis does not examine change over time.
50. Lazer et al., "The Parable of Google Flu."

51. D. T. O'Brien and R. J. Sampson, "Public and Private Spheres of Neighborhood Disorder: Assessing Pathways to Violence Using Large-Scale Digital Records," *Journal of Research in Crime and Delinquency* 52, no. 4 (2015): 486–510.

52. D. T. O'Brien and B. W. Montgomery, "The Other Side of the Broken Window: A Methodology That Translates Building Permits into an Ecometric of Investment by Community Members," *American Journal of Community Psychology* 55 (2015): 25–36.

53. J. Legewie and M. Schaeffer, "Contested Boundaries: Explaining Where Ethnoracial Diversity Provokes Neighborhood Conflict," *American Journal of Sociology* 122, no. 1 (2016): 125–161.

54. D. Quercia, R. Schifanella, L. M. Aiello, and K. McLean, "Smelly Maps: The Digital Life of Urban Smellscapes," in *Proceedings of the 9th International AAAI Conference on Web and Social Media,* ed. D. Quercia and B. Hogan (Palo Alto, CA: Association for the Advancement of Artificial Intelligence, 2015), 327–336; D. Quercia, N. K. O'Hare, and H. Cramer, "Aesthetic Capital: What Makes London Look Beautiful, Quiet, and Happy?," in *Proceedings of the 17th ACM Conference on Computer Supported Cooperative Work* (New York: ACM, 2014), 945–955; L. M. Aiello, R. Schifanella, D. Quercia, and F. Aletta, "Chatty Maps: Constructing Sound Maps of Urban Areas from Social Media Data," *Royal Society Open Science Journal* 3 (2016).

55. J. D. Boy and J. Uitermark, "How to Study the City on Instagram," *PLoS One* 11, no. 6 (2016): e0158161.

56. D. Lazer et al., "Computational Social Science," *Science* 323, no. 5915 (2009): 721–723.

3. Caring for One's Territory

1. M. Rawson, *Eden on the Charles* (Cambridge, MA: Harvard University Press, 2010).

2. G. Hardin, "The Tragedy of the Commons," *Science* 162, no. 3859 (1968): 1243–1248.

3. F. Alcock, "Bargaining, Uncertainty, and Property Rights in Fisheries," *World Politics* 54, no. 4 (2002): 437–461–; X. Basurto, "How Locally Designed Access and Use Controls Can Prevent the Tragedy of the Commons in a Mexican Small-Scale Fishing Community," *Society and Natural Resources* 18, no. 7 (2005): 643–659; A. Begossi, "Fishing Spots and Sea Tenure— Incipient Forms of Local Management in Atlantic Forest Coastal Communities," *Human Ecology* 23, no. 3 (1995): 387–406; F. Berkes, "Local-Level

Management and the Commons Problem: A Comparative Study of Turkish Coastal Fisheries," *Marine Policy* 10, no. 3 (1986): 215–229.

4. E. Ostrom, *Governing the Commons: The Evolution of Institutions for Collective Action* (Cambridge, MA: Harvard University Press, 1990).

5. S. F. Pires and W. D. Moreto, "Preventing Wildlife Crimes: Solutions That Can Overcome the 'Tragedy of the Commons,'" *European Journal on Criminal Policy and Research* 17, no. 2 (2011): 101–123.

6. P. Kollock and M. Smith, "Managing the Virtual Commons," in *Computer-Mediated Communication: Linguistic, Social, and Cross-Cultural Perspectives,* ed. S. H. Herring (Amsterdam: Benjamins, 1996), 109–128.

7. H. Demsetz, "Toward a Theory of Property Rights," *American Economic Review* 62 (1967): 347–359; O. E. G. Johnson, "Economic Analysis, the Legal Framework and Land Tenure Systems," *Journal of Law and Economics* 15 (1972): 259–276; R. J. Smith, "Resolving the Tragedy of the Commons by Creating Private Property Rights in Wildlife," *CATO Journal* 1 (1981): 439–468.

8. See, for example, W. Ophuls, "Leviathan or Oblivion," in *Toward a Steady State Economy,* ed. H. E. Daly,(San Francisco: Freeman, 1973), 215–230; R. L. Heilbroner, *An Inquiry into the Human Prospect* (New York: Norton, 1974); D. W. Ehrenfeld, *Conserving Life on Earth* (Oxford: Oxford University Press, 1972).

9. Ostrom, *Governing the Commons*; E. Ostrom, J. Burger, C. B. Field, R. B. Norgaard, and D. Policansky, "Revisiting the Commons: Local Lessons, Global Challenges," *Science* 284, no. 5412 (1999): 278–282; E. Ostrom, *Understanding Institutional Diversity* (Princeton, NJ: Princeton University Press, 2005).

10. Ostrom, *Governing the Commons.*

11. R. J. Sampson, *Great American City: Chicago and the Enduring Neighborhood Effect* (Chicago: University of Chicago Press, 2012); R. J. Sampson and S. W. Raudenbush, "Systematic Social Observation of Public Spaces: A New Look at Disorder in Urban Neighborhoods," *American Journal of Sociology* 105, no. 3 (1999): 603–651; R. J. Sampson, S. W. Raudenbush, and F. Earls, "Neighborhoods and Violent Crime: A Multilevel Study of Collective Efficacy," *Science* 277, no. 5328 (1997): 918–924; J. D. Morenoff, R. J. Sampson, and S. W. Raudenbush, "Neighborhood Inequality, Collective Efficacy, and the Spatial Dynamics of Urban Violence," *Criminology* 39, no. 3 (2001): 517–560.

12. R. J. Sampson and W. B. Groves, "Community Structure and Crime: Testing Social Disorganization Theory," *American Journal of Sociology* 94, no. 4 (1989): 774–802; P. E. Bellair, "Informal Surveillance and Street Crime: A Complex Relationship," *Criminology* 38 (2000): 137–170; B. D.

Warner and P. W. Rountree, "Local Social Ties in a Community and Crime Model: Questioning the Systemic Nature of Informal Social Control," *Social Problems* 44 (1997): 520–536; W. Steenbeek and J. R. Hipp, "A Longitudinal Test of Social Disorganization Theory: Feedback Effects among Cohesion, Social Control, and Disorder," *Criminology* 49 (2011): 833–871.

13. A. Bandura, *Social Foundations of Thought and Action* (Englewood Cliffs, NJ: Prentice Hall, 1986). See also R. Wickes, J. R. Hipp, E. Sargeant, and R. Homel, "Collective Efficacy as a Task Specific Process: Examining the Relationship between Social Ties, Neighborhood Cohesion and the Capacity to Respond to Violence, Delinquency and Civic Problems," *American Journal of Community Psychology* 52 (2013): 115–127.

14. Compare J. Coleman, *The Foundations of Social Theory* (Cambridge, MA: Harvard University Press, 1990).

15. See, for example, R. Boyd, H. Gintis, S. Bowles, and P. J. Richerson, "The Evolution of Altruistic Punishment," in *Moral Sentiments and Material Interests,* ed. H. Gintis, S. Bowles, and E. Fehr (Cambridge, MA: MIT Press, 2005), 3531–3535; H. Gintis S. Bowles, R. Boyd, and E. Fehr, "Explaining Altruistic Behavior in Humans," *Evolution and Human Behavior* 24, no. 3 (2003): 153–172; O. Gurerk, B. Irlenbusch, and B. Rockenbach, "The Competitive Advantage of Sanctioning Institutions," *Science* 312, no. 5770 (2006): 108–111; M. Milinski, D. Semmann, and H. J. Krambeck, "Reputation Helps Solve the 'Tragedy of the Commons,'" *Nature* 415, no. 6870 (2002): 424–426; E. Fehr and S. Gachter, "Altruistic Punishment in Humans," *Nature* 415, no. 6868 (2002): 137–140.

16. J. Elster, *Explaining Social Behavior: More Nuts and Bolts for the Social Sciences* (Cambridge: Cambridge University Press, 2007).

17. See, for example, R. Ardrey, *The Territorial Imperative* (New York: Atheneum, 1966).

18. G. Brown, "Claiming a Corner at Work: Measuring Employee Territoriality in Their Workspaces," *Journal of Environmental Psychology* 29 (2009): 44–52.

19. For a scientific analysis of this phenomenon, see M. Costa, "Territorial Behavior in Public Settings," *Environment and Behavior* 44 (2012): 713–721.

20. J. J. Edney, "Human Territoriality," *Psychological Bulletin* 81, no. 12 (1974): 959–975; I. Altman, "Territorial Behavior in Humans: An Analysis of the Concept," in *Spatial Behavior of Older People,* ed. L. A. Pastalan and D. A. Carson (Ann Arbor: University of Michigan Press, 1970), 1–24; B. B. Brown, "Territoriality," in *Handbook of Environmental Psychology,* ed. D. Stokols and I. Altman (New York: Wiley, 1987), 505–531; R. B. Taylor, *Human Territorial Functioning: An Empirical, Evolutionary Perspective on*

Individual and Small Group Territorial Cognitions, Behaviors and Consequences (Cambridge: Cambridge University Press, 1988).

21. J. L. Pierce, T. Kostova, and K. T. Dirks, "Toward a Theory of Psychological Ownership in Organizations," *Academy of Management Review* 26, no. 2 (2001): 298–310 at 299. See also G. Brown, T. B. Lawrence, and S. L. Robinson, "Territoriality in Organizations," *Academy of Management Review* 30, no. 3 (2005): 577–594.

22. C. M. Werner, S. Peterson-Lewis, and B. B. Brown, "Inferences about Homeowners' Sociability: Impact of Christmas Decorations and other Cues," *Journal of Environmental Psychology* 9, no. 4 (1989): 279–296; B. B. Brown and C.M. Werner, "Social Cohesiveness, Territoriality and Holiday Decorations: The Influence of Cul-de-Sacs," *Environment and Behavior* 17 (1985): 539–565.

23. M. O. Caughy, P. J. O'Campo, and J. Patterson, "A Brief Observational Measure for Urban Neighborhoods," *Health and Place* 7 (2001): 225–236.

24. Brown, "Claiming a Corner at Work"; Brown, Lawrence, and Robinson, "Territoriality in Organizations."

25. J. L. Pierce and I. Jussila, "Collective Psychological Ownership within the Work and Organizational Context: Construct Introduction and Elaboration," *Journal of Organizational Behavior* 31 (2010): 810–834.

26. B. B. Brown and I. Altman, "Territoriality and Residential Crime," in *Environmental Criminology*, ed. P. J. Brantingham and P. L. Brantingham (Beverly Hills, CA: Sage, 1981), 56–76.

27. Brown and Werner, "Social Cohesiveness, Territoriality and Holiday Decorations"; P. B. Harris and B. B. Brown, "The Home and Identity Display: Interpreting Resident Territoriality from Home Exteriors," *Journal of Environmental Psychology* 16 (1996): 187–203; B. B. Brown, D. D. Perkins, and G. Brown, "Incivilities, Place Attachment and Crime: Block and Individual Effects," *Journal of Environmental Psychology* 24 (2004): 359–371; R. O. Pitner, M. Yu, and E. Brown, "Making Neighborhoods Safer: Examining Predictors of Residents' Concerns about Neighborhood Safety," *Journal of Environmental Psychology* 32 (2012): 43–49.

28. https://dataverse.harvard.edu/dataset.xhtml?persistentId=doi:10.7910 /DVN/CVKM87&version=1.0, though it is important to note that the database is regularly updated. V1 is the one used in this book.

29. The methodology that follows was originally presented on a smaller corpus of data in D. T. O'Brien, "Custodians and Custodianship in Urban Neighborhoods: A Methodology Using Reports of Public Issues Received by a City's 311 Hotline," *Environment and Behavior* 47 (2015): 304–327.

30. City employees were identified as anyone who either had at least one report whose case type included "Employee" or "Internal" in the name,

had at least one report generated by the smartphone app that allows city
employees to manage their own work queue and report new cases, or had "
.gov" or ".ma.us" in their e-mail address. This amounted to 3,320 employees. There were also 26,781 accounts with zero reports that we exclude
from analysis here. This could happen because either the person made a
report that had no geographical reference, which means we excluded it
before analysis, or because he or she created an account when downloading
the city's smartphone app BOS:311 but never used it to make a report.

31. C. J. Coulton, J. Korbin, T. Chan, and M. Su, "Mapping Residents' Percep-
tions of Neighborhood Boundaries: A Methodological Note," *American
Journal of Community Psychology* 29, no. 2 (2001): 371–383; A. M. Guest and
B. A. Lee, "How Urbanites Define Their Neighborhoods," *Population and
Environment* 7, no. 1 (1984): 32–56; N. Sastry, A. R. Pebley, and M. Zonta,
"Neighborhood Definitions and the Spatial Dimensions of Daily Life in
Los Angeles" (paper presented at the Annual Meeting of the Population
Association of America, Minneapolis, MN, 2002).

32. L. D. Frank, T. L. Schmid, J. F. Sallis, J. Chapman, and B. E. Saelens,
"Linking Objectively Measured Physical Activity with Objectively
Measured Urban Form," *American Journal of Preventive Medicine* 28, no. 2,
Suppl. 2 (2005): 117–125; N. Colabianchi, M. Dowda, K. Pfeiffer, D. Porter,
M. J. Almeida, and R. R. Pate, "Towards an Understanding of Salient
Neighborhood Boundaries: Adolescent Reports of an Easy Walking
Distance and Convenient Driving Distance," *International Journal of
Behavioral Nutrition and Physical Activity* 4, no. 1 (2007): 66.

33. Sastry, Pebley, and Zonta, "Neighborhood Definitions and the Spatial
Dimensions of Daily Life in Los Angeles."

34. Density reachability and connectivity clustering, or DBSCAN. See
C. Hennig, *fpc: Flexible Procedures for Clustering* (Comprehensive R Archive
Network, 2014).

35. Density reachability and connectivity clustering used a minimum
distance of 300 m, approximating the diameter around the home for the
narrowest definition of neighborhood, or a radius of 150 m. This produced
clusters of reports for every custodian with at least two public reports
within 300 m of each other. Any reports that did not fit these criteria
were classified as one-case clusters. The nearest report to home in each
distinguished "home clusters" from those located in other places around
the city. This measure had a Poisson distribution, with an "elbow" at
300 m, suggesting this as the most appropriate cut point for home
clusters. The same threshold was then used to classify one-case clusters.
See Hennig, *fpc*.

36. A somewhat different analysis of these data for this question was originally presented in D. T. O'Brien, E. Gordon, and J. Baldwin-Philippi, "Caring about the Community, Counteracting Disorder: 311 Reports of Public Issues as Expressions of Territoriality," *Journal of Environmental Psychology* 40 (2014): 320–330.

37. There were 765 respondents (response rate = 21 percent), 743 of whom could be merged with a particular user account. Of these respondents, 674 completed all items used in the analyses.

38. W. A. Fischel, *The Homevoter Hypothesis: How Home Values Influence Local Government Taxation, School Finance, and Land-Use Policies* (Cambridge, MA: Harvard University Press, 2005).

39. W. Seo and B. von Rabenau, "Spatial Impacts of Microneighborhood Physical Disorder on Property Resale Values in Columbus, Ohio," *Journal of Urban Planning and Development* 137, no. 3 (2011): 337–345.

40. A repeated-measures analysis of variance (ANOVA) indicated that these differences were significant ($F = 360$, $p < .001$), and post-hoc tests confirmed this for all pairwise comparisons (Tukey's adjustment, $p < .001$ for all tests).

41. These analyses were limited to survey respondents having a home address associated with their account and living in a census tract from which at least three residents participated in the survey (final $n = 427$ individuals in 81 tracts). Models predicting reporting in different geographical contexts were limited to custodians only, meaning they could only include those custodians from census tracts with at least three other custodians represented in the survey sample ($n = 211$ individuals in 48 census tracts).

42. Derived from models with a logit link.

43. A version of the analysis that follows based on a smaller corpus of the data was presented originally in D. T. O'Brien, "Using Small Data to Interpret Big Data: 311 Reports as Individual Contributions to Informal Social Control in Urban Neighborhoods," *Social Science Research* 59 (2016): 83–96.

44. This is a hurdle model, with the two models specified independently. Again, demographic factors are controlled for and a logit link is used.

45. Before the analysis, outliers with more than 100 custodial reports (91 individuals; 0.2 percent of custodians) were removed, and both sets of counts were log-transformed to account for the Poisson distribution.

46. This approach is limited to the 2,549 custodians who made both types of reports and had home addresses on file.

47. Based on the binomial function, $\binom{n}{k} * a^{n-k} * b^k = 5 * .8^4 * .2^1 = .41$.

48. The total number of possible combinations was actually 8,933, but I limited the study to those in which the expected count was greater than .5 (i.e., could be rounded to 1 or greater).

49. $\% \text{ diff} = \dfrac{\text{obs.} - \text{exp.}}{\text{exp.}}$

50. The significance of this result was confirmed by a curvilinear regression, which found that the proportion of incivility reports was a positive, quadratic predictor of the percentage difference between observed and expected ($\beta = .74$, $p < .001$).

4. Division of Labor in the Commons

1. C. Hilbe, A. Traulsen, T. Röhl, and M. Milinski, "Democratic Decisions Establish Stable Authorities That Overcome the Paradox of Second-Order Punishment," *Proceedings of the National Academy of Sciences* 111, no. 2 (2014): 752–756; J. Henrich et al., "Costly Punishment across Human Societies," *Science* 312, no. 5781 (2006): 1767–1770.

2. M. A. McKean, "The Japanese Experience with Scarcity: Management of Traditional Common Lands," *Environmental Review* 6 (1982): 63–88; M. A. McKean, "Management of Traditional Common Lands (iriaichi) in Japan," in *Conference on Common Property Resource Management* (Washington, DC: National Academy Press, 1986), 533–589.

3. E. Ostrom, *Governing the Commons: The Evolution of Institutions for Collective Action* (Cambridge, MA: Harvard University Press, 1990).

4. McKean, "Management of Traditional Common Lands (iriaichi) in Japan," 559.

5. Ostrom, *Governing the Commons.*

6. This argument and the analysis that follows builds on ideas originally presented in D. T. O'Brien, "Lamp Lighters and Sidewalk Smoothers: How Individual Residents Contribute to the Maintenance of the Urban Commons," *American Journal of Community Psychology* 58 (2016): 391–409.

7. S. B. Sarason, *The Creation of Settings and the Future Societies* (San Francisco: Jossey-Bass, 1972).

8. E. Seidman, "Back to the Future, Community Psychology: Unfolding a Theory of Social Intervention," *American Journal of Community Psychology* 16 (1988): 3–24; E. Seidman, "Pursuing the Meaning and Utility of Social Regularities for Community Psychology," in *Researching Community Psychology: Issues of Theories and Methods,* ed. P. H. Tolan, C. Keys, F. Chertok, and L. Jason (Washington, DC: American Psychological Association, 1990), 91–100; E. Seidman, "An Emerging Action Science of Social Settings," *American Journal of Community Psychology* 50 (2012): 1–16.

9. The geographic range of reporting was estimated for those who had a home address on file as the farthest distance of a reported issue from the custodian's home (calculated using the Pythagorean equation, $\sqrt{(x_r - x_h)^2 + (y_r - y_h)^2}$, where the subscripts r and h indicate the location of the report and the home, respectively). Using three reports as a cut point generated a greater distinction between groups in geographic range ($t = 11.2$, $p < .001$) than using two reports ($t = 4.6$, $p < .001$) or four reports ($t = 10.6$, $p < .001$).

10. W. J. Wilson, *The Truly Disadvantaged* (Chicago: University of Chicago Press, 1987).

11. D. M. Kennedy, A. M. Piehl, and A. A. Braga, "Youth Violence in Boston: Gun Markets, Serious Youth Offenders, and a Use-Reduction Strategy," *Law and Contemporary Problems* 59, no. 1 (1996): 147-196.

12. T. D. Clear, D. R. Rose, E. Waring, and K. Scully, "Coercive Mobility and Crime: A Preliminary Examination of Concentrated Incarceration and Social Disorganization," *Justice Quarterly* 20, no. 1 (2003): 33-64.

13. Compare M. S. Granovetter, "The Strength of Weak Ties," *American Journal of Sociology* 78, no. 6 (1973): 1360-1380.

14. M. Small, *Villa Victoria: The Transformation of Social Capital in a Boston Barrio* (Chicago: University of Chicago Press, 2004); P. G. Foster-Fishman, C. Collins, and S. J. Pierce, "An Investigation of the Dynamic Processes Promoting Citizen Participation," *American Journal of Community Psychology* 51 (2013): 492-509.

15. For those 311 accounts without mappable home addresses, census geography of residence was estimated as the geography from which the individual made the most reports. This technique was accurate for those with known home addresses 93 percent of the time for census tracks and 91 percent of the time for block groups.

16. Because all measures of behavioral composition featured a positive skew, they were log-transformed before regression analysis.

17. To eliminate any shared variance between the interaction effect and the main effects, it was first regressed on the two component variables, a process known as residual centering, which is more effective than the traditional mean centering. See C. E. Lance, "Residual Centering, Exploratory and Confirmatory Moderator Analysis, and Decomposition of Effects in Path Models Containing Interactions," *Applied Psychological Measurement* 12, no. 2 (1988): 163-175; T. D. Little, J. A. Bovaird, and K. F. Widaman, "On the Merits of Orthogonalizing Powered and Product Terms: Implications for Modeling Interactions among Latent Variables," *Structural Equation Modeling* 13 (2006): 497-519. The residual (i.e., the unique variance of the interaction factor) was then entered into the equation.

18. For comparison, I ran two simpler models that did not differentiate between types of users, once with the total number of custodians as a lone predictor and again with custodians per square mile as the lone predictor. Though both were significant (total number: $\beta = .35, p < .001$; number per sq. mile: $\beta = .48, p < .001$), these models explained less variation than the full model with typical custodians, exemplars, and their interaction (ANOVA comparisons $p < .001$). This further justifies the division of custodians into two groups. See Appendix D for complete models.

19. The initial introduction of the interaction effect improved the model, explaining an additional 2 percent of the variance, but because of the small sample size, this was a nonsignificant change. It also made all predictors nonsignificant. Upon trimming the model, the interaction effect was the last remaining predictor. Note that the lower level of significance in this model results from the smaller sample size, $N = 54$.

20. For sidewalks, the parameters for the behavioral composition were nearly identical (typical custodians: $\beta = .38, p < .001$; exemplars: $\beta = .30, p < .001$; interaction: $\beta = .14, p < .05$). Of the new predictors, only Hispanic population marginally predicted greater reporting than accounted for by the three measures of the behavioral composition ($\beta = .16, p < .10$). For streetlight outages, the small sample size called for a stepwise regression. The four demographic variables were entered into the model first, none of which were significant predictors. The interaction was entered next as the strongest remaining predictor ($\beta = .31, p < .05$). The further introduction of either typical or exemplar custodians was nonsignificant, though they maintained their correlations with reporting when controlling for demographics (typical custodians: $\beta = .27$; exemplars: $\beta = .26$; both p-values <= .10).

21. https://dataverse.harvard.edu/dataset.xhtml?persistentId=doi:10.7910/DVN/CVKM87&version=1.0.

22. This maintains the previous ratio of ~10 percent of custodians being exemplars.

23. B. B. Brown and I. Altman, "Territoriality and Residential Crime," in *Environmental Criminology*, ed. P. J. Brantingham and P. L. Brantingham (Beverly Hills, CA: Sage, 1981), 56–76.

24. In addition to the predictors related to the main hypotheses, these models controlled for day of the week and season of the year, whether a report was for snow removal (often made by one-time callers), and street length.

25. The discerning and statistically savvy reader will probably note that, with this multivariate distinction between typical and exemplar custodians, it is possible to use cluster analysis to create a more sophisticated algorithm

for differentiating between the groups than the arbitrary dividing line of three reports of public issues. I have conducted such an analysis using total reports, estimated geographical range of custodianship, incivilities reported, reports made on main streets, and reports made on nonresidential streets as the defining variables for clusters. Surprisingly, the resulting clusters only muddy the waters. The ability to predict whether a person will engage in the types of tasks associated with exemplars was far greater with the dichotomy based on a simplistic reporting threshold than with the division based on a clustering algorithm. This seemed to result from the fact that the variance in estimated geographical range of reporting dominated the k-means clustering algorithm, obscuring to some extent deviations in the other forms of behavior.

26. For the case of exemplars, this is calculated as $length * \dfrac{issues}{m} * P(exemplar)$, where $\dfrac{issues}{m}$ is the expected count of issues per meter, specific to a road's zoning type (calculated from the entire database of all issues, excluding any duplicate reports), and $P(exemplar)$ is based on the road- and tract-level characteristics (e.g., zoning, main vs. side streets) and the parameters from the multilevel models in the previous analysis.

27. As before, we measure the latter in terms of the density of typical custodians and the raw number of exemplars.

28. It is important to note that for factors that are presumed to operate at the individual level, such as affluence, these conclusions are vulnerable to the ecological fallacy—that factors measured at the group level can be used as evidence of individual-level effects. See G. King, *A Solution to the Ecological Inference Problem* (Princeton, NJ: Princeton University Press, 1997). For example, while it might seem that individuals with greater access to resources are more likely to participate in 311, it is also possible that what really matters is living in a neighborhood with greater overall access to resources, regardless of one's own socioeconomic standing.

29. J. M. Darley and B. Latané, "Bystander Intervention in Emergencies: Diffusion of Responsibility," *Journal of Personality and Social Psychology* 8, no. 4 (1968): 377–383.

30. J. Jacobs, *The Death and Life of Great American Cities* (New York: Random House, 1961).

31. M. Pattillo-McCoy, *Black Picket Fences: Privilege and Peril among the Black Middle Class* (Chicago: University of Chicago Press, 2000).

32. Ibid.

33. Ostrom, *Governing the Commons.*

5. Partnering with the Public

1. Reported in D. T. O'Brien, D. Offenhuber, J. Baldwin-Philippi, and E. Gordon, "Uncharted Territoriality in Coproduction: The Motivations for 311 Reporting," *Journal of Public Adminstration Research and Theory* 27 (2017): 320–335.

2. W. Barnes and B. Mann, *Making Local Democracy Work: Municipal Officials' Views about Public Engagement* (Washington, DC: National League of Cities Center for Research and Innovation, 2009); K. A. McComas, "Trivial Pursuits: Participant Views of Public Meetings," *Journal of Public Relations Research* 15, no. 2 (2003): 91–115.

3. T. O'Reilly, "Government as a Platform," in *Open Government*, ed. D. Lathrop and L. Ruma (Sebastopol, CA: O'Reilly, 2010), 11–40; E. Ferro and F. Molinari, "Making Sense of Gov 2.0 Strategies: 'No Citizens, No Party,'" *Journal of eDemocracy* 2, no. 1 (2010): 56–68; B. S. Noveck, *Wiki Government: How Technology Can Make Government Better, Democracy Stronger, and Citizens More Powerful* (Washington, DC: Brookings Institution Press, 2009).

4. S. Goldsmith and S. Crawford, *The Responsive City: Engaging Communities through Data-Smart Governance* (San Francisco: Jossey-Bass, 2014).

5. J. S. Evans-Cowley, "Planning in the Age of Facebook: The Role of Social Networking in Planning Processes," *GeoJournal* 75, no. 5 (2010): 407–420; D. G. Freelon, T. Kriplean, J. Morgan, W. L. Bennett, and A. Borning, "Facilitating Diverse Political Engagement with the Living Voters Guide," *Journal of Information Technology and Politics* 9, no. 3 (2012): 279–297.

6. B. Barber, *Strong Democracy: Participatory Politics for a New Age* (Oakland: University of California Press, 1984).

7. R. B. Parks, P. C. Baker, L. Kiser, R. Oakerson, E. Ostrom, V. Ostrom, S. L. Percy, M. B. Vandivort, G. P. Whitaker, and R. Wilson, "Consumers as Coproducers of Public Services: Some Economic and Institutional Considerations," *Policy Studies Journal* 9 (1982): 1001–1011; E. Ostrom, "Metropolitan Reform: Propositions Derived from Two Traditions," *Social Science Quarterly* 53 (1972): 474–493; G. P. Whitaker, "Coproduction: Citizen Participation in Service Delivery," *Public Administration Review* 40 (1980): 240–246; C. H. Levine, "Citizenship and Service Delivery: The Promise of Coproduction," *Public Administration Review* 44 (1984): 178–187; S. Percy, "Citizen Participation in the Co-production of Urban Services," *Urban Affairs Quarterly* 19, no. 4 (1984): 431–436.

8. Y. Cabannes, "Participatory Budgeting: A Significant Contribution to Participatory Democracy," *Environment and Urbanization* 16 (2004): 27–46.

9. E. Gordon and J. Baldwin-Philippi, "Playful Civic Learning: Enabling Lateral Trust and Reflection in Game-Based Public Participation," *International Journal of Communication* 8 (2014): 759–786.

10. See, for example, J. Alford, "Why Do Public-Sector Clients Coproduce? Toward a Contingency Theory," *Administration and Society* 34 (2002): 32–56.

11. Parks et al., "Consumers as Coproducers of Public Services"; Ostrom, "Metropolitan Reform."

12. See, for example, Whitaker, "Coproduction"; Levine, "Citizenship and Service Delivery"; Percy, "Citizen Participation in the Co-production of Urban Services."

13. E. Ostrom, "Crossing the Great Divide: Coproduction, Synergy, and Development," *World Development* 24 (1996): 1073–1087 at 1079.

14. D. Osborne, "Reinventing Government," *Public Productivity and Management Review* 16, no. 4 (1993): 349–356; C. Hood, "A Public Management for All Seasons?," *Public Administration* 69, no. 1 (1991): 3–19.

15. S. P. Osborne and K. Strokosch, "It Takes Two to Tango? Understanding the Co-production of Public Services by Integrating the Services Management and Public Administration Perspectives," *British Journal of Management* 24 (2013): S31–S47; S. P. Osborne, "Delivering Public Services: Time for a New Theory?," *Public Management Review* 12 (2010): 1–10.

16. Ostrom, "Crossing the Great Divide."

17. Osborne and Strokosch, "It Takes Two to Tango?"; Osborne, "Delivering Public Services"; S. P. Osborne, Z. Radnor, and G. Nasi, "A New Theory for Public Service Management? Toward a (Public) Service-Dominant Approach," *American Review of Public Administration* 43, no. 2 (2012): 135–158.

18. E. Mayo and H. Moore, eds., *Building the Mutual State: Findings from the Virtual Thinktank* (London: New Economics Foundation / Mutuo, 2002).

19. T. Bovaird, "Beyond Engagement and Participation: User and Community Coproduction of Public Services," *Public Administration Review* 67, no. 5 (2007): 846–860.

20. A. Joshi and M. Moore, "Institutionalized Co-production: Unorthodox Public Service Delivery in Challenging Environments," *Journal of Development Studies* 40, no. 4 (2004): 31–49; Bovaird, "Beyond Engagement and Participation"; T. Brandsen and V. Pestoff, "Co-production, the Third Sector and the Delivery of Public Services: An Introduction," *Public Management Review* 8, no. 4 (2006): 493–501; D. Cepiku and F. Giordano, "Co-production in Developing Countries," *Public Management Review* 16, no. 3 (2014): 317–340.

21. D. H. Folz, "Recycling Solid Waste: Citizen Participation in the Design of a Coproduced Program," *State and Local Government Review* 23 (1991): 92–102; M. J. Marschall, "Parent Involvement and Educational Outcomes for Latino Students," *Review of Policy Research* 23 (2006): 1053–1076; K. J. Powers and F. Thompson, "Managing Coprovision: Using Expectancy Theory to Overcome the Free-Rider Problem," *Journal of Public Administration Research and Theory* 4, no. 2 (1994): 179–196.

22. This stands in contrast to more extensive efforts to uncover the motivations that characterize public-sector employees See B. E. Wright, "Public-Sector Work Motivation: A Review of the Current Literature and a Revised Conceptual Model," *Journal of Public Administration Research and Theory* 11, no. 4 (2001): 559–586; J. L. Perry, "Antecedents of Public Service Motivation," *Journal of Public Administration Research and Theory* 7, no. 2 (1997): 181–197. It also stands in contrast to such efforts to uncover the motivations behind volunteerism. See E. G. Clary and M. Snyder, "The Motivations to Volunteer: Theoretical and Practical Considerations," *Current Directions in Psychological Science* 8, no. 5 (1999): 156–159.

23. J. C. Thomas, "Citizen, Customer, Partner: Rethinking the Place of the Public in Public Management," *Public Administration Review* 73, no. 6 (2013): 786–796.

24. Osborne, "Reinventing Government"; Hood, "A Public Management for All Seasons?"

25. Levine, "Citizenship and Service Delivery"; Bovaird, "Beyond Engagement and Participation."

26. J. Fledderus, T. Brandsen, and M. Honingh, "Restoring Trust through the Co-production of Public Services: A Theoretical Elaboration," *Public Management Review* 16, no. 3 (2014): 424–443.

27. See, for example, M. J. Marschall, "Citizen Participation and the Neighborhood Context: A New Look at the Coproduction of Local Public Goods," *Political Research Quarterly* 57 (2004): 231–244.

28. Joshi and Moore, "Institutionalized Co-production."

29. J. A. Fodor, *Modularity of Mind: An Essay on Faculty Psychology* (Cambridge, MA: MIT Press, 1983); J. Tooby and L. Cosmides, "The Psychological Foundations of Culture," in *The Adapted mind: Evolutionary Psychology and the Generation of Culture*, ed. J. H. Barkow, L. Cosmides, and J. Tooby (New York: Oxford University Press, 1992), 19–136.

30. Alford, "Why Do Public-Sector Clients Coproduce?"; J. Alford, *Engaging Public Sector Clients: From Service-Delivery to Co-production* (Basingstoke: Palgrave Macmillan, 2009).

31. B. Y. Clark, J. L. Brudney, and S.-G. Jang, "Coproduction of Government Services and the New Information Technology: Investigating the Distri-

butional Biases," *Public Administration Review* 73, no. 5 (2013): 687–701; J. Fountain, "Connecting Technologies to Citizenship," in *Technology and the Resilience of Metropolitan Regions,* ed. M. A. Pagano (Champaign: University of Illinois Press, 2014), 25–51; J. R. Levine and C. Gershenson, "From Political to Material Inequality: Race, Immigration, and Request for Public Goods," *Sociological Forum* 29 (2014): 607–627; A. E. Lerman and V. Weaver, "Staying Out of Sight? Concentrated Policing and Local Political Action," *Annals of the American Academy of Political and Social Science* 651 (2014): 202–219; S. L. Minkoff, "NYC 311: A Tract-Level Analysis of Citizen-Government Contacting in New York City," *Urban Affairs Review* 52, no. 2 (2016): 211–246.

32. Clark, Brudney, and Jang, "Coproduction of Government Services and the New Information Technology"; Fountain, "Connecting Technologies to Citizenship"; Levine and Gershenson, "From Political to Material Inequality"; Lerman and Weaver, "Staying Out of Sight?"

33. The nine activities were sufficiently correlated to justify combining them as a single index of civic activities (Cronbach's $\alpha = .76$).

34. We linked survey respondents to the Boston voter file via exact and approximate (fuzzy) string matching in R. Exact matches were identified as unique combinations of name and address or name and phone number in both files. Next, a fuzzy string-matching algorithm was applied to unmatched sets of name and address fields, such that similar names (e.g., "Stephen" and "Steve") could constitute a match. We then manually checked all approximate matches for false positives. The analyses reported here include all fuzzy matches but were rerun restricting the analysis to exact matches, producing results that were qualitatively identical.

35. Z. L. Hajnal and P. G. Lewis, "Municipal Institutions and Voter Turnout in Local Elections," *Urban Affairs Review* 5 (2003): 645–668.

36. A. Lijphart, "Unequal Participation: Democracy's Unresolved Dilemma," *American Political Science Review* 91, no. 1 (1997): 1–14.

37. Final $N = 439$ individuals in 82 tracts in multilevel models.

38. There was no significant variation in custodians across neighborhoods, suggesting that people living in any neighborhood were about equally likely to have the opportunity to report at least one public issue ($ICC = .02; \chi^2_{df=81} = 90.95, p = ns$).

39. Both of these had Poisson distributions, requiring the use of a log-link model.

40. Limited to those custodians from census tracts with at least three other custodians represented in the survey sample ($N = 220$ individuals in 50 census tracts).

41. In contrast to the model predicting custodianship, both reports within the home neighborhood and size of home neighborhood had significant variation at the neighborhood level (reports: ICC = .08, p < .001; size: ICC = .10, p < .001), indicating the importance of controlling for similarity in reporting between neighbors owing to shared environment.

42. There was no significant neighborhood-level variation regarding whether someone reported in any of these three contexts.

43. Clark, Brudney, and Jang, "Coproduction of Government Services and the New Information Technology"; Fountain, "Connecting Technologies to Citizenship"; Levine and Gershenson, "From Political to Material Inequality"; Lerman and Weaver, "Staying Out of Sight?"

44. B. B. Brown, "Territoriality," in *Handbook of Environmental Psychology*, ed. D. Stokols and I. Altman (New York: Wiley, 1987), 505–531; D. D. Perkins, A. Wandersman, R. C. Rich, and R. B. Taylor, "The Physical Environment of Street Crime: Defensible Space, Territoriality and Incivilities," *Journal of Environmental Psychology* 13 (1993): 29–49; R. B. Taylor, *Human Territorial Functioning: An Empirical, Evolutionary Perspective on Individual and Small Group Territorial Cognitions, Behaviors and Consequences* (Cambridge: Cambridge University Press, 1988).

45. As described in Bovaird, "Beyond Engagement and Participation."

46. E. Melhuish and J. Barnes, *Towards Understanding Sure Start Local Programmes: Summary of Findings from the National Evaluation* (London: Department for Education and Skills, 2004).

47. Cepiku and Giordano, "Co-production in Developing Countries."

48. Gordon and Baldwin-Philippi, "Playful Civic Learning."

49. S. Haselmayer, "What Boston's Snow Crisis Can Teach Us about Solving Problems in New Ways," *The Atlantic CityLab*, February 19, 2015.

50. Ostrom, "Crossing the Great Divide."

51. Marschall, "Citizen Participation and the Neighborhood Context."

52. Alford, "Why Do Public-Sector Clients Coproduce?"

53. Perkins et al., "The Physical Environment of Street Crime"; B. B. Brown and C. M. Werner, "Social Cohesiveness, Territoriality and Holiday Decorations: The Influence of Cul-de-Sacs," *Environment and Behavior* 17 (1985): 539–565; P. B. Harris and B. B. Brown, "The Home and Identity Display: Interpreting Resident Territoriality from Home Exteriors," *Journal of Environmental Psychology* 16 (1996): 187–203. Note that I do not report it in this book, but this correlation also holds within our survey data. See D. T. O'Brien, E. Gordon, and J. Baldwin, "Caring about the Community, Counteracting Disorder: 311 Reports of Public Issues as Expressions of Territoriality," *Journal of Environmental Psychology* 40 (2014): 320–330.

54. Marschall, "Citizen Participation and the Neighborhood Context."
55. Osborne and Strokosch, "It Takes Two to Tango?"; Osborne, "Delivering Public Services."
56. See, for example, S. Shahrabani, U. Benzion, and G. Y. Din, "Factors Affecting Nurses' Decision to Get the Flu Vaccine," *European Journal of Health Economics* 10 (2009): 227-231.
57. Bovaird, "Beyond Engagement and Participation."
58. Levine, "Citizenship and Service Delivery."
59. M. Jakobsen and S. C. Andersen, "Coproduction and Equity in Public Service Delivery," *Public Administration Review* 73, no. 5 (2013): 704-713; R. Warren, M. S. Rosentraub, and K. S. Harlow, "Coproduction, Equity, and the Distribution of Safety," *Urban Affairs Review* 19, no. 4 (1984): 447-464.

6. Experiments in Coproduction

1. J. Q. Wilson and G. L. Kelling, "Broken Windows: The Police and Neighborhood Safety," *Atlantic Monthly* 127 (March 1982): 29-38.
2. D. Weisburd, J. Hinkle, A. A. Braga, and A. Wooditch, "Understanding the Mechanisms Underlying Broken Windows Policing: The Need for Evaluation Evidence," *Journal of Research in Crime and Delinquency* 52, no. 4 (2015): 589-608; R. B. Taylor, *Breaking Away from Broken Windows: Baltimore Neighborhoods and the Nationwide Fight against Crime, Grime, Fear, and Decline* (Boulder, CO: Westview Press, 2001); W. G. Skogan, *Disorder and Decline* (Berkeley: University of California Press, 1992); B. E. Harcourt and J. Ludwig, "Broken Windows: New Evidence from New York City and a Five-City Social Experiment," *University of Chicago Law Review* 73, no. 1 (2006): 271-320; B. E. Harcourt, *Illusion of Order: The False Promise of Broken Windows Policing* (Cambridge, MA: Harvard University Press, 2001).
3. R. J. Sampson and S. W. Raudenbush, "Systematic Social Observation of Public Spaces: A New Look at Disorder in Urban Neighborhoods," *American Journal of Sociology* 105, no. 3 (1999): 603--651.
4. T. Meares, "Law of Community Policing and Public Order Policing," in *Encyclopedia of Criminology and Criminal Justice,* ed. G. Bruinsma and D. Weisburd (New York: Springer, 2014), 2823-2827.
5. D. Weisburd and J. E. Eck, "What Can Police Do to Reduce Crime, Disorder, and Fear?" *Annals of the American Academy of Political and Social Science* 593 (2004): 42-65.
6. M. Jakobsen, "Can Government Initiatives Increase Citizen Coproduction? Results of a Randomized Field Experiment," *Journal of Public Administration Research and Theory* 23, no. 1 (2013): 27-54.

7. This experiment was also described as part of a discussion of the relevance of humans' evolved territoriality to the management of 311 systems in D. T. O'Brien, "311 Hotlines, Territoriality, and the Collaborative Maintenance of the Urban Commons: Examining the Intersection of a Coproduction Policy and Evolved Human Behavior," *Evolutionary Behavioral Sciences* 10, no. 2 (2016): 123–141.

8. Matched triplets were constructed via the following process. First, to control for regional characteristics, all three tracts had to be in the same planning district, large regions of the city with historical and social identity (e.g., Fenway, South Boston). Second, standardized measures of difference between the tracts composing all eligible triplets were calculated based on four demographic measures related to custodianship—prevalence of home ownership, level of median income, and proportion black and proportion Hispanic—and previous measures of custodianship at the neighborhood level. This produced an ordered list of the overall consistency in custodianship and relevant sociodemographics for all triplets of census tracts contained in the same planning district. A final selection of five triplets was then made, with two rules: (1) no planning district could produce more than one triplet, and (2) a triplet was included from each of the city's three most disadvantaged districts, which also have the lowest overall engagement with 311, in order to maximize the potential effect of the intervention.

9. We placed flyers within or against the front doorway of each building, with additional flyers at buildings with multiple units, distributed in such a way as to have one given for each unit if possible. We agreed with our public sector collaborators that we would not place the flyers in mailboxes, thereby keeping on the right side of federal law that allows only mail delivered by the U.S. Postal Service to be placed in mailboxes.

10. $\binom{n}{k} * a^{n-k} * (1-a)^k = 5 * \frac{1}{3}^4 * \frac{2}{3}^1 = .04$, where n is the number of times an event happens in k attempts, and a is the probability of the event.

11. A. Ryan, "Missing Link: App Will Connect Citizens," *Boston Globe*, October 12, 2010.

12. T. Trenkner, "Public Officials of the Year: Nigel Jacob and Chris Osgood," *Governing*, October 27, 2011.

13. C. McDowell and M. Chinchilla, "Partnering with Communities and Institutions," in *Civic Media: Technology, Design, Practice*, ed. E. Gordon and P. Mihalidis (Cambridge, MA: MIT Press, 2016), 461–480.

14. T. O'Reilly, "Government as a Platform," in *Open Government*, ed. D. Lathrop and L. Ruma (Sebastopol, CA: O'Reilly, 2010), 11–40; E. Ferro and F. Molinari, "Making Sense of Gov 2.0 Strategies: 'No Citizens, No Party,'" *Journal of eDemocracy* 2, no. 1 (2010): 56–68; B. S. Noveck, *Wiki*

Government: How Technology Can Make Government Better, Democracy Stronger, and Citizens More Powerful (Washington, DC: Brookings Institution Press, 2009); S. Johnson, *Future Perfect: The Case for Progress in a Networked Age* (New York: Penguin Books, 2012).

15. E. Morozov, "From Slacktivism to Activism," *Foreign Policy*, September 5, 2009.

16. E. Zuckerman, "New Media, New Civics?" *Policy and Internet* 6 (2014): 151-168.

17. For robustness, a reanalysis treating all General Requests as public issues produced practically identical results (e.g., the more inclusive approach found that 65 percent of custodians made only one report, rather than 68 percent).

18. D. T. Campbell and J. Stanley, *Experimental and Quasi-experimental Designs for Research* (New York: Rand McNally, 1963).

19. S. L. Morgan and C. Winship, *Counterfactuals and Causal Inference* (New York: Cambridge University Press, 2007).

20. This is mathematically equivalent to creating weighted match scores on a single categorical variable.

21. Certain supplemental analyses will, however, leverage those individuals who did have home addresses on file for more robust tests, albeit with a smaller sample.

22. The accuracy of this estimate was evaluated for the 38,830 individuals with home addresses. The estimates were found to be nearly identical statistically to the true maximum distance ($r = .999$).

23. The linear estimate was based on the regression equation *true range = est. range* $*$ $1.009 - 6.453$.

24. Log-transformed outcome variable in a backwards regression that also controlled for total population and traditional users.

25. Because both outcome measures of interest had a Poisson distribution, a logit link was used.

26. The regression predicted $log(diameter+1)$ in order to account for skew while also attending to diameters less than 1. The intercept for calls was 0.72 and that for geographic range was 3.05.

27. An alternative approach would be to analyze the 301 BOS:311 users with home addresses on file, thus creating a within-subjects design. For these individuals, the median true distance from home was 310 m. Again, this reflects an expansion in range but not an overwhelming one. Of these 301 individuals, 292 had actually made public reports using both the hotline and BOS:311, making for a within-subjects experimental design that compares the geographical range of their reports made via BOS:311 versus those made via traditional channels. The median maximum

distance from home for hotline reports for these individuals was 129 m; the same value for BOS:311 reports was 270 m.

28. New samples $n = 588$ custodians in 107 census tracts with three or more users and $n = 315$ custodians in 69 census tracts with three or more custodians. Using this expanded sample had no impact on the qualitative interpretations of models run in previous chapters and in fact generally strengthened all findings.

29. 4.6 vs. 3.6 public issues and 319 m vs. 500 m in range when comparing a white male of average education and age with average levels of territorial motivation. These estimates are notably higher than those of the full data set, but this is because of the greater levels of custodianship exhibited by those in the survey sample.

30. M. Dimock, C. Doherty, and A. Kohut, *Majority Says the Federal Government Threatens Their Personal Rights* (Washington, DC: Pew Research Center, 2013); American National Election Studies, *American National Election Studies Guide to Public Opinion and Electoral Behavior* (Ann Arbor: Center for Political Studies, Institute for Social Research, University of Michigan, 2012); R. Putnam, *Making Democracy Work: Civic Traditions in Modern Italy* (Princeton, NJ: Princeton University Press, 1993).

31. S. Mettler, *The Submerged State: How Invisible Government Policies Undermine American Democracy* (Chicago: University of Chicago Press, 2011).

32. R. W. Buell and M. I. Norton, "The Labor Illusion: How Operational Transparency Increases Perceived Value," *Management Science* 57, no. 9 (2011): 1564–1579; R. W. Buell, T. Kim, and C.-J. Tsay, "Creating Reciprocal Value through Operational Transparency," *Management Science* 63, no. 6 (2016): 1673–1695.

33. R. W. Buell, E. Porter, and M. I. Norton, *Surfacing the Submerged State: Operational Transparency Increases Trust in and Engagement with Government* (Cambridge, MA: Harvard Business School, 2016).

34. At the time, it was Citizens Connect, though for consistency we refer to it as BOS:311.

35. The sample is considerably larger than the number of registered 311 users who had made reports through BOS:311 presented in the previous section. This is because the app-based data can differentiate between individuals based on their device without the individual having created a registered account.

36. This is an average of 17 months per user. This is greater than the 14 months over which the messages were sent so that the panel models could capitalize on baseline behavior occurring in advance of the program.

37. True home address when available, or estimated home as in the previous section.

38. A. Fung, H. R. Gilman, and J. Shkabatur, "Six Models for the Internet + Politics," *International Studies Review* 15 (2013): 30–47.

7. Extending 311 across Massachusetts

1. N. Selwyn, "Reconsidering Political and Popular Understandings of the Digital Divide," *New Media and Society* 6, no. 3 (2004): 341–362.
2. U.S. Department of Commerce, *Falling through the Net III: Defining the Digital Divide* (Washington, DC: National Telecommunications and Information Administration, U.S. Department of Commerce, 1999).
3. J. B. Horrigan and M. Duggan, *Home Broadband 2015* (Washington, DC: Pew Research Center, 2015).
4. Controlling for income. See J. van Dijk and K. Hacker, "The Digital Divide as a Complex and Dynamic Phenomenon," *The Information Society* 19, no. 4 (2003): 315–326.
5. P. J. Tichenor, G. A. Donohue, and C. N. Olien, "Mass Media Flow and Differential Growth in Knowledge," *Public Opinion Quarterly* 34, no. 2 (1970): 159–170.
6. A. van Deursen and J. van Dijk, "The Digital Divide Shifts to Differences in Usage," *New Media and Society* 16, no. 3 (2004): 507–526.
7. J. van Dijk, *The Deepening Divide: Inequality in the Information Society* (London: SAGE, 2005); P. Dimaggio and E. Hargittai, "From the 'Digital Divide' to 'Digital Inequality': Studying Internet Use as Penetration Increases" (working paper, Center for Arts, Culture and Policy Studies, Princeton University, 2001); K. Mossberger, C. J. Tolbert, and M. Stansbury, *Virtual Inequality: Beyond the Digital Divide* (Washington, DC: Georgetown University Press, 2003); M. Warschauer, *Technology and Social Inclusion* (Cambridge, MA: MIT Press, 2003).
8. E. Hargittai, "Second-Level Digital Divide: Differences in People's Online Skills," *First Monday* 7, no. 4 (2002).
9. van Deursen and van Dijk, "The Digital Divide Shifts to Differences in Usage."
10. E. Kontos, K. D. Blake, W.-Y. S. Chou, and A. Prestin, "Predictors of eHealth Usage: Insights on the Digital Divide from the Health Information National Trends Survey 2012," *Journal of Medical Internet Research* 16, no. 7 (2014): e172.
11. M. Anderson and J. B. Horrigan, *Smartphones Help Those without Broadband Get Online, but Don't Necessarily Bridge the Digital Divide* (Washington, DC: Pew Research Center, 2016).
12. T. Newcombe, "Is the Cost of 311 Systems Worth the Price of Knowing?," *Governing*, March 2014.

13. D. Shemek, S. Winograd, and K. R. Vining, *Case Studies for Consolidated Public Safety Dispatch Center Feasibility Study: The Next Steps* (Cleveland: Center for Public Management, Maxine Goodman Levin College of Urban Affairs, Cleveland State University, 2011).

14. https://dataverse.harvard.edu/dataverse.xhtml?alias=Commonwealth _Connect.

15. https://worldmap.harvard.edu/maps/Commonwealth_Connect.

16. Note that the system did not start at a true "0," as some municipalities already had contracts with SeeClickFix, and in some areas constituents had used the SeeClickFix app even though their municipality did not have a contract.

17. 3/2010–2/2011, the first whole year with clean records. The system was introduced in 2008.

18. E. Ostrom, "Crossing the Great Divide: Coproduction, Synergy, and Development," *World Development* 24 (1996): 1073–1087.

19. Ibid.

20. K. Layne and J. Lee, "Developing Fully Functional e-Government: A Four Stage Model," *Government Information Quarterly* 18, no. 2 (2001): 122–136; M. J. Moon, "The Evolution of e-Government among Municipalities: Rhetoric or Reality?," *Public Administration Review* 62, no. 4 (2002): 424–433; D. M. West, "E-Government and the Transformation of Service Delivery and Citizen Attitudes," *Public Administration Review* 64, no. 1 (2004): 15–27.

21. B. S. Jimenez, K. Mossberger, and Y. Wu, "Municipal Government and the Interactive Web: Trends and Issues for Civic Engagement," in *E-Governance and Civic Engagement: Factors and Determinants of e-Democracy,* ed. A. Manoharan and M. Holzer (Hershey, PA: Information Science Reference, 2011), 251–271.

22. Moon, "The Evolution of e-Government among Municipalities."

23. C. J. Tolbert, K. Mossberger, and R. McNeal, "Institutions, Policy Innovation, and e-Government in the American States," *Public Administration Review* 68, no. 3 (2008): 549–563.

24. R. Eyestone, "Confusion, Diffusion, and Innovation," *American Political Science Review* 71, no. 2 (1977): 441–447; V. Gray, "Innovation in the States: A Diffusion Study," *American Political Science Review* 67, no. 4 (1973): 1174–1185; C. Knill, "Introduction: Cross-National Policy Convergence: Concepts, Approaches and Explanatory Factors," *Journal of European Public Policy* 12, no. 5 (2005): 764–774.

25. F. S. Berry and W. D. Berry, "Innovation and Diffusion Models in Policy Research," in *Theories of the Policy Process,* ed. P. A. Sabatier, 2nd ed. (Boulder, CO: Westview Press, 2007), 223–260.

26. H. J. Yun and C. Opheim, "Building on Success: The Diffusion of e-Government in the American States," *Electronic Journal of e-government* 8, no. 1 (2010): 71–82.

27. C. Z. Mooney, "Modeling Regional Effects on State Policy Diffusion," *Political Research Quarterly* 54, no. 1 (2001): 103–124.

28. M. Z. Sobaci and K. Y. Eryigit, "Determinants of e-Democracy Adoption in Turkish Municipalities: An Analysis for Spatial Diffusion Effect," *Local Government Studies* 41, no. 3 (2015): 445–469.

29. Massachusetts Department of Revenue, *Municipal Databank*, http://www.mass.gov/dor/local-officials/municipal-databank-and-local-aid-unit/databank-reports-new.html.

30. That is, free cash at year end. See Jimenez, Mossberger, and Wu, "Municipal Government and the Interactive Web."

31. L. Anselin, R. J. Florax, and S. J. Rey, eds., *Advances in Spatial Econometrics: Methodology, Tools and Applications* (Berlin: Springer, 2004).

32. Importantly, these are not formal spatial lag models based on maximum likelihood estimates. We were most interested in the question of how many neighborhood municipalities were also in the program, whereas a spatial lag model would explicitly predict outcomes based on the proportion of neighboring municipalities in the program. Theoretically, the former would better capture the magnitude of social influence. We also tested a model of "any neighboring municipality." In the end, the total count measure was the only one with predictive power for any of the outcome measures.

33. Ostrom, "Crossing the Great Divide."

34. Based on population density, with 3,000 people / sq. mile as the dividing point between rural and suburban and 10,000 people / sq. mile as the dividing point between suburban and urban.

35. This classification was only true for 5 of the 64 municipalities (1 suburban and 4 rural), none of which participated in the survey.

36. This stands somewhat in contradiction to SeeClickFix's records, which state that only 10 of these municipalities had robust buy-in and promotion. This could be a function of differing definitions of what constitutes a thorough launch effort or could reflect incomplete communication between municipalities and SeeClickFix.

37. S. Goldsmith and S. Crawford, *The Responsive City: Engaging Communities through Data-Smart Governance* (San Francisco: Jossey-Bass, 2014).

8. Whither the Community?

1. U.S. Department of Education, *Application for Grants Under the Promise Neighborhoods Program* (Washington, DC: U.S. Department of Education, 2010).

2. P. Tough, *Whatever It Takes: Geoffrey Canada's Quest to Change Harlem and America* (Wilmington, MA: Mariner Books, 2009).

3. U.S. Department of Education, *Application for Grants Under the Promise Neighborhoods Program.*

4. J. A. Johnson, "From Open Data to Information Justice," *Ethics and Information Technology* 16, no. 4 (2014): 263–274.

5. C. Martin, "Barriers to the Open Government Data Agenda: Taking a Multi-level Perspective," *Policy and Internet* 6, no. 3 (2014): 217–240.

6. M. Boychuk, M. Cousins, A. Lloyd, and C. MacKeigan, "Do We Need Data Literacy? Public Perceptions Regarding Canada's Open Data Initiative," *Dalhousie Journal of Interdisciplinary Management* 12 (2016): 1–26.

7. P. Vahey, L. Yarnall, C. Patton, D. Zalles, and K. Swan, "Mathematizing Middle School: Results from a Cross-Disciplinary Study of Data Literacy" (paper presented at American Educational Research Association Annual Conference, San Francisco, 2006). See also B. L. Madison and L. Steen, eds., *Quantitative Literacy: Why Numeracy Matters for Schools and Colleges* (Princeton, NJ: National Council on Education and the Disciplines, 2003).

8. Vahey et al., "Mathematizing Middle School."

9. *Policy Map,* policymap.com.

10. *Data USA,* datausa.io.

11. *Racial Dot Map,* http://demographics.virginia.edu/DotMap/.

12. *Detroit, MI Tax Parcel Map,* https://data.detroitmi.gov/Property-Parcels/Parcel-Map/fxkw-udwf/data.

13. *Crime Mapping,* crimemapping.com.

14. *City of Boston 311 Map,* https://data.cityofboston.gov/City-Services/311-Open-Service-Requests-Map/j2a7-cdyk.

15. *City of Chicago Open Grid,* https://chicago.opengrid.io/opengrid.

16. K. A. Lynch, *Image of the City* (Cambridge, MA: MIT Press, 1960).

17. See, for example, C. J. Coulton, J. Korbin, T. Chan, and M. Su, "Mapping Residents' Perceptions of Neighborhood Boundaries: A Methodological Note," *American Journal of Community Psychology* 29, no. 2 (2001): 371–383; C. E. Dunn, "Participatory GIS—A People's GIS?," *Progress in Human Geography* 31 (2007): 616–637; G. Brown, M. F. Schebella, and D. Weber, "Using Participator GIS to Measure Physical Activity and Urban Park Benefits," *Landscape and Urban Planning* 121 (2014): 34–44.

18. R. Bhargava, *Data Therapy*, 2016, datatherapy.org.

19. K. O'Connell, Y. Lee, F. Peer, S. M. Staudaher, A. Godwin, M. Madden, and E. Zegura, "Making Public Safety Data Accessible in the Westside Atlanta Data Dashboard" (paper presented at Bloomberg Data for Good Exchange Conference, New York, 2016).

20. M. P. Johnson, "Data, Analytics and Community-Based Organizations: Transforming Data to Decisions for Community Development," *I/S* 11, no. 1 (2015): 49–96.

21. Ibid.

22. R. Stoecker, "The Research Practices and Needs of Non-profit Organizations in an Urban Center," *Journal of Sociology and Social Welfare* 34, no. 4 (2007): 97–120.

23. D. Hackler and G. D. Saxton, "The Strategic Use of Information Technology by Nonprofit Organizations: Increasing Capacity and Untapped Potential," *Public Administration Review* 67, no. 3 (2007): 474–487.

24. Johnson, "Data, Analytics and Community-Based Organizations."

25. M. Gurstein, "Open Data: Empowering the Empowered or Effective Data Use for Everyone?," *First Monday* 16, no. 2 (2011).

26. A. S. Taylor, S. Lindley, T. Regan, D. Sweeney, V. Vlachokyriakos, L. Grainger, and J. Lingel, "Data-in-Place: Thinking Through the Relations between Data and Community," in *Proceedings of the 33rd Annual ACM Conference on Human Factors in Computing Systems* (New York: ACM, 2015), 2863–2872.

27. M. P. Johnson and S. Jani, "Measuring Success: Community Analytics for Local Economic Development, 2017, https://works.bepress.com/michael_johnson/70/. This project received seed funding from the Boston Area Research Initiative.

Conclusion: The Future of the Urban Commons

1. New York City Department of Transportation, *Making Safer Streets* (New York: New York City Department of Transportation, 2013).

2. E. Fishman, "Bikeshare: A Review of Recent Literature," *Transport Reviews* 36 (2016): 92–113.

3. T. O'Reilly, "Government as a Platform," in *Open Government*, ed. D. Lathrop and L. Ruma (Sebastopol, CA: O'Reilly, 2010), 11–40.

4. J. B. Carr and J. L. Doleac, *The Geography, Incidence, and Underreporting of Gun Violence: New Evidence Using ShotSpotter Data*, (Washington, DC: Brookings Institution, 2016); Y. Irvin-Erickson, N. G. La Vigne, N. Levine, and S. Bieler, "What Does Gunshot Detection Technology Tell Us about Gun Violence?," *Applied Geography* 86 (2017): 262–273.

5. O'Reilly, "Government as a Platform."
6. E. Ostrom, *Governing the Commons: The Evolution of Institutions for Collective Action* (Cambridge, MA: Harvard University Press, 1990).

Appendix A

1. A distinction created by the Boston Redevelopment Authority for administrative purposes but based on historically salient regions, many of which are once-independent municipalities that were annexed. Using an analysis of variance (ANOVA), the planning districts account for about 50 percent of the variation in ethnic composition and median income across census tracts.
2. S. W. Raudenbush, A. S. Bryk, Y. F. Cheong, and R. T. Congdon Jr., *HLM 6: Hierarchical Linear and Nonlinear Modeling* (Lincolnwood, IL: Scientific Software International, 2004).
3. This number diminishes with some measures that allow greater time between identification of an outage and reporting, being that those reported by city employees in that time span were removed.

Acknowledgments

Though this book is formally a sole-authored work, it is deeply collaborative at its heart. Indeed, new ideas typically require colleagues, collaborators, friends, and family who can help to refine the insights, place them in proper context, and synthesize them with other lines of thought. This is especially true when part of the focus is the emergence of a new field—a collective enterprise that, in this case, promises to alter the shape of urban science and policy. One does not pontificate on such things without having had many dozens of conversations with others who are concerned with the very same phenomenon. Here I attempt to give credit to the many people who have contributed to this work, either directly or indirectly.

First and foremost, my colleagues at the Boston Area Research Initiative (BARI) deserve much credit not only as collaborators but for making this work possible in the first place. This includes the founding directors, Robert J. Sampson and Christopher Winship, for spearheading the effort; David Luberoff for sharing with me his own vision of city-university partnerships and for being a mentor and friend in building BARI; Nancy Hill and David Lazer, as original members of BARI's steering committee; and Rebecca Wassarman and Deans Barbara Grosz and Liz Cohen of the Radcliffe Institute for Advanced Study at Harvard University and its Academic Ventures program for seeing the promise of BARI and investing in it when we had nothing but an aspirational idea for a new approach to urban science and policy. Others who have invested resources in the work reported in this book include the National Science Foundation (SMA-1338446 from the Research Coordination Network program and SES-1637124 from the Resource Implementation for Data-Intensive Research program), John D. and Catherine T. MacArthur Foundation, and the Herman and Frieda L. Miller Foundation.

Other collaborators who contributed to one or more of the studies summarized in the book include Jessica Baldwin-Philippi; Ryan Buell; Eric Gordon; Mauro Martino; Dietmar Offenhuber; Michael Norton; Ethan Porter; and Melissa Sands. A rotating team of data-savvy students over the years—all of whom have moved on to bigger and greater things or will soon do so—also has made the work possible. These students include Akua Abu, Armin Akhavan, Matthew Blackburn, Alex Ciomek, Gabriel Cunningham, Chelsea Farrell, Henry Gomory, Jeremy Levine, and Barrett Montgomery. The impressively dedicated students who helped conduct the neighborhood audits reported in Chapters 2 and 4 were Beijien Balata, Evan Cutler, Norris Guscott, Spencer Hall, Michael Hrovat, Ben Lynch, Emily Simpson, and Jacey Taft. The students of Advanced Experimental Methods: Social Psychology at UMass Boston in Spring 2012 were crucial to the execution of the "flyer study" reported in Chapter 6. I also have to give much thanks to Samantha Levy, who has kept BARI's trains running on time since November 2016 and without whom this book would never have reached fruition.

My colleagues in the public sector have been vital partners not only in the specific projects described in the book but also in developing the philosophy of how research-policy collaborations work best in the modern digital age. These include my friends Nigel Jacob, Chris Osgood, and Kris Carter of the city of Boston's Mayor's Office of New Urban Mechanics and their team; Bill Oates, Curt Savoie, Jascha Franklin-Hodge, Andrew Therriault, and Patricia Boyle-McKenna, all of the city of Boston's Department of Innovation and Technology; Justin Holmes and Jerome Smith, in their own custodianship of Boston's 311 system; and Holly St. Clair and Tim Reardon of the Metropolitan Area Planning Council's Data Services team. (It is worth noting that the project has gone on for long enough that many of the people listed together are each other's respective predecessor and successor, and that in other cases some who are not listed together have since begun to work with each other at other agencies.) I am also grateful to Cari Tate and the team at SeeClickFix for making data available for the evaluation of Commonwealth Connect reported in Chapter 7.

I also need to thank those who were less directly involved in the research projects described in the book but have been active partners in thinking through the emerging world of urban informatics and research-policy collaboration. Many of these individuals also commented on early versions of this manuscript. These include Michael Johnson of UMass Boston's URBAN.Boston network, Ben Levine of the MetroLab Network, Katharine Lusk of Boston University's Initiative on Cities, and Cathy Wissink and Aimee Sprung of Microsoft's Office of Civic Engagement and Technology. I also am indebted to Mercè Crosas and the Dataverse team at the Institute of Quantitative Social Science, and Ben Lewis and the WorldMap development group at the Center for Geographic Analysis, both at Harvard University, for their partnership in building the Boston Data Portal and making it possible to publicly share the data and metrics developed for this book. I also want to thank Thomas Embree LeBien for his editorial advice and for helping me establish my voice in this book.

Last, I am grateful to my family, especially my wife, Leslie, for their enthusiasm, insights, advice, and endless patience as this project went from an initial idea, to a loose constellation of studies, to a full thought that I could share with those who are not obliged to listen to me.

Index